Healthy Housing

Healthy Housing

A practical guide

RAY RANSON

Published by E & F N Spon on behalf of
the World Health Organization Regional
Office for Europe

E & F N SPON
An Imprint of Chapman & Hall

World Health Organization

**Published by E & FN Spon, an imprint of Chapman & Hall, 2–6
Boundary Row, London SE1 8HN**

Chapman & Hall, 2–6 Boundary Row, London SE1 8HN, UK

Van Nostrand Reinhold Inc., 115 5th Avenue, New York NY10003, USA

Chapman & Hall Japan, Thomson Publishing Japan, Hirakawacho Nemoto
Building, 7F, 1-7-11 Hirakawa-cho, Chiyoda-ku, Tokyo 102, Japan

Chapman & Hall Australia, Thomas Nelson Australia, 102 Dodds Street,
South Melbourne, Victoria 3205, Australia

Chapman & Hall India, R. Seshadri, 32 Second Main Road, CIT East,
Madras 600 035, India

First edition 1991

© 1991 E & FN Spon

Typeset in 10½/12pt Baskerville by Mews Photosetting, Beckenham, Kent
Printed in Great Britain by St Edmundsbury Press, Bury St Edmunds, Suffolk

ISBN 0 419 15400 0   0 442 31430 2 (USA)

A catalogue record for this book is available from the British Library

Library of Congress Cataloging-in-Publication data available

91-3993
CIP

Contents

Contents

Acknowledgements

Many organizations and professionals have contributed to these guidelines. In particular I would like to thank the following agencies for their comments on earlier drafts: The Institute of Hygiene and Epidemiology, Prague; The National School of Public Health, Portugal; The Higher Institute of Sanitation, Rome; The General Council of Bridges and Roads, Paris; The Child Accident Prevention Trust, UK; The UK Building Research Establishment; The School of Public Health at Yale University; and Greater London Scientific Services.

I would like to thank Ornette Prentice and Audrey Castle for typing the original drafts of the manuscript, and Elaine Grandjean at the World Health Organization (WHO) Regional Office for Europe for her painstaking sub-editing of those drafts. Thanks also to my friend Derek Walker for collecting statistical information, and for proof-reading endless rewrites.

Finally, I must thank Eric Girault, formerly Regional Officer for Environmental Health Management and Ecology at the WHO Regional Office for Europe, for his effort in getting the project off the ground and giving active encouragement and support throughout.

Perhaps it goes without saying, however, that the responsibility for the text and any inaccuracies contained therein rest with the author.

We are grateful to the following for permission to reproduce photographs on the indicated pages:
p. 5, Janet Moore; p. 6, Barrett Special Project; p. 22, Institute of Environmental Health Officers (IEHO); p. 48, Rentokil; p. 49, Rentokil; p. 54, Janet Moore; p. 61, IEHO; p. 68, Rentokil; p. 74, Rentokil; p. 77, Metropolitan Police; p. 121, IEHO; p. 139, Rentokil; p. 142, Vent-Axia; p. 151, Caradon Everest; p. 163, British Gas; p. 184, Tony Sleep; p. 185, Chubb Fire; p. 189, Tony Sleep; p. 195, Tony Sleep; p. 196, Tony Sleep; p. 207, Habinkeg Housing Association; p. 219, IEHO.

Foreword

Healthy housing, together with clean water, sanitation, food and clothing, is a basic human requirement. This has been the case since humans sought caves for protection against wild animals and external elements. Some 20 000 years later, we still need refuge against the outside world and housing that provides a safe and healthy environment in which to live.

The relationship between health and housing has long been recognized. In England, for example, the Victorians clearly recognized an association between poor housing and ill-health, albeit they wrongly explained it in terms of the miasma theory (transmission of diseases by bad odours). Nevertheless, their solutions (slum clearance and improved sanitation) did much to improve health. Indeed, improvements in death rates from infectious diseases such as cholera and typhoid, and to some extent tuberculosis, owed as much to improved standards of housing as to microbiology and antibiotics. As our knowledge of communicable diseases and illness has grown, so has our awareness of the importance of housing and the environment to physical and mental well-being.

This importance is reflected in this book, which represents the most recent in a long series of efforts by the WHO Regional Office for Europe to promote housing hygiene. Other work includes health aspects related to indoor air quality, prevention of accidents in the home, noise control in buildings, environmental health aspects of human settlements, health aspects of indoor air quality, and the impact of indoor climate on the health of the elderly. The results of these efforts have provided governments and professionals alike with invaluable tools to help them implement the European health for all movement, which includes targets for provision of safe and healthy housing.

This movement comes none too soon. Information generated during the International Year of Shelter for the Homeless in 1987 indicated that more than 1000 million people live in grossly inadequate shelter and that 100 million have no shelter whatsoever. Further, the housing situation in the developing countries is worse now than it was ten years ago. This situation is exacerbated by exponential population growth and rapid urbanization. According to United Nations figures the world population is expected to reach 6122 million by the year 2000, and 8206 million by 2025, an increase of 26% between 1985 and 2000, and a further 34% between 2000 and 2025.

Much of this population growth is being centralized in cities and other urban centres. Thus the urban population of the world is likely to reach 2854 million by the year 2000 (an increase of 44%) and 4932 million by 2025 (a further increase of 73%). Such rapid growth is not confined to capital cities and large metropolitan areas, but also affects secondary and tertiary cities, often outstripping the ability of urban services to keep pace and forcing large sections of their populations to live in poverty and squalor.

The challenges that these developments present to governments, communities and professionals are enormous, but many countries are actively working towards meeting these demands. This book has been written to aid such efforts.

In this book, Ray Ranson, a consultant for the WHO, has brought together the basic principles of health and housing that can be applied to new and existing housing and the housing environment. Although intended mainly for industrialized countries, many of the conclusions also apply to developing countries. Many practical suggestions are given on healthy housing design that should be of great interest to architects, builders, sanitarians and environmental health officers. Attention is also given to the organizational and policy factors that need to be considered in a healthy housing strategy. However, the book is not a textbook, nor is it intended to be prescriptive. Individuals, governments, ministries, housing professionals and communities must come to their own conclusions about technical remedies, standards, legislation and policy. Nevertheless, acceptance of the basic principles of healthy housing indicated in this book provides a useful framework for preventing costly housing failures in the future.

In 1984, the governments of the European Region of WHO adopted a common policy on health with 38 targets. Target 24 specifically address the housing issue:

By the year 2000, all people of the Region should have a better opportunity of living in houses and settlements which provide a healthy and safe environment.

In 1986, the WHO Regional Office for Europe initiated the Healthy Cities Project to implement the policy of health for all at city level. The Project now includes 31 Healthy Cities in 18 European countries, 17 national networks and three international networks encompassing more than 500 cities and towns in the industrialized parts of the world. As laid out in this volume the principles, which show clearly the link between better health and healthier housing, are highly relevant to the goals of the Healthy Cities Project.

It is the intention of this book to increase motivation in countries to implement this target in a more forceful way, and to provide guidance on how it can be achieved.

Dr J.E. Asvall
Regional Director for Europe
World Health Organization

Preface

This guide is an update of *Guidelines for Healthy Housing* (Environmental Health 31), published by the WHO Regional Office for Europe in 1988. This guide focuses on the health requirements of 'housing' which in the context of this book means the home or shelter and the immediate residential neighbourhood. This geographical cut-off means that wider environmental health considerations which indirectly relate to housing have had to be excluded. However, many WHO and other publications are available on this subject as reference material when planning human settlements, particularly important in the current ecologically and environmentally conscious climate. The wide disparities in geography, culture, social habits and political priorities towards housing mean that this book is inevitably very generalized. However, for those readers who are not familiar with the principles underlying healthy housing then these guidelines should provide a practical introduction to a subject which transverses many disciplines from human ecology, sociology, and urban planning to building science. A lot of reference material has been drawn from many different sources, principally from WHO publications, some of which have had limited distribution or are now no longer available. However, the references in this book are by no means exhaustive and so I apologize in advance for significant omissions.

The main difficulty in writing a guide to healthy housing is not knowing where to **start** but knowing where to **finish**. I hope this book will at least provide you with a framework to make that start in applying health principles to housing in your respective countries and organizations.

SCOPE

The book is divided into three chapters. Chapter 1 deals with some general considerations applicable to basic housing hygiene. Chapter 2 outlines the fundamental technical and social requirements for housing hygiene including health implications, suggested control measures and a few examples of standards. These requirements are set out within a series of broad parameters outlining the basic requirements for housing in relation to health needs. This part should be of particular interest to architects, environmental health officers, hygienists and technical personnel. Chapter 3 summarizes some of the operational and organizational priorities and constraints for implementing a basic healthy housing strategy. This section is mainly aimed at the appropriate policy-makers within ministries, institutions and other housing agencies who may be unaware of the health dimensions of their housing activities.

GENERAL APPROACH

Housing and health is not and never will be an exact science. As yet, scientifically determined parameters for healthy housing are generally unavailable, and there are difficulties in using empirical evaluation techniques for assessing the effects of housing conditions on health. However, the absence of definite measurements does not denote the absence of a relationship between housing and health, it just means that a relationship cannot always be proven. Fortunately, that does not stop us from proposing parameters for healthy housing which reflect many thousands of years of experience in designing and living in housing. It is wrong to assume therefore that healthy housing is a new subject. It has, like food, water and clothing, always been a major preoccupation of mankind, if only for survival against harmful external elements or dangerous animals. However, we now know a lot more about other factors which are important to healthy housing, e.g. sanitation, home safety, and the significance of indoor air quality and climate to health. Indeed experience from developed, developing and Third World countries seems to show a remarkable consistency in delineating basic health needs as they relate to housing. Thus a number of parameters for healthy housing are proposed in this book as minimum targets for human occupation which arguably could and should be applied to housing anywhere in the world. The basis of this approach is that healthy housing needs are more or less universal throughout the world and that healthy housing is a basic human need which, with food and water, should not be denied to the world's population. These parameters also include the special needs of children, the elderly, disabled people and the chronically sick who may have different health and thus different housing needs compared with the wider community. The technical parameters thus provide health goals for housing design, planning, assessment of fitness for human habitation as well as resource materials for training and health education.

Ray Ranson

1

General considerations

1.1 HEALTHY HOUSING – AN INTERPRETATION

Throughout recorded history mankind has been concerned with provision of adequate shelter against the elements and the development of a safe and comfortable physical environment in which to live. The degree of success in achieving this has been largely determined by prevailing socio-economic conditions and the influence of environmental changes arising from, for instance, industrialization or technological pursuits. As a result many parts of the developing world have a serious housing problem as expressed by homelessness, slum and poor quality housing, ostensibly contributing to hazards to health and well-being. For instance, disease, accidents and fires are all more prevalent in slum areas; psychological and social disturbances are also partly attributed to sub-standard housing.

'**Healthy housing**', '**healthful housing**' or '**housing hygiene**' are the terms which are generally used to describe the conditions which will provide a safe and healthy housing environment for its inhabitants. So what is healthy housing? The World Health Organization Regional Office for Europe has defined it in one sentence (219 words long!) as follows:

A human habitation that is structurally sound and relatively free from accidental injury hazards, provides sufficient space for all normal household activities for all members of the family, has readily and easily available an adequate supply of potable and palatable water, has a sanitary means of collection, storage and disposal of all liquid and solid wastes, is provided with appropriate installed facilities for personal and household hygiene and cleanliness, is sufficiently weatherproof and watertight, provides proper protection from the elements, especially for those persons who may be particularly susceptible, for physical and/or physiological reasons to these potentially adverse environmental conditions, provides a hygrothermal indoor environment which is healthful and comfortable, is free from excessive noise from both interior and exterior sources of the structure, has natural and

1

artificial means of illumination that are safe and adequate in quality and quantity for the fulfilment of all normal household activities and functions, is free from toxic and/or noxious odours, chemicals and other air contaminants or pollutants, has adequate but not excessive microbial and thermal characteristics, provides sufficient but not excessive solar radiation, provides adequate protection from insects and rodents which may be reservoirs and/or vectors of disease agents, and is served by the necessary and/or desirable health, welfare, social, educational, cultural and protective community services and facilities.

However, healthy housing is not just concerned with the sanitary and hygienic design of the shelter but with the whole health spectrum of physical health, mental health and social well-being both within the dwelling and in the residential environment. Healthy housing is thus not just about avoidance of illness but is about providing a living environment for betterment of health. This concept has long been a major goal of the World Health Organization's strategy and indeed it is now generally recognized that healthy housing can only be effectively tackled if it forms part of a wider public health policy such as the WHO 'Health for all by the year 2000' strategy which has been formally adopted by most of the world's governments.

A number of targets relating to housing and health are included in the health for all policy. For example, target number 24 states: 'By the year 2000, all people of the Region should have a better opportunity of living in houses and settlements which provide a healthy and safe environment'. Target number 11 mentions the need to reduce deaths from accidents, including accidents in the home, by 25% by the year 2000. These goals have been criticized as being too idealistic. However, the intention of 'Health for All 2000' is to provide a focus for national and local authorities to establish achievable healthy housing targets commensurate with the resources available. Without such ideals no housing improvements are likely to be achieved.

1.2 THE CHALLENGE OF SLUM HOUSING

There is no doubt that slum housing is both widespread and presents an enormous challenge to public health. Despite the scale of the housing problem in many countries, much is being done to improve housing hygiene albeit that change is often slow and not always visibly obvious in the poorer areas. For example, in a recent review, Yew described experience in six cities (Bangkok, Hong Kong, Jakarta, Kuala Lumpur, Manila and Singapore) and draws the conclusion that it is unrealistic for the large countries of south-east Asia to expect to solve their housing problems in the present decade, given the rate of urban population growth and the rapid increase in slum and squatter areas. [10] Such problems are not confined to any one region of the world. For example, in Mozambique as elsewhere in Africa, the major source of urban growth is the rapid influx of migrants from rural areas which accounts for 66% of urban population growth. Maputo had about one million inhabitants in 1985 and an annual growth of 80%. This has increased overcrowding and facilitated the transmission of infections and parasitic diseases.

However, health problems associated with slum housing are not confined to Third World countries. In Europe, for example, most of the older cities, towns and other human settlements have pockets of housing that have deteriorated into slums through lack of maintenance and rehabilitation. In addition, most of the less developed countries within the European Region are undergoing fundamental demographic and social changes as a result of rural–urban drift and the accompanying increase in their urban populations is seriously affecting housing

Densely built housing.

conditions in these countries. More and more people are moving from essentially rural societies based on agrarian pursuits to urban societies built upon industrial and commercial activities. This trend is most pronounced in developing Mediterranean countries where at least five different types of slum housing can be identified: traditional slums, industrial slums, shanty-town and self-build slums, modern slums and rural slums.

Thus, while they vary in degree and extent, many of the health problems attached to urban centres of developing countries are the same or similar to those in developed countries. Common problems include:

- lack of effective land management

- an insufficient supply of low-cost housing

- unauthorized residential expansion outpacing and impeding the provision of an adequate infrastructure and public services

- unemployment, poverty and all that follows in their wake.

The distinction between the problems of developed *vis-à-vis* developing countries, although real, may also be exaggerated. The problems of homelessness, unhealthy housing and otherwise poor housing are pandemic. It is precisely for these reasons that policy-makers must examine their responses to the housing targets set out in 'Health for All 2000' in the light of their own situation and practicable targets for achieving improvements.

1.2.1 Traditional slums

In the inner city areas of older towns, overcrowding, industrialization, air pollution and poor environmental amenities has meant that the more affluent members of the population have often moved out of the centre to the more spacious housing at the urban periphery, leaving poorer, older and less mobile groups behind. Poor maintenance and lack of housing investment have created large areas of 'traditional slum' housing in the older inner city areas. Martin and Oeter [8] described these areas as

> . . . at best a threat to the health of the inhabitants due to overcrowding, defective physical structure of the building resulting in dampness, sanitary defects, increased home accidents and lack of suitable outdoor areas for children with a consequent increase in street accidents and in children being kept indoors. At worst, the influence of less desirable members of the population results in an increase in crime, juvenile delinquency and immobility.

1.2.2 Industrial slums

These are frequently to be seen in many inner city areas where the industrial population increased greatly in the late nineteenth and early twentieth centuries. In these cases, poor quality ribbon development and terraced back-to-back insanitary housing were erected with little thought to urban planning or long-term health effects. These houses rapidly deteriorated and, like the first group, were frequently occupied by the poorer members of the population, including immigrant workers often of different ethnic origins and with different social cultures and customs. Industrial slum areas are characterized by poor environmental conditions, overcrowding, industrial pollution, poor design and layout, low levels of basic amenities and serious disrepair.

1.2.3 Shanty-town and self-build slums

Shanty-town, self-build, squatter and mobile housing (such as caravans)

Most industrial cities have pockets of slum housing.

can frequently be seen at the edge of cities where land is relatively cheap, sometimes adjacent to industrial areas or just outside the administrative control of the city authority. These make-shift dwellings are usually constructed of salvaged materials, such as wood and corrugated iron, completely lack indoor water supplies, drainage and sanitation (including provision for waste disposal), and have no proper access roads. Indoor space requirements and air quality are poor, and inadequate building materials fail to compensate for changes in temperature and other climatic factors during the year. Basic housing hygiene conditions are usually appalling and communicable diseases endemic.

The scale of the shanty-town slum is difficult to comprehend. For instance, in Ankara, Turkey, 72% of the population live in squatter shanty-town housing despite attempts by the Turkish Government to deal with the problem through municipal housing projects and planning controls. The problem is largely economic in two ways: the impoverished shanty-town occupants cannot afford to own or rent housing in the planned sections of the cities; and they need to be near the city centre for employment. A third problem relates to the lack of security, which often tends to discourage investment in basic sanitation, infrastructure and other improvements.

1.2.4 The modern slum

The modern slum is perhaps the most tragic and certainly the most difficult type to deal with. These slums resulted from cheap, quickly-built, high-density, system-package developments erected in the 1950s, 1960s and 1970s to 'solve' the housing problem. Far from solving the housing problem, they often worsened it. They consist mostly of slab-block or high-rise buildings frequently overlooking each other and with little thought given to the planning, layout, internal design, maintenance and public health/social consequences within the context of urban planning and healthy housing principles. Planners and architects seemed either unaware or insensitive to the fact that people actually had to live in these buildings. Many of the designs are totally inappropriate to the climatic and socio-economic conditions. As a result, many of these apartments are damp, badly lighted, often completely lacking in through ventilation, infested with vermin (which because of the design cannot be exterminated), very hot in the summer and very cold in the winter because of poor insulation and inappropriate heating methods, inadequately protected against noise, and in a poor state of repair because of unsuitable building materials and design. These conditions are in addition to the adverse social and mental health consequences created by high-density, high-rise developments. They are often

Many comparatively modern housing developments have become slums.

characterized by vandalism, excessive rent arrears and difficulty in renting simply because nobody wants to live in them. In many cities, they are being pulled down because this solution is cheaper than rectifying inherent defects in their design and construction.

1.2.5 Rural slum housing

Part of the reason for rural–urban drift is the belief (often mistaken) that housing conditions and employment opportunities are better in towns than in indigenous rural areas. Information on rural housing in many countries is often scarce, but rural areas of developing countries frequently lack piped water supplies or sanitation and are overcrowded. Water supplies are often inadequate, polluted or not reasonably accessible. Invariably, facilities for disposal of solid waste, surface water and waste water are unavailable. For instance, in a study of 10 rural towns in Bosnia and Herzegovina in Yugoslavia, almost half (48.7%) of the occupants had 6–10 m² of housing surface area and nearly 90% lived in overcrowded conditions. In addition, most houses had inadequate disposal of human and animal excreta and sometimes no form of toilet at all. [11] Offset against this, rural areas are usually quieter and less affected

7

by air pollution; they also have more open space for recreational pursuits and a healthier outside environment.

A definite cause-and-effect relationship exists between slum housing conditions and incidence of disease, particularly enteric diseases such as infantile diarrhoea and parasitic infections and respiratory diseases such as tuberculosis, pneumonia and other chest infections, and above-average numbers of home accidents. The combination of poor housing, poverty, malnutrition and ignorance in slum areas is largely responsible for increased infant mortality rates and high morbidity indices for the target population. These themes are common to all countries where housing hygiene is poor.

1.3 HOUSING AND HEALTH

To date, many thousands of studies have attempted to show some relationship between housing and its possible association with health. However, the empirical evaluation of housing and health has proved difficult for the following reasons:

- Housing and health studies have usually failed to separate or take into account the multifactorial non-housing variables that affect health (e.g. poverty, ignorance, poor nutrition and lack of medical care). Even less clear is whether or not these various factors are equally important and how they should be evaluated in a research programme.

- The direction of a cause-and-effect relationship pertaining to housing and health variables also is often unclear. Thus, if a particular housing factor is shown to be associated with a disease, the question arises whether or not the disease has given rise to the factor or whether a third set of determinants is responsible.

- Indices for measuring health and the hygienic quality of housing are often too insensitive, inappropriate and/or lack universal acceptability. This is a particular problem when assessing the intangible or aesthetic effects of housing on social well-being, in determining comfort levels or measuring qualitative aspects such as quality of life.

- In many cases, no epidemiological studies into the effect of particular housing factors on health have been conducted. As a result the causal factors of potential housing-related illnesses are often unknown or insufficiently corroborated.

Commenting on these drawbacks, the first WHO Expert Committee on the Public Health Aspects of Housing [12] concluded the following:

The lack of definite measurements does not denote the absence of a relationship between housing and health. By deductive measuring a strong relationship can be established. Since the residential environment consists of many elements of the overall environment, with each element capable of exerting individual detrimental effects upon health and wellbeing, it can be deduced that the effect of the residential environment upon health is the sum of the individual factors.

1.4 COLLECTION OF DATA

To reach a better understanding of the aetiology of housing and health, we need to know as much as possible about the relationship between housing hygiene and its effects on health. A less piecemeal approach towards data collection and epidemiology is needed, and better coordination of housing/health information between the various agencies and professions involved (e.g. architects, doctors, sanitarians, social workers and other professionals) would prove invaluable to epidemiologists, health statisticians, planners and policy-makers in understanding the aetiology of housing-related diseases.

One model for achieving this goal is described in the recommended protocol of the European study of public health aspects of the indoor environment of human habitations. [12] This protocol proposes epidemiological methods to identify and evaluate health hazards with the objective of ascertaining the relationship between various elements and components of human habitations and the health of the occupants. The study requires an interdisciplinary approach using various health scientists and others to design, plan, implement and monitor the research programme and to analyse results. This is in line with recommendations of a WHO Expert Committee on Housing and Health in 1974 proposing that multidisciplinary teams be set up to examine the aetiology of housing and health. [13]

1.5 INTERACTION OF HOUSING CONDITIONS AND DISEASE

In determining the inter-relationship between housing conditions and specific diseases, account should be taken of the interaction of three factors on which the hazard potential for causing toxic, traumatic or pathogenic effects on humans depends:

- the **dose** of the causative agent as measured by the intensity, frequency and/or duration separately or in combination with other agents and factors

- the susceptibility of the **host** to the causative agent

9

- the **environment** in which the interaction between host and agent may increase or decrease the toxicity, injury potential or pathogenicity of the potentially harmful chemical, physical and biological agent. [12]

The major diseases possibly related to a poor housing environment can be crudely divided into **communicable** diseases and **non-communicable** diseases, which have a greater or lesser effect on physical health, mental health and social well-being.

Most housing and health studies have dealt specifically with the effects of housing on physical health and only a few with psychological illness or social well-being. For instance, by 1962, of 14 selected European studies dealing with some aspect of physical health, eight investigated solely the relationship between housing and tuberculosis, five analysed general morbidity rates, death rates, birth rates and infant mortality caused by respiratory diseases, and one studied the height of preschool children. By contrast, of 24 selected American studies, 10 dealt with physical diseases and studies of general morbidity while the remaining 14 studies dealt with social and psychological matters with a marked interest in a single topic. Of the 14 studies, seven dealt solely with juvenile delinquency.

Most of the findings showed a marked positive association between housing and health: poor housing correlated with poor health, and better housing with better health. Some mixed, ambiguous or null findings and a very small number of actual negative findings were reported. Of 24 studies reviewed (14 European and 10 American) involving physical morbidity, 15 showed positive findings, seven seemed ambiguous or showed no relationship between housing and health, and two arrived at negative results. Of 16 studies dealing with some aspect of social adjustment, 11 found a positive relationship to housing, four gave ambiguous or null results and one was negative. [14]

The difficulties in establishing a relationship (if any) between housing and mental health or psychosocial disorders lie in the subjective nature of the symptoms and the indeterminate influence of other factors. As a result, clear cause-and-effect relationships based on facts are difficult to establish. [13]

In many Eastern European countries, health and housing administrations are required to lay down specific environmental standards. This requirement has resulted in extensive research data dealing with the potential toxic effects of new chemicals used in housing and house furnishings, the efficiency of heating and ventilation systems, and insulation and housing design as they affect indoor microclimates. However, more information is needed about the potential carcinogenic or other adverse health effects due to use of certain construction materials, and the role of ergonomic housing design on comfort and well-being.

Detailed epidemiological studies into the causes of home accidents also are needed. Similarly, little research has been carried out on the effects of indoor air quality on health, although considerable information is available on the chronic effects of outdoor air pollution on respiratory diseases such as bronchitis and lung cancer. Various research programmes into these problems are currently being undertaken by the WHO Regional Office for Europe in collaboration with research institutions. The information from these sources and from individual Member States will then be distributed and exchanged, to help avoid costly mistakes caused by poor planning and housing design in the future.

Member States are encouraged to establish their own coordinating centres from which information resources can be collated, if necessary, with WHO collaboration.

1.6 PARAMETERS OF HEALTH

Before an analysis can be made of healthy housing requirements, clarification is needed on the meaning of the term 'health', which can be interpreted in various ways. The WHO defines health as 'not merely the absence of disease and infirmity, but a state of complete physical, mental and social well-being'. [15]

Health has also been described as 'an absolute condition of well-being' or alternatively 'an optimum capacity of effective performance of value tasks'. [16] These different views of health have an important bearing on health models and subsequent health care services, standards and policies. In general terms, though, health is normally assessed by reference to deviant behavioural indicators, such as physical, mental or social pathologies. However, these indicators are often difficult to apply to 'well-being' as many doctors fail to recognize them, treat them symptomatically, or are unwilling or unable to remedy the underlying cause.

Examination of current health models confirms the limitation of diagnostic and prognostic methods in dealing with physical, mental and social health needs. At present, developing countries are concerned mainly with biomedical conditions, while the developed countries are turning to biopsychosocial models of ill-health. The main reasons for this difference are changing patterns of disease and consumer expectations: developed countries have largely eradicated infectious, nutritional and other acute diseases through preventative and remedial action but are left with unabated degenerative, chronic and psychosocial diseases, which have a more complex aetiology.

In terms of housing, information about epidemiology and identification of causal factors rarely includes psychosomatic and social pathologies. As a result, little is known about the contribution made by housing in causing stress-related diseases such as hypertension, migraine, depression, neurosis, alcoholism and social diseases manifested by pathologically derived antisocial behaviour (e.g. crime, violence, street mugging, vandalism, child abuse, and mental or sexual disorders). Without detailed cause-and-effect studies, remedial action cannot be precise, and symptomatic medical treatment is likely to be the only course of action available to sufferers of bad housing. However, this assumes that no account is taken of intuitive or pragmatic considerations which often guide patients, doctors and others in coming to certain decisions about the causation of particular illnesses. Thus, in many cases, patients ascribe their state of ill-health partly or wholly to the state of their housing. For example, common colds and chest conditions are often blamed on damp and cold housing. However, intuitive considerations alone are often suspect as patients may be unaware or unwilling to accept concomitant ill-health factors that are often present. Conversely, patients, doctors and health officials may be unaware of the aetiology of a particular housing-related illness or be unable to help abate causal factors. Thus, unless healthy housing policies form part of a primary health care programme, and an interdisciplinary approach towards intervention housing and medical practitioners are unlikely on their own to be able to prevent housing-related illnesses. Clearly, people suffering from illnesses and disease need medical treatment while at the same time the insanitary housing and environmental conditions that caused them need to be removed. Unless this is done, re-exposure to the conditions will merely cause reinfection or recurrent illness resulting in recommencement of the treatment cycle.

1.7 GENERAL HEALTHY HOUSING NEEDS

We spend an estimated two thirds of our life within the home and its immediate surroundings. The health of each occupant is potentially at risk from an insanitary or otherwise unhealthy housing environment. However, the groups who spend most time in the home are children, mothers with young children, the elderly, disabled persons, the chronically sick and the unemployed. These groups can be expected to be disproportionately affected by poor housing conditions and may also have special health and housing needs. Thus, housing suitable for general needs may not necessarily be suitable for these groups. In addition, considerable variation in healthy housing needs can be expected within these groups, a factor that would need to be taken into account in technical and policy requirements.

Nevertheless, common human health requirements **can** be identified in relation to housing. These are generally described in terms of the negative effects of the residential environment on health rather than in terms of the positive effects of 'good' housing in maintaining and promoting **good** health.

Thus, poor housing may affect **physical health** in at least three ways:

- it may facilitate the transmission of communicable diseases

- it may interfere with physiological needs

- its design or construction may cause injury to health.

The maintenance and promotion of mental health and social well-being is more difficult to define but since housing provides the scenario for family life, recreation, rest, sleep and social interaction, it follows that many aspects of poor housing, such as overcrowding, noise, air pollution, bad odours or dampness, give rise to considerable dissatisfaction and annoyance and perhaps contribute to poor health. Conversely, comfortable, pleasant surroundings aid satisfaction and facilitate the maintenance of friendly interpersonal relationships. Housing also forms part of the wider social setting whereby communities are formed and institutionalized. Community infrastructures are thus extremely important to individuals and the community alike, particularly in times of hardship or illness.

A healthful environment must therefore do more than merely limit the occurrence and spread of physical diseases and infections. It must permit individuals of all ages to conduct useful household activities without undue fatigue and without putting an excessive burden upon any organ of the body. The housing environment also should be comfortable, pleasant and provide a social setting for active and passive recreation, rest and exercise. [12] These goals have therefore incorporated into relevant parameters for healthy housing adopted by WHO, as described in these guidelines.

2

Technical and social requirements

The technical and social requirements of housing can be defined by a number of parameters likely to be relatively consistent with basic healthy housing needs anywhere in the world. For example, as long ago as 1939, the American Public Health Association devised a set of housing principles that were widely adopted for housing hygiene policies in a number of countries and are still largely applicable today. [18] However, the detailed control measures, standards and policies have changed and will vary in accordance with national, political and economic considerations. Wide differences in technical and social requirements also exist between rural and urban areas.

In developing countries, financial constraints largely determine what can be provided; inevitably the interest tends to be in minimal rather than optimal requirements and solutions. Control measures that require heavy capital expenditure are therefore to be discouraged.

In some cases, the technical and social requirements set out in this chapter could be included in several different categories, and each requirement should therefore be considered as part of an overall programme. For instance, the impact of physical factors upon social well-being means that technical and social factors often cannot be divorced. Similarly, the overlap between purely 'health' considerations as opposed to 'safety' provisions makes any distinction arbitrary. Nevertheless, providing that a holistic approach is taken, the basic framework should serve as a useful guide for tackling the problems of unhealthy housing.

2.1 HOUSING LAYOUT REQUIREMENTS

2.1.1 Provision of housing of suitable height to enable normal family use and social activities to be performed

(a) High-rise flats
In the post-war period, many countries built tall housing blocks

as part of high-density developments, usually in response to an acute housing shortage or as part of redevelopment programmes. Shortage of building land and the need for housing within reasonable travelling distance of the workplace and city centres have meant that residential densities are often very high, although, in theory, reasonable **indoor** space norms can be achieved by building blocks of flats that much higher. However, high-rise flats are generally not socially suitable for family housing, and capital and maintenance costs are usually higher than for low-rise housing.

In many cases, high-rise flats were system-built and erected using cheap and unsuitable building materials with little or no consideration given to healthy housing design, indoor air quality and indoor climate. As a result, living conditions are often extremely poor and a new generation of slums has been created.

(i) Health effects

A number of studies have examined the health effects of living in flats compared with houses or other types of development. For instance, an increase in illness has been found in flats: twice as many upper respiratory infections were found in children below the age of 10 years who lived in flats as compared with house dwellers.

These findings were supported by research by Fanning [19] who studied two groups of families of members of the US armed forces stationed in the former Federal Republic of Germany, one group living in flats and the other in houses. The morbidity of families living in flats was 57% greater than of those living in houses. The greatest differences were seen in the incidence of respiratory infections in young women and children and of psychoneurotic disorders in women. The reasons for the differences in respiratory infections were felt to be due to the relatively small space available in a flat compared with that in a house and confinement of the family within the flat. This confinement and the resulting social isolation were thought to be the reasons for the increase in psychoneurosis in the women. Fanning suggests that further investigation is needed into the effects of flat life, particularly the individual causal factors that might account for the differences in morbidity patterns.

Factors in flats that might affect the **physical** health of occupants include poor indoor air quality and climate (which depend upon ventilation requirements, adequacy of heating methods and thermal insulation), inappropriate home safety design, insufficient indoor space provisions, and use of toxic or otherwise unsuitable building materials. The risk of children being killed or severely injured by falling from windows and balconies is much higher in homes above the first floor, and children's play activities are more restricted by multistorey living. The lack of access to fresh air and a garden by children and mothers alike means that they spend more time indoors, thereby increasing the risk of contracting respiratory infections and other communicable diseases. Other health problems associated with flats include residential noise, difficulties associated with solid waste disposal and inadequate drainage systems, and finally pest infestation in ventilation and service ducts (especially cockroaches).

Factors that might affect **mental** health of flat dwellers are much more diverse and difficult to define, particularly as they are usually inter-related with other factors not necessarily peculiar to flats or which might be applicable to one flat development but not another (e.g. location in relation to the town centre, transport, recreation facilities and hospitals).

Numerous research studies have shown that the mental health of flat dwellers varies considerably with the type of development in terms of access (e.g. stair access, balcony access, deck access or tower block access), noise insulation provision, number and ages of children, income level, marital status, proximity to friends and family, satisfaction with area and design of living accommodation. In fact, no generalizations can be made as some people like living in flats. Indeed, many single, working or childless couples prefer flats to traditional housing where additional maintenance responsibilities, gardening, etc., may be a source of worry. For many people, flats (or indeed any housing) are only used as a place to sleep, with all meals and social activities taking place outside the home. Other advantages of high-rise flats are that they can, if they are well planned, provide good views, privacy and solitude from busy and noisy city areas below.

However, numerous social studies of **families** living in flats have shown a disproportionate dissatisfaction with living on the upper floors (normally considered to be above the fourth floor level) and that this can in many cases adversely affect mental health. For instance, a major survey into the effects of flat-living on families carried out by the UK Government between 1977 and 1978 highlighted the effects that mothers felt this had on their health and emotional state as well as identifying the perceived causes of dissatisfaction. [20] The study showed that two fifths of mothers of families who had moved from higher storeys to lower floors of multistorey blocks said their health, particularly their emotional health, had improved. Those with children over 5 years of age felt they had benefited less — a reflection perhaps that some health problems connected with looking after toddlers are transitory and improve as the children get older. Mothers who moved down claimed that they were less irritable, slept better, and were less affected by nerves, depression, feelings of loneliness or a sense of being cut-off, compared with when they lived on the higher storeys. In all cases, this change was more directly related to the age and number of children, size of income and type of access provided to the flats. A greater improvement in health was felt by low-income mothers with younger, larger numbers of children compared with other groups who also had previously lived on the upper storeys of flats, particularly tower blocks, which were the most unpopular form of housing in terms of mental illness. These health problems did not necessarily disappear when the people moved to lower storeys, but mothers and children were able to identify particular benefits that had eased worry and anxiety.

The UK study came to a number of conclusions that have been shared by several other countries:

- Mothers' dissatisfaction with housing and mental illness increases the higher up they live, which in turn adversely affects their children's development.

- Fear of being trapped in lifts prevents many school-age children from going out to play. This in turn can isolate them and reduce their ability to make friends. This applies particularly to children under 5 years who are probably more adversely affected by their mother's dissatisfaction with the housing than the older age groups.

- The risk of a child being killed falling from his home is 57 times higher if he lives above the first floor level than if he lives on the ground or first floor.

- Mothers with preschool children, particularly those with more than one child, are most dissatisfied with living off the ground and feel more cut off, isolated and depressed compared with mothers of school-age children.

- There is no evidence of an increase in management problems arising from transfers of high-rise families with children to lower floors.

- The allocation of dwellings on the lower floors of flats is more likely to be acceptable to families if lift access is available. There is some indication that maisonettes rather than flats are more satisfactory for family living, possibly because of increased opportunity to segregate the living area in the same way as in a house (e.g. putting children upstairs to bed). However, some countries have found that additional indoor space can help alleviate tension by providing more opportunity for privacy to individual family members.

In general, the psychosocial problems of living on the upper floors of high-rise buildings appear to be caused mainly by the lack of opportunity for contact between residents (this is true in all high-rise buildings but is exaggerated in tower blocks where the lift is usually the only common point of contact with neighbours). The social isolation felt by women in high-rise flats was described by Stewart [21] who had interviewed women who said they had not seen a neighbour for three to four weeks and reported going to the rubbish chute twice a day in the hope of meeting somebody. However, the need for such contact depends partly upon the individual, how much time is spent in the building and how much social contact is made outside. Thus, working people with plenty of contact with people during the day may welcome the sanctitude and solitude of an apartment socially isolated from other dwellings. On the other hand, house-bound single people, such as the elderly, may become depressed by the loneliness and the lack of contact with others. Children undoubtedly need the stimulation of and opportunities for mixing with other children, often denied to them in high-rise housing.

In addition, some evidence shows that children living in high-rise flats fail to acquire a sense of security, curiosity and later ability to explore and experiment, thus impairing normal personality development. [22]

(ii) Control measures

Several measures have been put forward to counteract the problems of high-rise living.

- Many countries have decided to restrict the building of new high-rise residential buildings. For instance, the Netherlands is attempting to limit residential buildings to six storeys and in the Republic of Ireland, the Building Corporation has decided to build no more dwellings higher than three storeys. However, in practice, a trade-off may have to be made depending on land resources, housing demand and degree of homelessness.

- In general terms, high-rise blocks of apartments are not normally suitable for housing families with young children or for housing single elderly persons who do not want or are unable to cope with the difficulties of high-rise living. This should be taken into account when planning new housing developments and in allocating public housing. Preferably, young families should not be allocated flats at all but should be housed in traditional single- or two-storey housing with a garden, but where this is not possible, allocation on the **lower** floors of multistorey blocks is preferable (i.e. below the sixth floor). In these cases, lift access should be provided.

- Housing managers should be aware of the management problems of rehousing people accustomed to living in single-storey housing, into flats. This applies particularly to rural immigrants with close community ties who often have great difficulty adjusting to living in high-rise housing.

- To make the best use of resources, local housing services, education, recreation, health and social service departments and voluntary organizations should collectively review the adequacy of services available to multistorey families. In this way, gaps can be identified and consideration given to remedying deficiencies.

- Community facilities must be situated as near as possible to the flats. In some cases, community halls have been successfully provided by converting flats on intervening floors above ground level, a common practice in Eastern Europe.

- Existing high-rise flats in central areas may be useful to accommodate some office workers and business executives who are single or married without children (assuming the wife also holds a job outside the home).

- In all cases, sufficient attention must be given to avoiding the difficulties created by high-density housing through good housing design and management. This can be done by ensuring that the following amenities are sufficient: play facilities for children; noise insulation of flats; facilities for drying clothes; space for parking cars, bicycles, etc.; facilities for hobbies; arrangements for waste disposal; fire protection; and social arrangements to help people adjust to high-rise living, particularly the elderly and young families. Regular inspection and maintenance of lifts are especially important to keep them in good working order, and security arrangements must be adequate.

(b) Low-rise, high-density housing

Low-rise, high-density housing provides a useful alternative to high-rise, high-density developments. These schemes overcome some of the problems associated with high-rise apartment buildings, such as the need for reliance on lifts (which can break down), and they engender a greater sense of security. Mothers of young children show a marked improvement in mental health when moved to lower storey flats. [20] Low-rise, high density development also is somewhat less expensive in terms of capital and management costs.

The disadvantages of these schemes are that they do nothing to alleviate the problems of density and space. In fact, pressure on space at ground level becomes even more intensive with low-rise buildings because a higher percentage of the site is covered with buildings. This means that open space, greenery, play space and recreational facilities are provided at a premium, causing poor environmental conditions. The situation becomes particularly difficult if provision has to be made for parking cars. Nevertheless, in overcrowded city areas where land for building is in short supply, low-rise, high-density housing often fulfils a useful role by accommodating small families and childless couples and, if properly allocated, could cater for the majority of housing needs of the wider community.

(c) Traditional housing

Traditionally built single- or two-storey terraced, detached or semi-detached housing is the most common form of housing development in many developed and developing countries; although it is gradually being superseded by high-rise or low-rise flats and apartments in urban areas where land is at a premium. Traditional housing is generally popular with residents because it allows a variety of design and construction materials, uses relatively simple building techniques, offers easy maintenance and cleaning, and brings independence from communally shared amenities. Compared with multistorey developments, traditional housing generally has less nuisance from transmitted noise, easier means of escape in case of fire, easier refuse disposal arrangements, and when a garden is provided, greater opportunities for recreation and play. The problems of

Terraced housing can provide excellent homes in many communities.

alienation, loneliness and distorted sense of perspective of the outside environment is also thought to be less compared with multistorey housing.

In general terms, traditional housing is most suitable for families, provided that reasonable housing density requirements can be met. Obviously, terraced housing offers better opportunities for obtaining higher housing densities compared with detached or semi-detached dwellings, which are also costlier to build, maintain and heat. However, dwelling size, mix and type also depend upon other factors, including consumer demand, age distribution of the population, desirability of the neighbourhood, and location in relation to cities, towns and employment.

2.1.2 Provision of housing with suitable dwelling size mix to enable community and social interaction

Many authorities faced with acute housing shortages have successfully adopted mixed development schemes comprising two- or three-storey houses for very large families, four-storey maisonettes for families with two to four children and tall blocks for the remainder. The ratio of each development depends upon the overall density to be achieved and the need/demand for a particular type of housing. If properly planned, reasonably high densities often can be achieved by using mixed developments without sacrificing basic healthy housing principles.

The main advantage of mixed development schemes is in encouraging a diversification of residents in terms of age groups, interests, and socioeconomic and cultural backgrounds, which in the long-term usually results in better community and social interaction. This point is particularly important to elderly or disabled people who are often based in nursing homes or hospitals and effectively cut-off from the wider community.

2.1.3 Provision of sufficient space between housing blocks so as not to intrude upon view, privacy or impede insolation and air circulation

Providing adequate space between buildings is of central importance when planning the micro-environment. The principal features of badly spaced housing include intrusion of view and privacy, overshadowing (which reduces sunlight and daylight) and interference with air circulation around buildings, and reduced ventilation to rooms. Poor spacing standards are usually (but not always) associated with high residential densities and overcrowding.

(a) Health effects
The indirect health effects of badly-spaced buildings concern those

Insufficient space between housing causes overshadowing and invades privacy.

diseases and conditions associated with poor natural lighting, sunlight deficiency and gloominess due to the absence of view; also, those conditions which are related to poor ventilation, poor indoor air quality and climate. In addition, fire has a higher chance to spread across narrow streets or to neighbouring buildings.

(b) Control measures

- Spacing standards can be applied as a legally enforceable planning control for new housing developments and also as a factor in assessing slum clearance options. Spacing standards should be applied with flexibility and consideration for other factors that might necessitate their relaxation. For example, in some countries, cultural factors are largely responsible for close space between housing blocks. In other cases, selective demolition of buildings causing overshadowing will alleviate the situation.

- A spacing standard widely used in England and Wales recommends that a general width of 21.5 m should be provided between parallel rows of dwellings to safeguard privacy, sunlight and daylight [23]. This standard is appropriate mainly for housing with a private front garden (or space for cars). It stipulates a minimum distance of 6 m between the footpath and house, assuming that the verge is 2 m in width with a 6 m-wide carriageway. Earlier spacing standards prescribed a spacing of 1 m along new streets, where front entrances opened directly onto the footpath.

- Current Scottish Building Regulations set a minimum horizontal distance of 18 m between mutually visible habitable room windows of one dwelling and those of another and lesser minimum distances down to 2 m, where such windows are set at an angle to each other. The main intention of this requirement is to preserve privacy. [24]

- In practice, spacing standards vary considerably with layout, concern for privacy and daylight requirements. For instance, a spacing standard [25] applied for development control purposes by one UK planning authority requires that 'if a living room is overlooked from an opposing dwelling or curtilage, the minimum eye to eye distance shall be 35 m'. (This applies in the private zone side, normally the rear of the dwelling.)

- The overall objectives of these design measures should be to ensure that buildings do not overshadow neighbouring property and that buildings in a proposed housing layout are so spaced as to satisfy not only the requirements of sunlight and daylight but also that they are not too near to each other as to intrude on privacy. On the other hand, the close-knit character of an old town centre may justify closer spacing of new buildings than would normally be desirable.

2.1.4 Provision for good orientation of buildings compatible with climatic conditions

The orientation of houses and other buildings is an important factor in the planning and design of new housing developments. In hot countries, correct orientation helps ensure that buildings are not overheated by the sun and that at least one cool, shady room is available within the house. Conversely, in cooler regions, orientation is a factor in encouraging radiation to warm dwellings by facing main living rooms towards the sun. Orientation planning also has to take account of other climatic factors such as wind direction and strength, which in cold regions can cause excessive infiltration of outside air. In these cases, wind-breaks and technical measures should be employed while concurrently maximizing sunlight into living quarters through correct orientation. Marked differences will inevitably occur in orientation of buildings in warmer and cold climates, but orientation also depends upon site arrangement and the purposes for which rooms are used. In particular, orientation is important in ensuring good natural lighting to rooms.

The ideal orientation of housing allows all sides of the building to be exposed to the sun for some period of the day. Living rooms should receive maximum sunlight, but in hot climates, orientation could help keep these rooms from becoming excessively hot. In hot countries, housing is usually planned for coolness by designing rooms oblong in shape with the short axes running NS or NNE and SSW. [26]

2.2 SPACE AND DENSITY REQUIREMENTS

2.2.1 Provision of housing built to suitable residential housing densities compatible with good environmental conditions and social and recreational needs

Space and density levels in many ways offer a crude but useful indicator of healthy housing provision in a given area. Many factors, not least indoor air quality, indoor climate, home safety, sanitation and environmental considerations, are dependent upon well-planned spacial control of residential densities. Different ways can be used to express residential housing densities as a measure of housing hygiene in a particular area. The objective of residential density norms is to prescribe limits for occupation of residential land compatible with good environmental conditions and planning criteria.

The gross density of an area is the product of the area and population of the neighbourhood, but housing densities are frequently expressed in terms of the **net residential density** or the number of habitable rooms per hectare. Another way of expressing density is by using persons per hectare, which has the advantage of giving direct numbers for planning environmental amenities, institutions and services, etc. A further distinction can be made between family housing and non-family housing and the need to define **child densities** in individual housing developments. Other indices of population and construction density and open space include the following: total residential floor area in relation to average height of buildings and the total area occupied by buildings

24

and space surrounding buildings; ratio of vacant lots to total number of lots in neighbourhood units and the density of structures or arrangement interfering with light, solarization, ventilation and circulation; percentage of neighbourhood devoted to playgrounds, parks and other open areas for recreation and relaxation; and nearness of residential neighbourhoods to major parks, beaches and other major outdoor open spaces and green belts. High-rise, high-density developments theoretically provide more open space per person within a given area compared with low-rise developments with similar occupancy levels. A distinction, therefore, has to be made between these individual environmental physical planning requirements and indoor space densities within the shelter itself.

(a) Health effects

High residential density within a given area often leads to unhygienic conditions and the spread of a number of communicable diseases as well as increased road traffic accidents (particularly where road traffic is not separated from pedestrian areas). However, reports on the relationship between population density and disease are ambiguous: some studies

High residential density presents a number of housing hygiene problems.

show a relationship between population density and health status, particularly overall mortality, lung cancer and cardiovascular diseases, while others do not.

However, noise levels are higher in areas with high residential densities, which can aggravate stress-related diseases. High densities of children in housing developments and parental dissatisfaction with housing are inter-related. However, whether any correlation exists between high densities and emotional disorders or whether this is merely an artifact of other unrelated factors is not known.

Certainly there are several examples where settlements have very high residential densities where stress or related illnesses do not appear to be a problem. This may be due to more effective patterns of social control and adaptation to high-density environments.

(b) Control measures

- Residential density standards can be usefully incorporated into planning briefs for new housing development plans and comprehensive redevelopment or area improvement schemes. However, the problems in achieving optimum density standards cannot be overcome by planning controls alone. Problems of enforcing densities in over-crowded regions are inextricably linked with the available supply of suitable housing and the demand for accommodation. When demand outstrips supply, high residential densities inevitably result.

- A number of countries have incorporated guidelines on desirable density norms into long-term development plans. For instance, the Greater London Development Plan recommends the following density standards for local authorities in the region:

  In schemes with a housing mix with dwellings for families with children and in schemes designed for non-family households, the overall density should not normally exceed 250 habitable rooms to the hectare and should provide low-rise dwellings for occupation by families wherever possible.

  Schemes that are mainly for family housing should be at somewhat lower densities and should not normally be above 210 habitable rooms to the hectare.

  To avoid the wasteful use of land for housing and infrastructure resources, the minimum density should be 175 habitable rooms to the hectare.

  Higher densities that would not otherwise be permitted may be

26

suitable for non-family housing up to a maximum of 350 habitable rooms to the hectare in locations with mixed developments of housing and commerce. [27]

2.2.2 Provision of housing of suitable size and usable floor area to satisfy human requirements for health, safety, family life, privacy, rest and domestic, recreational and social activities

The indoor space requirements for households depend upon the cultural, social and economic status of the population involved. There is little consensus concerning space requirements or the way in which space is appropriated within a dwelling unit despite the known importance of indoor space in satisfying human requirements for health, safety, family life, privacy, rest, and domestic, recreational and social activities. Indicators of indoor space are normally expressed in terms of crowding indices or at low-space levels in terms of over-crowding. Indoor space (i.e. the living area within the dwelling unit) is normally divided into **dwelling space** areas, such as living rooms, bedrooms and kitchens, and **ancillary** space, such as corridors, stairs and storage areas. The size, shape and number of rooms should be able to accommodate the activities normally carried out in these rooms, minimize the spread of infection, ease mental stress and accommodate the social needs of the household, i.e. an ergonistic approach. For example, young children require less space than teenagers, teenagers of different sexes should ideally not have to share bedrooms, and the husband and wife or other sexual partners would normally prefer bedroom accommodation separate from other family members. Indoor space may also be used for non-residential purposes, such as outwork or small cottage industries; separate non-residential shelter may be needed to house domestic animals. This may severely restrict the space available for residential use.

Indoor space levels are often extremely low in many developing countries throughout the world, particularly in urban centres, as a result of rapid urbanization, rural–urban migration and uncontrolled population growth.

For example, in Turkey, which has one of the highest occupancy rates in the Mediterranean area the annual increase of the urban population was 4% between 1975 and 1980. According to the 1980 census, the ratio of the urban population to the total population increased from 18.4 to 45% between 1950 and 1980. [28] This is much higher than the growth level of industrial development and has created problems of unemployment, low-income levels, squatter settlements, **overcrowding** and above all **poverty**. The true relationship between overcrowding and poverty

Table 2.1 Density of occupancy in selected developing countries [29]

Country	Average no. of persons/room			% of persons 1.5+ per room			% of persons 2.0+ per room			% of persons 3.0+ per room			Year
	R	U	T*	R	U	T	R	U	T	R	U	T	
Morocco	2.6	2.1	2.1	84.7	69.8	78.8	77.3	61.4	71.0	47.4	34.4	42.3	1971
Turkey	NA	NA	2.2	NA	NA	66.9	NA	NA	52.3	NA	NA	28.1	1970
Yugoslavia	1.5	1.3	1.4	53.8	39.8	47.8	36.3	23.5	30.8	11.4	6.1	9.2	1971
Rumania	1.4	1.3	1.4	45.8	38.5	43.1	30.5	23.3	27.8	11.0	6.7	9.4	1966
Bulgaria	1.1	1.3	1.2	31.8	47.0	38.4	18.8	28.6	23.1	5.7	8.9	7.1	1965
Czechoslovakia	1.1	1.0	1.1	22.4	21.6	21.9	14.6	7.5	10.4	3.0	1.2	1.9	1970

*R = rural; U = urban; T = total.
NA = no information available.

was illustrated by a survey of 60 houses in Ankara, where 72% of the population lives in squatter housing.

Table 2.1 gives examples of occupancy densities in developing European countries. In many of these countries, a family of perhaps four to six persons may live in one room.

(a) Health effects

Epidemiological studies have shown a positive association between crowding and respiratory diseases spread by transmission of infectious pathogens through air by droplet infection or aerosols. Crowding increases the risk of volatile infections (measles, rubella, rhinoviruses, influenza), droplet-transmitted (coughing, sneezing) infections, such as tuberculosis, pertussis, diptheria, cerebrospinal meningitis, viral meningitis, and colonization of endogenous pathogens producing pneumonia and bronchopneumonia.

Research studies carried out at the Budapest National Institute of Hygiene in Hungary have shown an added correlation between increased frequency of respiratory infections, such as bronchitis, rhinopharyngitis and tonsillitis in children aged 1–3 years living in overcrowded housing, especially if subjected to environmental air pollution (P. Rudnai, personal communication, 1985). This has been explained by the adverse effect of air pollution on the defence mechanism of the organism and the increased possibility of pathogen transmission which overcrowding brings.

Enteric diseases also are often more frequent in overcrowded housing. This can be partly explained by the increased opportunity for cross-infection through person-to-person contact and by indirect contact with the poor sanitary conditions associated with overcrowding.

However, it is not true to say that crowding elicits infectious diseases or that these diseases would not be spread in uncrowded conditions: the relationship is multilevel and complicated, but crowding increases vulnerability to possible infections by increasing frequency, duration and mode of contact between people and infectious agents. Thus, a sufficient dose of the pathogenic agent in respiratory illness (e.g. influenza, pneumonia and bronchitis) is readily spread, usually through air, in crowded and ill-ventilated rooms where people are coughing, sneezing or merely talking. [30] The sharing of beds by family members increases the transmission of airborne infections, and risks are exacerbated by the large variety of respiratory infections typically found in public places and the limited acquired immunity of the ambient population to respiratory diseases.

Studies by Stein in Edinburgh and Glasgow show a clear link between **tuberculosis** and the very severe degree of overcrowding in these two cities. [31] However, in addition to bad housing, poverty, malnutrition and poor environment have long been linked with tuberculosis. In addition, there are difficulties in distinguishing the significance of income, nutrition, occupational hazards and social class from poor housing in the aetiology of the disease. [32] In the developed countries, the spread of tuberculosis is now primarily linked with the presence of infectious diseases, and, although overcrowding is a subsidiary factor in the spread of the disease, it is no longer used as an index of housing deprivation. However, in developing countries with poor medical treatment facilities and poor sanitary conditions related to serious overcrowding, the association may still be prominent and relevant, and the number of cases of tuberculosis, especially among children, is still unacceptably high.

In general terms, **children** form the group most at risk from the effects of density and crowding on health. One study revealed retarded skeletal malnutrition in crowded children [33] and another reported a correlation

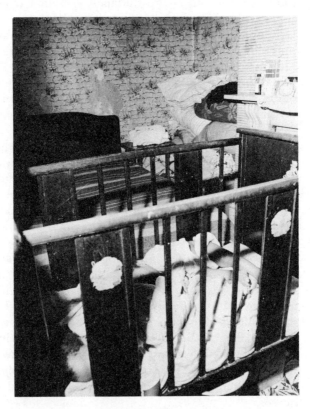

Overcrowded housing facilitates spread of respiratory and enteric diseases and contributes to accidents.

between psychoneurotic disorders in later life and living in crowded dwellings in childhood. [34] Also, the housing conditions in a UK national child development study showed that children in crowded homes missed more school for medical reasons (mainly bronchitis), that boys from crowded homes were slightly shorter than non-crowded boys and that children from crowded homes had lower scores for both reading and maths attainment at the age of 16. [35] No reasons are suggested for these findings, but educational attainment probably depends partly on the home environment. For example, Wilner *et al.* [36] noted that one consequence of crowding was lack of sleep for family members. Thus, lack of sleep may cause a child to be regarded as backward and incompetent in school, and have an adverse effect on his/her education. Burn and scald injuries to children are higher in crowded houses, particularly those without separate cooking and lavatory accommodations for each family and without adequate indoor playing space. [37]

Overcrowding also may promote disturbances in **mental health** by creating confusion, noise and lack of privacy, which may lead to low self-esteem, depression, feelings of annoyance and interpersonal conflicts. For instance, Brandon [38] has suggested that overcrowding, lack of privacy and lack of housing facilities may create a situation where violence may erupt when some triggering factor operates. Overcrowding also may increase promiscuity and incestuous relationships, which can add further tension and stress within the family. However, adaptive mechanisms help to compensate for the adverse health impact of crowding on social organization and stress responses can be expected to depend on socioeconomic and cultural factors. This may explain why in some regions of the world where crowding indices are very high (e.g. Hong Kong and parts of S.E. Asia) there is no obvious evidence of any causal relationship between crowding and illness.

(b) Control measures

In the developing countries, space norms and crowding indices are primarily an artefact of socioeconomic and cultural status. Short-term remedies for controlling overcrowding are complex, costly and often intrinsically insoluble. Policy-makers are often confronted with the problem of dealing with the underlying causes, that is, in stemming uncontrolled population growth and urbanization. Any long-term comprehensive planning strategy must therefore address these issues by improving rural conditions, employment opportunities and fiscal support measures aimed at discouraging further urbanization or setting up family planning schemes and other measures to encourage birth control and restrict family size. At a local level, the optimum design and allocation of indoor space at the formative planning stage could enable additional housing space to be added at a later date when the economic conditions improve or the demands for space decrease, e.g. provision of one or two rooms with a facility to extend or 'bolt on' additional rooms or storeys at a later date. This practice is favoured in many Mediterranean countries and in the USSR and other Eastern European countries planned increases in space standards are incorporated into each five-year plan. However, this does little to increase current provision of space levels where demand exceeds supply despite rigorous management and legal control over space allocation.

In reality, good space planning is a compromise between functional and performance requirements and minimum overall floor areas for the dwelling that are themselves dependent upon space availability. Ergonistic space planning (which is based upon the size of the family and the activities the occupiers want to pursue within the home) assumes a detailed knowledge and understanding of people's housing needs and is much to be preferred to standardized numbers, sizes and layout of housing units – providing of course that sanitary design norms can be maintained (e.g. by ensuring that lavatories do not interconnect with other rooms or that kitchens are kept separate from living room areas).

Overcrowding in urban areas is caused chiefly by a shortfall between the supply and demand for housing that people can afford to rent or buy (i.e. occupancy rate decreases in proportion with an increase in income levels). Thus, in the high-income groups, the family is smaller and the number of rooms increases, resulting in a lower occupancy rate, while in the low-income groups, the family is bigger and can afford fewer rooms, which subsequently have a much higher occupancy rate.

This situation does not necessarily improve as economic conditions get better, because in this situation land prices and rents are pushed up and the poor have to pay more for the same or (depending on demand) less living space. The economics of the market place thus determine occupancy rates and can only be compensated through social intervention in the market to provide uncrowded housing space at a price that people can afford to rent or buy. In fact, space standards in the developing countries are likely to be a balance between a number of economic and planning factors, as reflected by housing investment resources, land availability and political/social/cultural constraints. However, in some communities, 'crowding' is not perceived as being detrimental to health or family enjoyment but is an established part of the way of life and social tradition. In these cases, removal or control of the negative effects of overcrowding (i.e. unhygienic conditions) would be preferred to family disintegration, compulsory removal or insensitive resettlement policies. Examples of suitable action to control overcrowding are detailed below.

- The negative effects of crowding, such as transmission of certain communicable diseases and increased likelihood of home accidents, can be controlled by maintaining satisfactory indoor air quality, sanitation and home safety measures.

- Large-scale provision of suitably designed low-cost housing which low-income groups can afford to rent or buy should be encouraged. Such buildings should be built to basic space standards with the facility to enlarge or add on further rooms as the need arises or as economic conditions improve. The long-term aim should be to optimize space standards to enable occupants to work, rest and play in reasonable conditions of comfort.

- Housing should be regarded as part of the whole environment. Where environmental air pollution is high, consideration should be given to requiring higher space standards to compensate for this impact.

- The renting of dwelling space in public and privately rented housing above permitted occupancy standards as prescribed by housing codes and implemented through a licensing scheme or tenancy agreement should be prohibited. However, careful consideration would need to be given to how this might be enforced.

- Social intervention in the housing market may be necessary to prevent land prices and rents from exceeding the ability of low-income groups to pay for uncrowded housing space. This may be achieved by publicly subsidizing new house building, regulating land prices, controlling rent levels, providing housing benefit payments to low-income groups to assist with house purchase or rent, or providing interest-free loans or cheap building materials to prospective house builders.

- To reduce crowding in urban areas, new towns and urban satellites could be created, which can also provide employment opportunities.

- Areas of overcrowded slum housing could be redeveloped and densities reduced through change of dwelling size mix.

As yet, no minimum standards based on meeting human health needs have been developed, although a number of countries have instituted their own based on pragmatic and economic considerations. The following are examples of space standards endorsed by international agencies or adopted by countries for legislative action.

- A WHO Expert Committee on the Public Health Aspects of Housing [12] proposed that one of the fundamentals of a healthful residential environment should be 'a safe and structurally sound, adequately maintained, separate, self-contained dwelling unit for each

Table 2.2 Minimum floor space by family size proposed by the United Nations [39]

Room	Index of capacity* (in m²)								
	2/3	2/4	3/4	3/5	3/6	4/6	4/7	4/8	5/8
1. Living space									
Dining area	5	5	5	6	6	6	7	8	8
Living room	13	13	13	14	16	16	17	18	18
2. Kitchen	6	7	7	7	8	8	8	8	8
3. Bedroom (parents)	14	14	14	14	14	14	14	14	14
4. Bedroom 2	8	12	8	12	12	12	12	12	12
5. Bedroom 3	–	–	8	8	12	8	12	12	12
6. Bedroom 4	–	–	–	–	–	8	8	12	8
7. Bedroom 5	–	–	–	–	–	–	–	–	8
7. Bathroom with WC	4	4	4	4	4	4	4	4	4
7. Bathroom, no WC	–	–	–	–	–	–	–	–	–
7. Separate WC	–	–	–	1.2	1.2	1.2	1.2	1.2	1.2
7. Extra washbasin	–	–	–	1	1	1	1	2	2
8. Storage space	1.5	1.5	1.5	2	2	2	2.5	2.5	2.5
9. Additional bedroom (optional)	–	–	–	–	–	–	–	(8)	(8)
Total	51.5	56.5	60.5	69.2	76.2	80.2	86.7	93.7	97.7

*The first number refers to the number of bedrooms, the second to the number of occupants.

household, if so desired, with each dwelling unit providing at least the following:

(a) A sufficient number of rooms, usable floor area and volume of enclosed space to satisfy human requirements for health and for family life consistent with the prevailing cultural and social pattern of that region and so utilized that living or sleeping rooms are not overcrowded.

(b) At least a minimum degree of desired privacy:
  (i) for individual persons within the household; and
  (ii) for the members of the household against undue disturbance by external factors.

(c) Suitable separation of rooms as used for:
  (i) sleeping by adolescent and adult members of the opposite sex except husband and wife; and
  (ii) housing of domestic animals apart from the living room of the dwelling unit.'

These needs can be expressed in terms of space requirements to perform household activities and/or for occupancy standards.

- A United Nations report [39] on the use of space in dwellings proposed minimum floor space (in m^2) according to the size of family (Tables 2.2 and 2.3).

- The UN report also concluded that, based on the calculations that a double bed required $7.6\,m^2$ of space for movement on three sides and a wardrobe closet required $1.5\,m^2$ for itself plus another $1.5\,m^2$ for movement, the minimum area of a bedroom for two persons is $10.6\,m^2$.

Table 2.3 Minimum floor space requirements for family of three to five proposed by the United Nations [39]

Room	m^2
Living plus dining room space	18.6
Kitchen	7.0
First bedroom	13.9
Second bedroom	12.0
Third bedroom	8.0
Total usable floor space	59.5*

*This can be compared with the average total floor area of 50 m^2 for aided self-help housing in Columbia.

- Another set of standards setting out minimum inhabitable surfaces for rooms in the European countries, prepared jointly by the International Union of Family Organizations (IUFO) and the International Federation for Housing and Town Planning [40], is given in Table 2.4.

- A survey by Lebegge [41] on room sizes in European countries found considerable variation in crowding standards. He concluded that a number of reasons accounted for these differences, including climate, way of life, ideas concerning internal arrangement and economic considerations. His data showed the minimum, maximum and average 'inhabitable surface' in the European Region at the time (Table 2.5).

- The American Public Health Service/Centres for Disease Control of the US Public Health Service recommended the following housing maintenance and occupancy ordinance. [42]

  1. Maximum occupancy of any dwelling unit shall not exceed the lesser of the following two requirements:
      (i) First occupant, at least $14.2\,m^2$ habitable floor area; second and subsequent occupants, at least $9.4\,m^2$.
      (ii) Permitted number shall be less than 2 times the number of habitable rooms within the dwelling unit.

Table 2.4. Minimum inhabitable surface per size of family [40]

Room	\multicolumn{9}{c}{Index of capacity* (in m^2)}								
	2/3	2/4	3/4	3/5	3/6	4/6	4/7	4/8	5/8
Day rooms									
Kitchen–dining	6	7	7	8	8	8	8	8	8
Dining room	5	5	5	6	6	6	7	8	8
Living room	13	13	13	14	16	16	17	18	18
Total area	24	25	25	28	30	30	32	34	34
Sleeping rooms									
For parents	14	14	14	14	14	14	14	14	14
For one child	8	12	8	12	12	12	12	12	12
For two children	–	–	8	8	12	8	12	12	12
For three children	–	–	–	–	–	8	8	12	8
For four children	–	–	–	–	–	–	–	–	8
Total area	22	26	30	34	38	42	46	50	54
Total	46	51	55	62	68	72	78	84	88

*The first figure refers to the number of bedrooms, the second to the total number of persons normally accommodated.

Table 2.5 Minimum and maximum inhabitable surface (in m^2) in the European Region

	Type 1	Type 2	Surface* Type 3	Type 4	Type 5
Minimum	20.7	35.9	49.5	60.6	42.9
Average	32.9	53.0	64.3	78.6	61.5
Maximum	48.2	82.3	97.9	104.7	96.8

*Key:
1. One floor residence (flat or bungalow with one bedroom) for an elderly couple.
2. Flat in a building without a lift (or in a two-storey house) for a family of four in an urban zone.
3. Flat in a building with a lift (or in a two-storey house) for a family of five in an urban zone.
4. Two-storey house or apartment for a family of seven.
5. House for a family of five in a rural zone.

2. Every dwelling of two or more rooms occupied for sleeping purposes by one occupant shall contain at least 6.6 m^2 of floor space for the first floor occupant and every room occupied for sleeping purposes by more than one occupant shall contain at least 4.73 m^2 of floor space for each occupant thereof.

Non-habitable floor space and storage space for personal effects of each permissible occupant also are defined in the ordinance.

- In the UK, recommended standards for floor space in public housing have been laid down and often serve as a basis for granting loan sanction and approving housing subsidy (Table 2.6).

Table 2.6 Recommended standards for floor space in new public housing in the UK [43]

	6	5	Number of people 4 3		2	1
			Minimum net floor area (in m^2)			
3-Storey house*	97.53	93.8	–	–	–	–
2-Storey terrace	92.00	84.5	74.13	–	–	–
2-Storey semi or end	92.00	81.7	71.5	–	–	–
Flat	86.4	79.0	69.7	–	–	–
Single-storey house	83.6	75.2	66.9	56.7	44.6	29.7
General storage						
Houses**	4.6	4.6	4.6	4.18	3.7	2.8
Flats and maisonettes	1.39	1.39	1.39	1.11	0.92	0.74
Inside	–	–	–	–	–	–
Outside	1.85	1.85	1.85	1.85	1.85	1.85

* Figures require modification with a built-in garage.
** Some of this may be on an upper floor but at least 2.3 m^2 should be at ground level.

- In the Soviet Union, the 'norm' for rationing living space is expressed in terms of specified floor space per person, rather than in numbers of persons per room. In the Russian Soviet Federation Socialist Republic, the sanitary norm for dwellings is the minimum permitted by civil codes, is $9\,m^2$ per person irrespective of age and sex. The significance of the norm is described in a Soviet housing textbook [44] as follows:

  > The establishment of a living space norm does not mean that a person may not be assigned a larger or smaller living space than a stipulated norm, providing that a person occupies space within the limits of the norm, it may not be taken away from him without his consent. If he occupies space less than the standard norm and is required to vacate it, he is entitled to alternative accommodation, but it may also be less than the norm.

- The Uniform Building Code of the International Association of Building Officials recommends that at least one room in a dwelling unit has an area of $11.3\,m^2$. In addition, every room used for sleeping purposes must have an area of $8.5\,m^2$ and no kitchen must have an area of less than $4.7\,m^2$. [40]

- The WHO Regional Office for Europe recommends that $12\,m^2$ of habitable space per person be provided in housing.

2.2.3 Provision of sufficient open space for active and passive recreation and aesthetically pleasing environment

Open space can provide some of the resources needed for active and passive recreation and also can contribute to a sense of well-being by providing aesthetically pleasing settings. Open space not only helps reduce residential densities but also facilitates the vital role played by green plants in oxygenation and controlling carbon dioxide. The report of a WHO Expert Committee on Environmental Health Aspects of Metropolitan Planning and Development [2] also drew attention to the other roles played by open green space in metropolitan planning:

(a) *Protective*: Green belts serve as living barriers between residential areas and industry: they protect against noise and fumes from motor traffic and they control expansion and divide urban areas from one another. Green belts are neither rigid barriers nor are they screens to hide ugliness: they act as a protection against the undesirable spread of noise, dust and fumes, and against wind and excessive cold or heat. They also are a microclimate regulator against the dangers of pollution.

(b) *Recreational*: Open space provides for a wide variety of recreational needs, such as activity for small children, who should be able to play near home, and for older children, who generally prefer more noisy games but whose playgrounds should be in the immediate neighbourhood. Open space also provides for sports and unorganized games for teenagers and young adults. Allotments also are a valuable use of open space in urban areas for growing food crops and flowers. Kitchen gardens are an important feature of many developing countries in the European Region.

(c) *Other needs*: Open space around schools, day nurseries, hospitals and health centres is necessary for calm and tranquillity. Important ecological considerations also relate to the role of open space in the conservation of natural resources that are important not only at a microlevel but also at a macrolevel through farmland, parks, game preserves and forests. They help to maintain the balance of nature and prevent reduced agricultural output of soil after deforestation, erosion and pollution.

In terms of the housing environment, open space makes the best use of fresh air, circulation and sunshine and, if properly controlled, can prevent encroachment into rural or agricultural outer regions. The protection of nature and open space usually requires positive action by the state through its land policy and planning laws. Such plans not only protect existing open space but can make open space available in urban areas as part of an overall redevelopment programme.

2.3 SOCIAL REQUIREMENTS

One of the primary objectives of balanced economic and social planning is to achieve high total production and a corresponding increase in the standard of living, while creating a condition in which the social values and culture of a society can be best expressed. The achievement of this dual objective, however, depends on the rational location of production, consumption and services in an efficient, healthful, comfortable and pleasing environment.

The report of a WHO Scientific Group on the Development of Environmental Health Criteria for Urban Planning acknowledges that certain sociophysical factors in the environment of predominantly residential areas are essential to promoting and enhancing the physical well-being of the residents. [2] This concerns the way individuals and communities form relationships either formally in clubs, associations, or civil, political and cultural groups or informally from day-to-day contact in shops, at work or when using transport. The role of these relationships for personal and social well-being and for reducing stress and anxiety cannot be overstated.

2.3.1 Provision of facilities for normal family life, hobbies, recreation, play and social activities

The shelter as a social setting has to accommodate individual and different interests and activities involving any or all of the family, with or without visitors. It must be designed to provide reasonable individual and group privacy as well as facilities for family life as part of a community of friends and relations. The shelter should therefore provide for children's play, homework, sewing and reading, hobbies, entertaining friends and callers, and making love in reasonable conditions of privacy from other family members. The adequacy and design of indoor space are two crucial factors in achieving this objective.

2.3.2 Provision of facilities for normal community and wide social life

The WHO Scientific Group on the Development of Environmental Health Criteria for Urban Planning [2] drew attention to the importance of sociophysical planning aspects of residential areas as stated by planning criteria as follows:

1. Urban planners should consider people not only as residents of large cities but also as members of communities, neighbourhoods and networks within those urban areas.

2. Such communities should be planned or maintained as residential units with recognizable spatial limits, so that people can identify themselves with their locality.

3. The residential clusters – neighbourhoods, districts, subcommunities – should have easy communal contact routes within and between them.

4. A range of facilities – schools, stores and buildings for recreational and assembly purposes – should be provided to encourage the development of interacting community units.

5. Through-traffic should, as far as possible, be kept from straining or severing community interactions and relationships.

6. Provision should be made for safe and easily identifiable access to units in a residential neighbourhood and for a balance between the opportunities for privacy and for interaction

of the individual and the family within the residential environment.

A number of social studies have supported these goals – people need roots, and the importance of the shelter as part of a wider social setting cannot be overstressed.

The many links with the district where members live, including friends, schools, familiar haunts, associations and memories of a lifetime, offer people a dimension in their lives the value of which cannot be measured. This is particularly important to elderly people who often cannot easily adapt to moving to a completely different environment. Enforced moves to new, unfamiliar housing because of slum clearance, employment opportunities etc., often have an adverse effect on social adaptation to new settings, particularly where people are moved from traditional housing to high-rise accommodation or new settlements.

2.3.3 Provision of facilities for rest and recuperation from sickness or ill-health

The home is not just a place to sleep and eat; it also is a refuge from the rigours of work, school or other activities, and a place to recover from sickness or ill-health. Therefore, peaceful, pleasant surroundings with sufficient indoor space and provision for privacy are important considerations in healthy housing and personal enjoyment.

Community care facilities for people recovering from sickness or illness should be an integral part of any housing hygiene policy. Good housing with family or community support provides a suitable environment for convalescence (see section 2.10.4).

Efforts to preserve and enhance physical and mental well-being of accident-prone people, such as the sick, chronically ill and disabled, are a necessary accompaniment to the more immediate work of accident prevention, e.g. avoidance of drugs which could affect balance or other faculties; attention to good vision, good muscle strength and agility; good footwear and foot care; proper nutrition; good general health care; building of self-confidence; maintaining family and social contacts; and freedom from financial worries. [45]

Non-housing requirements such as these can be provided only through social policies designed to help those who, because of sickness and poor health, cannot help themselves. However, doctors and health officials can help by ensuring that patients who, because of illness are prone to home accidents, are properly treated and for example, referring people to ear specialists, opticians and chiropodists where necessary. Medical care facilities, such as burn and poison units, and other care services, should also be made available.

2.3.4 Provision of reasonable conditions of privacy

Privacy or 'freedom from what is felt as unwanted intrusion by other people' can be expressed by different factors including visual, aural and social criteria. People's reaction to privacy depends as much on their own attitudes as on physical facts. Intrusion relates mainly to being seen, noise, social contact and communication. [46] The subjective reaction of people to each of these situations means that control measures and standards are extremely difficult to define, and little research has been conducted into the benefits and disbenefits of privacy or its effects on mental health and well-being. Clearly, cultural and adaptive aspects need to be considered. In some cultures, all family members share the same room (and sometimes bed) for sleeping whereas in other cultures, private sleeping quarters separated from the rest of the family are preferred. Similarly, in most cultures, people prefer privacy during personal toilet and washing activities while in others, this is not considered important or in some cases achievable. The need for privacy of the dwelling in relation to other dwellings and the wider community also varies significantly. Privacy must be considered in relation to a number of benefits, some of which may be incompatible with other housing hygiene requirements, e.g. large windows increase daylight, but could reduce privacy and security by making interiors visible from outside; easy access to a housing development reduces privacy in gardens and front rooms; low-rise, high-density development multiplies the chances of intrusions of all kinds. Design measures can only partly compensate for imbalances between opposing factors such as these.

A report by the UK Department of Environment [46] noted that research is needed to analyse physical conditions and people's reactions to them to help establish privacy requirements. This would include such factors as distance and lighting to degrees of perception, the recognition of a person's physical attitude (standing, sitting) and his facial expression. It should relate the extent of view into rooms with the characteristics of the window, the position of the viewer and the angle of view. It also should study the effect of curtain meshes and the two-way loss of light and vision through the curtain, the movement of passers-by in terms of angle and duration of the intrusive views and the effectiveness of screening by vegetation.

Existing privacy standards are based mainly on spacing and visual standards, which may not always be relevant to sensible town planning. Reducing the spacing between buildings by imaginative screening and design measures is often possible without compromising on privacy requirements. However, crude space norms should not be the sole basis for privacy standards. Where privacy requirements are applied, these should be incorporated into design briefs at the planning stage after having taken into account the various social and cultural needs.

2.3.5 Provision of opportunities for achieving aesthetic satisfaction in the home and its surroundings

A number of studies indicate that residents tend to judge the value of their home and housing environment largely by appearance and perceived visual impressions of various kinds. This may make a sizeable contribution to their moods, i.e. whether they feel contented or depressive. The matter though, is largely conceptual, housing is often a status symbol, a sign of wealth, achievement or otherwise. In the surroundings of the house, **view** is an important factor, but the aesthetic nature of view means that it is somewhat difficult to measure or define. What is known is that the benefits of view can be assessed by examining the main components of the visual field and evaluating those factors which by common consent have a pleasing or unpleasing appearance. The total impression of view is affected by the magnitude of pleasant and unpleasant elements but also takes into account shape, size, lighting, movement, colour, patterns, texture, detail and variety of the outside environment. Even small changes to one of these factors can influence satisfaction of view. These same factors apply equally to aesthetic satisfaction within the home. In these cases, provisions such as furnishings and consumer appliances are important and relevant to perceived satisfaction.

(a) Health effects
The importance of view for engendering a sense of well-being and satisfaction with the housing environment, as well as being a therapeutic tool in aiding recovery from sickness, should not be underestimated. A gloomy outside environment tends to make people feel shut in or oppressed. Aesthetic satisfaction in the home will also benefit mental health and well-being although there are differences in placing a 'health' value on aesthetic considerations that are indeterminate and dependent upon social, cultural, economic and individual factors.

(b) Control measures
There are many difficulties encountered in defining how to achieve aesthetic satisfaction in the surroundings of the home. Much depends upon the topography, climate and presence of natural geographical

features that can be used to give a pleasant perspective from the home. Location of industrial and commercial activities in relation to the home is also important, as accompanying noise, pollution and unsightliness may adversely affect health and well-being. However, physical planning and design measures such as control of new industrial developments can be engineered to create a pleasing outlook. These considerations should not be overlooked when designing new housing or when evaluating existing housing for redevelopment or improvement.

- Enclosed backyards should be avoided wherever possible. Gardens, where provided, should be open to view from the house. Any screen used to secure privacy or roofed yard space should be so placed as not to obstruct this view or cause undue enclosure. Huts, garages and outbuildings also should be so positioned as not to impede views from windows of principal living areas.

- Aesthetic satisfaction is increased considerably by design measures that maximize brightness of the external environment, e.g. avoidance of overshadowing from neighbouring buildings, good orientation to facilitate sunshine to outside areas and maximize daylight within rooms, and use of bright, visually appealing colours in buildings. Anything in fact that serves to make the micro-environment attractive. Similar factors apply to the indoor environment, particularly choice of wall coverings and furnishings.

- Within the immediate environment, the view should extend not only beyond the line of opposite buildings in a narrow street but also provide some perspective immediately outside the building. Even a small gap between buildings (in view) through which open country is visible can be extremely valuable in creating an impression of openness. The prospect of providing distant horizons is usually limited by the topography and elevation of the site. Housing on flat sites shuts off 10° or so of altitude from the horizon in which views of distance tend to be concentrated, but conversely views from upper storeys or on elevated sites can bring unpleasant views into the foreground as well as pleasant ones in the distance.

- Ideally, a distant view of the countryside or some other pleasant landscape and depth in the relatively short view will mitigate unpleasant impressions of building and road surfaces. [46]

- The view inside the layout is strongly inter-related with sunlight and privacy, recreational space, access and parking, private garden area, maintenance arrangements for public amenities, soft surface play areas and landscaping. [46] Ecologically sound urban designs which

44

combine nature and buildings (e.g. setting the development in deep countryside and giving it an inner texture of greenness) will often please residents. Vegetation (bushes, creepers and trees) also can be effectively planted to fill in solid angles in the field of view. The colour and movement of vegetation are both important to aesthetic satisfaction with housing surroundings.

2.3.6 Provision of opportunities to enable work activities to be carried out at home

In some countries, one or more members of the family often use the home as a place of work. Small cottage industries are a normal part of the financial infrastructures of rural communities. In many cases, the women and children undertake this work to supplement family income, which is often insufficient to pay for food, clothing, heating/cooking fuel and other basic necessities. In shanty towns, home work has become institutionalized with small industries serving fringe activities for street vendors and servicing the shanty towns themselves. Therefore, opportunities must be made available to enable low-income groups to carry out work activities at home. However, the adaptation of traditional housing for some work activities may not always be possible, although in many cases, a spare room can be easily converted into a suitable workroom. Huts or garages also are easily converted for a number of applications. It is also a trend in developed countries for more and more people to work from home, partly because of the increase in use of computer and information technology. However, the suitability of housing for carrying out work activities must depend upon the nature of the work, which might be a source of additional home accidents, including poisoning, asphyxiation or fire. Many industrial processes use chemicals and propellants that could adversely affect air quality. Other work activities (e.g. needlework) will require additional natural and artificial lighting to avoid eye strain. No hard-and-fast rules can be made for controlling home work activities, although in some cases special workshops can be provided in the settlements themselves. Where possible work activities in the home should be monitored in order to advise on any necessary safety or health precautions or to regulate operations through other control procedures.

2.4   SHELTER REQUIREMENTS

Shelter is a synonymous term for the individual home, flat, dwelling or rental unit: in fact, any residence or structure where people live. At a basic level, the shelter must protect against hostile elements in the immediate and wider environments, such as adverse climatic features, dangerous animals or external air pollutants. In addition, it must normally provide security against human intrusion. At a more sophisticated level, the shelter is also a social setting and a place of refuge and rest from the rigours of work, school or other activities. Its value therefore cannot be assessed in narrow hygiene terms but must be seen as part of a much more overall function in satisfying social, aesthetic and intangible human needs.

2.4.1 Provision of suitable shelter to ensure that housing is windproof and weathertight and otherwise protected from external elements and natural hazards

Different climatic and geographical factors in the various subregions and countries of the world mean that shelter requirements in relation to external elements and natural hazards differ widely from one area to another. Geographical considerations, such as ambient temperature, seasonal characteristics, sunlight, rainfall, snowfall and any susceptibility to natural hazards (e.g. earthquakes, volcanoes, cyclones, lightning, drought, flooding and landslip), are all important to housing design and planning.

For example, Mediterranean countries have very long hot summers, but their winters can be cold with moderate rain and snowfall. The southern European Region also is characterized by high seismic activity and earthquakes, which are not problems in western and northern Europe. In the latter regions, colder winters and higher rainfall, snow, frost and wind are major factors affecting the built environment.

Information on climate is thus integral to any healthy housing policy; it enables planners to choose or evaluate a site that will not be unduly affected by adverse weather conditions or natural hazards. This information is also important when considering design factors for ameliorating unfavourable climatic conditions (e.g. by providing shelter from strong sunshine or wind) while at the same time taking advantage of beneficial climatic and geographical features. For example, outside ambient temperatures can be used when evaluating thermal requirements and a knowledge of rainfall patterns helps in assessing surface water drainage requirements.

In many cases, civil engineering and housing design measures now make possible the adaptation of the housing environment to minimize the effects of adverse climatic conditions and natural hazards. Therefore, in assessing the consequences of external elements and natural hazards, an evaluation should be made of local conditions, including seismic and wind forces, meteorological and hydrological data, vectors and disease-transmitting organisms, and other climatic and natural conditions that could affect the health and comfort of the occupants. [3] Housing which is situated in areas subject to natural hazards such as regular flooding, earthquakes, volcanic disturbance, landslip or other geographical phenomena should be adequately protected where possible. Alternatively, settlements should be resited in a safer location. Preferably, restrictions should be made on building permits in these areas after consideration of past history and site information.

(a) Rainfall and penetrating dampness

Rainfall is clearly important to housing hygiene not just because it is the source of water supplies but is also the cause of most penetrating dampness in housing (including flooding). It is therefore important to have information on mean annual rainfall to determine water collection and storage requirements and for calculating surface water drainage and anti-flooding measures (e.g. in calculating surface run-off from roofs, gutters, yards, roads and concreted areas). Information on annual mean driving rain indices can also indicate resistance of different housing designs to rain penetration. Rainfall can cause housing dampness either directly through penetration of the shelter or indirectly by adding to condensation and water vapour levels inside the shelter (see section 2.7.1f).

Structural dampness can be a serious source of building damage and cause for complaint. It is usually caused by poor design, poor building maintenance, use of unsuitable building materials, dampness rising from the ground or by penetration of rainfall through defects in the structure.

(i) Health effects

Although epidemiological studies are contradictory, damp housing is generally considered a contributory factor to rheumatism, arthritis or respiratory diseases such as pneumonia, bronchitis and upper respiratory infections. Dampness can also affect mental health by causing stress to people worried about high heating bills (which are higher in damp houses) and destruction of clothes, furnishings, etc. Dampness may also affect social well-being by reducing the attractiveness of the home as a social venue, such as occurs when walls become damp or covered in unsightly mould. In other cases, dampness becomes a stigma that may give rise to feelings of shame, depression, alienation or a sense of injustice. In addition, some physiological effects may be brought about by changes in the thermal environment aggravated by dampness (see section 2.8.1). This can be critical in people with impaired thermoregulatory controls, such as children and the elderly.

Typical tidemark associated with rising dampness.

(ii) Control measures

- A damp-free environment should be regarded as a first priority by policy-makers. Housing codes and ordinances should be formulated to ensure that housing is constructed of suitable materials and of a design that protects against rainfall and penetrating dampness.

- Penetrating and rising dampness can be prevented by good housing design and construction techniques. In existing housing, penetrating dampness should be remedied by appropriate repair measures. Table 2.6 illustrates some possible causes of housing dampness and suitable remedial measures.

- Built-up areas, particularly residential areas, should not be subject to flooding, even at infrequent intervals.

- Flood prevention measures and improved surface water drainage should be adequate especially in low-lying areas. These include the

(con't on p. 52)

Damp-proof courses can be installed through silicon injection to exterior walls.

Table 2.7 Causes and remedies of penetrating dampness

Situation and form of dampness	Probable cause	Suitable remedy
Roofs		
Dampness localized	1. Cracked or defective roof coverings	1. Repair or renewal
	2. Faulty or absent flashings around vent pipes, chimney, etc.	2. Replace to appropriate detail
	3. Inadequate damp course	3. Replace
	4. Leaking or blocked gutters	4. Repair, renew or unblock

Technical and social requirements

Situation and form of dampness	Probable cause	Suitable remedy
Dampness fairly extensive but mainly linear	1. Faulty valley gutters or faulty gutters behind parapet walls	1. Remove and renew
	2. Inadequate damp course to parapet walls	2. Insert new one
	3. Faulty skirtings to flat roofs	3. Replace to appropriate detail
	4. Underfelt to pitched roofs incorrectly finished at eaves	4. Refix to be watertight
	5. Eaves details allow rain or snow to enter	5. Weatherproof eaves
Dampness fairly widespread	1. Drying out of construction water (May last several years in certain conditions)	1. Provide suitable heating and ventilation
	2. Unsuitable roof covering	2. Renew with suitable alternative
	3. Inadequate pitch or lap for type of weatherproof finish and degree of exposure	3. Relay roof covering to proper pitch and lap
Walls		
Dampness localized	1. Roof faults as above but where moisture is accessible to walls	1. See above
	2. Faulty wall jointing	2. Repoint joints
	3. Defective window sills or reveals	3. Repair or replace
	4. Cracked walls or rendering	4. Repair or rerender
	5. Cavity wall ties bridged by mortar	5. Clean off mortar
	6. Wall cavities obstructed	6. Remove obstructions
	7. Water leaking from dripping overflow pipe, leaking gutters, downpipes or drains	7. Remedy cause of overflow. Repair or renew leaking gutters. downpipes or drains
	8. Leaking pipes or joints in ducting or chased into wall	8. Repair
	9. Hygroscopic salts in walls or rendering	9. Treat walls or rerender
	10. Dampness to ceilings above flat roofs	10. Provide cross-ventilation to roof space and improve insulation

Shelter requirements

Situation and form of dampness	Probable cause	Suitable remedy
Dampness mainly in linear form	1. Rising dampness caused by absence of damp-proof course (DPC)	1. Provide suitable horizontal DPC
	2. DPC deteriorated in old buildings, incorrectly placed too near ground, with outside obstructions or incorrectly positioned floor slabs, etc.	2. Renew DPC. Remove outside obstructions
	3. Horizontal DPC over lintels incorrectly detailed	3. Replace to correct detail
	4. Wall panel joints not waterproof	4. Waterproof them
	5. Expansion joints not waterproof	5. Waterproof them
Dampness fairly widespread	1. Drying out of wet construction	1. Provide suitable heating and ventilation
	2. Presence of hygroscopic salts	2. Treat walls and rerender
	3. Walling porous, inadequately thick or protective against rain in exposed conditions	Remove and replace with impervious alternative
	4. Cavity filled with insulation that is not waterproof	4. Line-out walls with vertical damp-proof membrane and/or render outside walls
Floors	1. Dampness fairly equal over solid ground floor caused by lack of adequate damp-proof membrane or slow drying out of construction water	1. Provide damp-proof membrane to floors to correct detail or assist drying out process through heating and ventilation
	2. Suspended ground floors with insulation on underside of joists may have condensation in airspace if insulating material forms a vapour barrier	2. Provide cross-ventilation to floor space

51

following: civil engineering measures to raise the height of river banks and other water courses; providing surface water drainage systems, storm water relief sewers and flood barriers; adopting planning control measures to prohibit housing development in areas prone to flooding; and design measures, such as constructing housing on stilts or elevating them in some other way above flood levels.

- In highly exposed places, tall buildings should be adequately protected against the effects of lightning by lightning conductors and other preventive measures. Low-rise buildings usually do not require special precautions.

(b) Strong winds

The main structural elements of a building, such as walls, windows, roofs and outbuildings (e.g. huts and sheds) should be strong enough to resist typical wind speeds in a given situation. Wind speed usually increases with height above ground and also varies with ground roughness. These factors should be considered when planning new housing developments.

(i) Health effects

Excessive wind can lower thermal comfort, particularly if the building is draughty, in poor repair or poorly insulated. Strong winds are also frequently associated with driving rain, which can cause penetrating dampness. Housing situated in areas exposed to hurricanes and excessive wind gusts risk collapse and structural instability, which can be a major source of injury.

(ii) Control measures

Control measures against the effects of wind include:

- Making the shelter sufficiently windtight to prevent excessive draught or infiltration.

- The degree of exposure of buildings to prevailing winds will depend largely upon their location and position in relation to topography and wind strength.

- When assessing the wind loading on a building, account should be taken of the likely high wind speeds through and under access openings, which can create considerable pressure differences between the front and rear faces of the building. In these cases, suction loadings can damage glazing and claddings.

- Low-pitch roofs (15°) are particularly vulnerable to wind suction. This vulnerability decreases until the pitch reaches about 30°, but even in these cases, roof coverings can be dislodged near the ridge if not securely fastened.

- Wind-loading tables and maps should be consulted when designing buildings in areas prone to strong winds.

(c) Snowfall
Roofs must be designed to withstand snowloads which, if excessive, can cause severe structural damage. The shelter also needs to be protected against snow penetration which can lead to dampness. Planning factors also should acknowledge that snowfall frequently cuts off remote settlements from the rest of the community.

Appropriate control measures include the following:

- The shelter must be sufficiently wind- and weathertight to prevent the entry of snow.

- Roof design must have sufficient structural strength to withstand snowloads. Recent Swedish studies indicate that snowloads on pitched roofs may be appreciably higher than on flat roofs due to redeposit of snow from windward slopes to leeward slopes of the former.

- Average and peak snowfalls should be taken into account when planning the location of human settlements, and arrangements need to be made for snow removal on access roads.

(d) Frost damage
The depth to which the ground freezes depends upon the kind of soil, the kind of cover (i.e. vegetation or snow) and on the weather conditions. In hot countries, frost is extremely rare during the winter, but in colder climates frost can seriously damage fresh concrete or brickwork. In certain ground conditions, frost can cause 'heave' to foundations, pavements and concrete slabs, resulting in subsidence and cracking. Frozen water pipes can burst on thawing and frozen drainage pipes can fracture. A given site will freeze much more readily if it is waterlogged than if well drained (e.g. very fine sand, silts or chalk soils). A cover of grass or a layer of snow will afford good insulation and reduce the rate at which the ground freezes. In cold climates, foundations and underground drainage and water supply pipes should be laid sufficiently deep to be protected from frost damage.

2.4.2 Provision for admission of direct sunlight and protection against excessive insolation

(a) Health effects
Sunlight is important to housing hygiene for many reasons. It provides significant physiological and psychological benefits to health and well-

being. It is a source of warmth that may be pleasant in cold climates but conversely unpleasant in very hot climates, where it can cause thermal fatigue and sunstroke. It also directly influences natural daylighting to rooms as well as the character of exterior views. The sun's rays are especially important in sanitary compartments, where it has a bactericidal effect.

Sunlight is also significant to town planning; for example, recreation areas may need to be **sunny** while car parking areas need to be **cool**. Sunlight provisions have to be considered in relation to site density, orientation of buildings and spacing between apartment blocks. Finally, sunlight can degrade external paints, chemicals, sealants, other building materials and furnishings that may then emit unpleasant or toxic odours.

(b) Control measures

The main aim of planning authorities is to ensure enough sunlight and daylight on and between the faces of buildings for good interior and exterior conditions. The main aim of architects should be to ensure that sunlight and daylight can be had just where it is wanted (e.g. in gardens). Also, sunlight and daylight should be safeguarded for land that is likely to be developed or redeveloped in the future and in any existing building or buildings affected by a house building proposal.

In hot countries housing should be protected from excessive insolation.

In hot countries the main priority is to protect against excessive insolation. The following factors are particularly important in planning and design:

- Buildings should be orientated so that doors and windows do not face the midday sun and take advantage of prevailing summer winds. Good orientation also assists warming in winter (see section 2.1.4).

- Green belts, trees (especially large deciduous trees), shrubs, climbing plants and window boxes etc., as well as water reservoirs (e.g. on flat roofs), will help reduce temperatures of walls and roofs. Greenery on balconies and loggias reduces air temperature by an estimated 5° C and radiant temperature by 20° C. [12]

- Light-coloured paint on walls should be used to reflect as much solar radiation as possible.

- Buildings should be constructed of materials that do not absorb heat quickly.

- To reduce solar penetration, housing should be designed with living rooms that are long in relation to width. A width to length ratio of 1.4:1.6 is optimum. A ceiling height of 3.5 m is optimum for reducing radiant heating. [12]

- Flat roofs should have a ventilated space between roof deck and ceiling.

- Devices for producing shade, such as venetian blinds, broad canopies, window shutters, screens, deflectors and awnings, can be used to control sunlight penetration.

- Houses with verandas are particularly useful for preventing adjacent rooms from overheating. Shaded gardens are invaluable in providing a cool place to rest and relax.

- Window areas should be about one tenth of floor area and capable of providing cross-ventilation to all rooms. Reflective glass will reduce air temperature in insolated rooms by 3–4° C.

- Bright engineering metallized lavsan film on windows will effectively reduce solar penetration and brightness.

- The open area of windows should extend close to ceilings to allow hot air in the upper part of the room to escape.

- Natural night ventilation is especially effective in reducing air temperature during hot weather.

- Air conditioning is effective in maintaining a constant indoor air temperature but is expensive to install and run. Circulating and extract fans are effective for cooling rooms and assisting air movement.

2.4.3 Protection against seismic activity

Many regions are affected by seismic activity culminating in a number of earthquakes each year. The high density of urban areas (which often comprise old, historic towns) and the way in which building units are sometimes grouped, contribute to considerable loss of human life and property when earthquakes occur.

Appropriate **control measures** include the following:

- Regional investigations should be carried out in areas affected by seismic activity based on the geotechnical structure of the region, and active and potential faults. This should be followed by a study of the earthquake phenomenon and ground motions so that intensity, frequency, amplitude and recurrence period can be assessed.

- Control measures need to be implemented that provide optimum protection against seismic movement in new and existing buildings (particularly old buildings and town units built of stone and other traditional materials). The aim of all control measures, however, should be to ensure that buildings have sufficient seismic resistance and ductility based on probability studies to determine projections of vulnerability.

- Earthquakes are normally categorized into three levels of seismic activity: level 1, for an expected earthquake effect-and-return period of 50–100 years (light and moderate earthquakes); level 2, for an expected earthquake effect-and-return period of 200 years (strong earthquakes); and level 3, for a maximum probable earthquake (catastrophic earthquakes). Such defined parameters represent the basis for determining the individual criteria as well as stability criteria. [28]

- For level 1 earthquakes, the structure should be designed to reach the elastic range without any change to the basic structural system and minimum damage to non-structural elements, with no assumed intervention after the earthquake.

- For level 2 earthquakes, the structure should be designed to behave beyond the elastic range into the non-linear range. This means that structural elements are moderately damaged and non-structural elements considerably damaged. However, damage is assumed to be repairable and the structure usable again.

- For level 3 earthquakes, the building should be designed so that no structural collapse occurs although the structural elements may be severely deformed; heavy damage to and partial failure of the secondary infill elements is expected.

- In all cases, construction codes need to be drawn up detailing the design measures for each category. The redesign, repair and strengthening of buildings in seismic regions is detailed in a report by the United Nations Economic and Social Council. [47]

- Typified, prefabricated or industrialized housing systems should not be grouped together.

2.4.4 Protection against external air pollutants

The housing environment has a continuous but variable influx of air pollutants from the outdoor air to indoors. Important pollutants in this category are suspended particulates, sulphur oxides, nitrogen oxides, hydrocarbons, carbon oxides, photochemical oxidants and lead. [5] The shelter is only partially able to provide protection against external air pollutants, which are best controlled at source whenever possible. The close proximity of busy main roads to housing is a major public health problem in many cities, particularly those subject to temperature inversion and photochemical smog. This can severely restrict natural ventilation to habitable rooms. The planning of housing away from industrial operations, busy roads and other pollution sources is therefore essential to reduce exposure within the shelter.

(a) Sulphur oxides and suspended particulates
Sulphur oxides and suspended particulates (smoke) are common byproducts of fossil fuel combustion (from industrial processes and motor vehicles) and are found together in the atmosphere with several other pollutants, particularly in urban areas. The temperature of the gases, the exhaust gas velocity and chimney height of the chimney are important factors in emission dispersal. Sulphur dioxide (SO_2) will form sulphuric acid in the presence of moisture or as a result of catalytic or photochemical action, falling to the ground as sulphuric acid deposition ('acid rain'). Indoor levels of SO_2 can be absorbed by many building materials (e.g. SO_2 can react with formaldehyde where it often acts as a scavenger on particle board). [48]
(i) Health effects
Sulphur oxides and suspended particulates become heavily diluted in the ambient air and pose little threat to health except in extreme cases of poor dispersal such as would occur in fog or temperature inversion.

In these circumstances, mortality and morbidity curves and air pollution are closely related. A notorious example of this occurred in London in 1952 when fog, coupled with smoke and sulphur dioxide pollution, claimed 3500–4000 excess deaths, mostly in the very old or very young. Respiratory or cardiac conditions were the principal causes of death. [49]

Bronchitis, pneumonia and other respiratory infections have been correlated with daily levels of smoke and SO_2, regardless of atmospheric conditions. [50] These pollutants also may increase pulmonary airway resistance [51] and have been associated with asthma and dyspnoea. However, other studies have failed to demonstrate the influence of air pollution on respiratory disease or to distinguish the exact causal pollutant agents. [52] For instance, the adverse health effects of sulphur dioxide cannot normally be distinguished from those of particulates in smoke, as both are generally found together. Also, climatic and geographical differences make direct comparisons between the adverse health effects of air pollution in different countries difficult to make.

Sulphur oxides also can contaminate water, soil and crops, which in turn can give rise to significant exposure via ingestion of contaminated food. Other effects of air pollution include the possible reduction in 'well-being' in polluted areas due partly to reduction in the penetration of the sun's rays. The loss of ultraviolet radiation due to smoke and general air pollution in industrial towns can be 30% or more. [53]

(ii) Control measures

Control measures for such pollutants include:

- Pollution control measures and legislation to ensure the efficient burning of coal, oil and other fossil fuels and the dispersion of gases by tall chimneys. Old, inefficient fuel-burning plants should be gradually replaced by more efficient equipment.

- Smokeless zones and prohibition of coal burning in domestic fires have been largely responsible for reducing domestic pollution in many countries.

- Improvements to motor vehicle emission standards and siting of housing or re-routeing of roads away from residential areas may help reduce SO_2 levels.

- A WHO task group on sulphur oxides and suspended particulate matter [53] concluded that for long-term exposure, annual mean concentrations of SO_2 of 100 $\mu g/m^3$ and of smoke of 100 $\mu g/m^3$ were the lowest concentrations at which adverse health effects in the general population might be expected.

(b) Airborne lead

Sources of airborne lead include scrap metal yards, lead smelters, battery manufacturing plants and lead oxides from petrol-driven motor vehicles.

(i) Health effects

See section 2.5.3(c).

(ii) Control measures

- Measures should be taken to keep the annual mean concentration of lead in air to less than $2 \, \mu g/m^3$ in places where people are liable to be exposed continuously for long periods. These measures may include reducing emissions, relocating industry or housing, or traffic management schemes.

- Allotments and vegetable gardens should be planned so that they are not adjacent to busy roads or near to lead facilities such as smelters or scrap yards.

- Streets, playgrounds and other areas frequented by children should be swept regularly to remove dust and road dirt containing lead.

2.4.5 Protection against radioactive emissions

Sources of exposure to natural radiation include cosmic rays, terrestrial gamma rays and radioactive materials in the body. Sources of artificial radiation include fallout from weapons testing, certain occupational practices, radioactive consumer goods and radioactive waste. [54] However, the largest contribution to population exposure arises from the inhalation of the decay of **radon** products in indoor air. Radon is a chemically inert, dense radioactive gas with a half-life of 3.8 days; it is derived from uranium-238 deposits in the ground. This U-238 breaks down into other radioactive materials at a virtually constant rate, and one of these materials is radon gas. Radon gas can penetrate the materials in which it is found and pass into building materials and indoor air. Radon usually exists at low concentrations in the open air but at more elevated concentrations within buildings – usually between two and ten times the concentration in the open air. In most instances, the dominant source of radon within buildings is the subjacent ground. However, building materials also contribute to radon concentrations in indoor air and in some circumstances may be the major source. [55]

Building materials such as granite, alum shale stone, clay bricks, concrete containing uranium mine tailings, phosphate slag or aerated alum shale and gypsum board are potential sources of radon. Domestic water, natural gas, underlying soil and ground water can release substantial amounts of radon to the indoor atmosphere in certain regions. Radon levels vary considerably between different regions, depending upon concentrations of uranium deposits in the soil and ground water.

(a) Health effects

The potential consequence of irradiation is the induction of lung cancer and a resultant reduction in life expectancy. For instance, in one survey conducted in Schneeberg, where large concentrations of radon gas were present, 75% of the deaths among miners were caused by lung cancer. For the average person, the lifetime risk of lung cancer from radon exposure is estimated to be 1% of the risk of lung cancer from all causes. [56] A report by the UK National Radiological Protection Board [55] concluded that 'where the induction of cancer has been shown to be the consequence of exposure to ionizing radiation at high doses or dose rates, it is assumed that this effect will also occur at low doses or dose rates but with reduced frequency' and that exposure to products of radon-222 might be responsible for some of the lung cancer incidence in the general population.

Radon itself decays to produce two types of polonium, another radioactive substance. Polonium attaches itself to dust particles in a room, which are then inhaled by the occupants. Decaying polonium gives off alpha particles that, once in the lung cavity, are able to penetrate through the protective layers of tissue to damage living cells. Also, residual radon produced from building materials gives off gamma rays which, unlike polonium, deliver a dose to the entire body.

(b) Control measures

- The radon level is an important consideration when siting and designing new housing, particularly in areas where radon ground levels are high. Where high levels are suspected, radiological monitoring should be undertaken.

- In the developed countries, energy-conserving measures, such as draught-proofing and double glazing, are known to increase significantly the amount of radon within the building. Radon concentrations can be reduced significantly by increasing ventilation rates in buildings (both under the floor and within rooms).

- Building materials that do not contain deposits of radioactive materials should be used wherever possible.

- Where radon is diffusing into buildings through the ground, exposure can be reduced significantly by installing a vapour barrier between the ground and the living space above, or sealing floors and walls so as to prevent radon emissions.

- In the UK, the suggestion has been made that action should be taken to reduce annual doses of radon greater than 25 mSv and that doses between 5 and 25 mSv justify further investigation. New buildings should be designed within a dose limit of 5 mSv per year, [57] which is in line with proposals of the International Commission on Radiological Protection.

2.4.6 Protection against excessive noise and vibration from within and outside the dwelling

Noise is transmitted inside buildings through air and by vibration through structural components. Outdoor sources of noise include aircraft, traffic (both rail and road), factories, road repairs, building site operations, street noise, animals, and children playing. Common causes of noise complaints indoors include amplified music systems, radios, television, loud conversation, children crying, door banging, maintenance operations, and noises from appliances (e.g. plumbing installations, lifts and refuse chutes). The increase in high-density, multiple-housing schemes, together with mechanization and urbanization, means that noise is a serious problem in most human settlements throughout the world.

Road traffic is a major source of noise nuisance to houses.

Noise (or unwanted sound) is identified by two physical characteristics: frequency (expressed in hertz) and loudness (usually expressed in decibels). The average adult of 25–30 years of age can hear sounds ranging from 20 to 20 000 cycles per second, but this range decreases with age and is often accompanied by perceptible hearing losses within the limits of the range.

(a) Health effects

Many ill-health effects are associated with exposure to noise. These include permanent and temporary loss of hearing at intensive or long-term noise levels greater than 110 dB(A), with sleep disruption and psychological/hormonal disturbances at lower levels. The reaction of people to unwanted sound is extremely variable and complex, depending on a number of social, economic and other factors, including state of health and age. [58]

However, long-term exposure to certain sounds in the home can lead to functional disturbances of the central nervous system in some people. Such disturbances may manifest themselves in various ways, causing fatigue and reduced activity of the cortical processes, especially when rest and sleep are interrupted. For example, noise intrusion can interfere with falling asleep and can awaken people who are asleep. Studies indicate that the disturbance of sleep is worse when noise levels exceed about 35 dB(A) L_{eq}. The probability of subjects being awakened by a peak sound level of 40 dB(A) is 5%, increasing to 30% at 70 dB(A). [58] Fatigue caused by long-term exposure to low-frequency, low-intensity sound is thought to result from many warning signals which evoke a stress reaction related to fear or uneasiness.

In other cases, the level of sound in the home may be so high that it plays an important part in the development of cardiovascular, nervous and psychological disorders. Other studies have shown that a high intensity of background noise in urban areas apparently affects the developing foetus and that exposure to high intensities of sound affects communication and learning (including the acquisition of language), often leading to annoyance and aggressive behaviour. However, the interaction of noise with other environmental factors means that the adverse health effects of noise do not lend themselves to straightforward analysis. For instance, people accustomed to high levels of noise often have difficulties adjusting to a low-noise environment. [59]

(b) Control measures

Because sound-reducing methods in existing housing are often expensive, impractical or too complex for normal usage, prevention is much more effective than cure. The best preventive action lies in intelligent planning precautions taken *before* new building development begins and adopting technical, educational and enforcement action to control noise in existing housing, where noise is a problem.

(i) Outdoor noise

The following measures should be taken in planning, constructing and organizing human settlements to reduce noise in residential areas:

- Urban areas should be divided into zones that separate industry and transport from residential areas with buffer belts, parks, public gardens etc.

- Highways should be so planned that through-traffic bypasses residential areas.

- Housing should be separated from main streets by wide green belts of thickly planted trees (strong-leafed varieties and conifers) and bushes so that house fronts are at least 15 m from the road.

- Urban main streets should be widened with protective belts of greenery to separate different zones.

- Vehicular traffic should be prohibited or reduced in residential streets, particularly at night.

- Public transport (ground and air) needs to be strictly controlled. This would include aircraft movements and location of airports. Railway cuttings and solid embankments can be provided in built-up areas and housing planned away from marshalling yards or railway lines.

- Paving and other hard surfaces should be avoided where possible to minimize ground reflection. Grass areas can be used to help reduce noise.

- As far as practicable, play areas for children should be planned away from but preferably within sight of the dwelling.

- Industrial buidings and machinery should be insulated against noise at source.

(ii) Indoor noise

The planning of the residential environment and the internal planning of housing should ensure that noise from outside and inside the building is separated from living and bedroom areas. Public health personnel, architects, planners, builders and others should be aware of the principles of noise reduction when designing or vetting new housing. In particular, multiple dwellings need careful planning. From the acoustical standpoint, the best arrangement is a series of detached buildings, whereas the least favoured arrangements are single large building blocks with inward facing central courtyards, or tall buildings overlooking narrow streets.

- Rooms with shared walls and shared floors should preferably be of similar use. This ensures that bedrooms are not exposed to noise from adjoining living rooms.

- The staircase, hall and kitchen should preferably adjoin each other on either side of shared walls, thus providing a noise buffer between living rooms.

- Bedrooms should not be planned next to balconies and preferably not beneath them, certainly not without soundproofing the floors.

- The water closet (WC) should not be located over living rooms and bedrooms, whether within the same flat or over other flats.

- Partitions between WC compartments and living rooms or bedrooms should have a sound-reducing factor against airborne sound of not less than 35 dB.

- WC cisterns should not be fixed on partitions next to bedrooms or living rooms and should be fitted with silencer pipes.

- Drain pipes should not be carried in ducts next to living rooms or bedrooms without a solid wall in between.

- Refuse chutes should not be placed next to living rooms or bedrooms, and hoppers should be fitted with effective sound-deadening gaskets. Metal refuse chutes and containers should have sound-deadening linings.

- Main staircases in blocks of flats often reverbrate noise. Some of the surfaces (e.g. soffits, stair treads and linings) should be finished with sound-absorbing materials.

- Lift motors should be mounted on resilient supports, and access doors from machine rooms to internal staircases should be well fitting and of solid construction.

- The banging of entrance and garage doors should be limited by suitable devices.

- The structure of the dwelling should be adequately insulated against noise from outdoors or from adjacent dwellings. This can usually be achieved by good design and layout and use of building materials that provide a high degree of sound insulation to walls, floors and ceilings.

- Cavity walls require great attention to detail if they are to improve sound insulation: cavities must be fairly large in area ($>10\,m^2$) and have a minimum 5 cm cavity width (preferably up to 30 cm). Wall ties will reduce sound insulation values. Indirect sound transmission can be reduced by using heavy solid walls or boxed cavity construction with sound-absorbing materials in the cavity.

- Wall linings are more useful for sound insulating light-weight walls rather than heavy walls. Linings should not be too stiff and must not be porous. They are usually fixed onto plastered walls with battens at least 400 mm apart.

- Sound entering buildings through open windows will be reduced by 4–10 dB, depending on the degree of open window and absorbent conditions within the room. Ordinary closed single windows reduce incoming noise by about 20 dB (25 dB if airtight). Heavy glass further reduces noise to about 30 dB. Well-designed double windows should have an airspace gap of 200–300 mm with sound-absorbent linings to sides. Opening the windows or providing permanent ventilation to them substantially reduces sound insulation and has to be balanced against the need to secure good ventilation and indoor air quality.

- The main factors determining the sound insulation value of single doors is the mass of the door and the air leakage around its edges. Main entrance doors to common balconies should be designed to a high standard of sound insulation, including effective door closers.

- Floating floors are an effective method of reducing noise transmission in existing and new multiple-housing schemes. Usually an independent raft float is laid over a structural floor but separated from it by a suitable layer of resilient material such as plain wool quilt. Wood rafts are used for wood joist floors and usually a concrete screed for solid floors.

- The minimum weight of puggings (loose-fill usually inserted between floor joists to add mass to the floor and to dampen sound vibrations) should be 15 kg/m², but for the higher values of insulation obtainable with joist floors, the weight should not be less than about 75 kg/m². Materials used for puggings include sand (about 1600 kg/m³), ashes (about 800 kg/m³) and slag wool (100–200 kg/m³).

- Suspended ceilings are of benefit chiefly in raising the sound insulation of a concrete floor with a soft floor finish. The airspace above the ceiling should not be less than 25 mm deep, and the ceiling membrane should be moderately heavy (not less than 25 kg/m²) and airtight. (Plastered expanded metal or ceiling boards are often used.)

- Box structures within a room are sometimes used to isolate rooms from floors, ceilings and outer walls, and provide a high degree of sound insulation (i.e. 60–70 dB). Their main use in housing is to insulate rooms immediately adjacent to extremely noisy rooms (e.g. lift rooms).

- Ventilation ducts can be very potent conductors of airborne noise within a building, often entering through main inlet or extract ventilation openings or being created within the duct system by the fan, motor or other mechanical equipment. Noise can often be reduced through use of duct linings and quieter fans. Ventilation fans should be designed to be as large as possible and to run at the lowest possible speed. Noise also should be reduced along all strategic parts of the duct system. Special attention should be given to sound insulation of the duct walling, and ducting should be adequately lined with absorbent material between openings.

- Generally, sound absorption can best be achieved by increasing the mass of structural building elements, which is particularly effective at lower frequencies. However, porous absorbents, such as mineral wool, felts, acoustic tiles and soft furnishings, are effective for absorbing noise at higher frequencies. Resonant panels are effective only for noise in the range of 50–200 Hz and are therefore not applicable to most general noise problems. Sound insulation of stud partitions can be improved by staggering studs, infilling with mineral felt or sand, and properly sealing the stud cavity with plasterboard.

- Fans, compressors, lift motors, power-driven saws, steam hammers, drills and motor exhausts are examples of industrial machinery and equipment so designed, maintained and situated that they do not cause noise nuisance in residential areas.

- Where possible, quieter processes should be substituted for more noisy operations, such as welding for riveting.

- Legislation to prevent noise nuisance from factories, machinery, building operations or housing is often effectively used in many countries. Such legislation may be applied at the planning stage for new buildings and noise abatement legislation for existing noise sources. Courts should be empowered to ban noisy operations and to impose penalties on offenders.

- Tenancy agreements should stipulate the conditions for the playing of radios, musical instruments etc., and noise from these sources should be prohibited during night-time hours.

- Building regulations and ordinances should stipulate noise insulation values for new industrial and residential construction. These should be enforced by building or architect departments of the local health administration.

- The general public, building operatives, factory managers and others need to be fully informed about preventive measures to reduce noise emissions.

- The WHO Task Group on Environmental Health Criteria for Noise [58] recommended that for good speech intelligibility indoors, background levels of less than $45\,dB(A)\,L_{eq}$ are required and $35\,dB(A)\,L_{eq}$ in bedrooms. The group further recommended that outdoor noise levels of less than $55\,dB(A)\,L_{eq}$ be maintained during the day and $45\,dB(A)\,L_{eq}$ at night.

- A WHO Working Group on Noise Control in Buildings [7] made recommendations on maximum permissible sound levels, appropriate airborne sound insulation and impact sound levels, and reverberation time in dwellings. These standards should be consulted when designing new housing.

2.4.7 Provision of suitable shelter against disease vectors, pests and vermin

(i) General health effects
Many insects and mammals are important to housing hygiene and public health because of their ability to transmit disease, cause nuisance or otherwise adversely affect health. Many of these animals have a parasitic relationship with humans and/or have a life cycle where pathogens spend part of their time in an intermediate invertebrate host, and so spread disease by this route. Other biological vectors indirectly cause disease by transferring pathogens onto food or into water by contact with their wings, feet or body. Others carry pathogens in their alimentary tract and cause disease by urinating or defaecating onto food or into water.
(ii) General control measures
In terms of shelter requirements, sanitary design, housing maintenance and good housekeeping must be adequate to discourage insect and other animal disease vectors, for example, by thorough, regular vacuum cleaning to remove food debris and dirt, regular inspection of void spaces such as lofts and cupboards, rotation of food stocks, keeping food in sealed containers, good design and maintenance of the structure to eliminate gaps or holes, and prompt, efficient disposal of all waste and rubbish. Three general factors must always be considered in controlling pests and vermin: elimination of breeding places, destruction of the pest or its offspring, and preventing the vector from reaching humans. However, much depends upon environmental conditions, disease patterns, and a detailed understanding of the habits and life cycles of animal and disease

vectors with particular reference to their relationship with humans and the housing micro-environment.

(a) House flies

(i) Health effects

The house fly and many of its relatives are common agents for transmitting numerous infectious diseases. The mouth parts, numerous body spines and the sticky pads on the feet can carry many pathogens that cause human disease, including typhoid fever, cholera, bacillary and amoebic dysentery, tetanus and anthrax. Disease is spread by flies feeding on excrement, sputum, open sores or putrefying matter, which is then transferred to food, milk, mucous membranes or uncontaminated wounds.

Many studies have shown a causal relationship between flies and enteric disease. One American study demonstrated that effective fly control in areas with a high fly population reduced the prevalence of *Shigella* infections and other diarrhoeal diseases [60]. Similar results were observed by a WHO team studying diarrhoeal diseases in Venezuela.

House flies transmit a number of food-borne and enteric diseases.

Another American study [61] showed that construction of sanitary privies reduced the access of flies to the faecal material, hence breaking the chain of transmission for enteric disease.

(ii) Control measures

- The transmission of disease by house flies can be controlled by preventing access of flies to human faeces by constructing sanitary conveniences and providing sanitary drainage arrangements for disposal of liquid and solid waste.

- Adequate measures also need to be taken to keep flies out of dwellings and in particular from contaminating food. This can be partly achieved by screening doors and windows to larders and other food storage cupboards with fine wire mesh, and ensuring that food is not left uncovered in food preparation areas. Dirt, grease and other food debris should be removed daily.

- Environmental health measures, such as the sanitary disposal of household refuse, waste food and animal manure, should be implemented.

- Insecticides, such as dichlorvos, slow-release resin strips or pyrethrins, distributed either by hand-operated spray guns or aerosol sprays are effective for house fly control, although as with all insecticides great care must be taken with their use in food rooms.

(b) Mosquitoes
(i) Health effects

Several species of mosquitoes are known transmitters of encephalitis, malaria, filariasis, dengue fever and yellow fever. In infected areas, these diseases are spread by mosquitoes biting infected persons and then transmitting the disease to non-infected persons through biting. As with other biting insects, mosquitos also affect comfort and efficiency through severe annoyance, itching, loss of sleep and nervousness. Some people also are allergic to insect bites.

(ii) Control measures

- Mosquito control is best accomplished at the aquatic stage of the life cycle. Breeding sites are removed in several ways: emptying standing water in tanks, cisterns, tins and other containers; clearing blocked gutters, gullies, drains and ditches; draining ponds and swampy areas; and making adequate provision for surface water drainage.

- Biological controls can also be employed by introduction of natural predators into ponds and lakes.

- Larvicidal agents also are effective in some cases to control mosquitos.

- Adult mosquitoes within buildings are killed quickly by pyrethrins synergized or boosted with piperanyl butoxide.

- Protection while sleeping in infested areas can be achieved by mosquito nets or doors and windows mosquito-proofed with fine-gauged mesh of bronze wire, plastic or nylon.

- Detailed measures for controlling mosquitoes are set out in numerous WHO douments and publications, which should be consulted before carrying out mosquito control programmes.

(c) Cockroaches

Cockroaches harbour in cracks, crevices, and heating and ventilation ducts of dwellings. They are particularly fond of warmth, dampness and darkness and are thus commonplace in insanitary or poorly designed housing. They commonly infest kitchens and areas where waste food is found.

(i) Health effects

Cockroaches impart an unsavory odour and taste to food they infect. They carry organisms causing enteric diseases such as diarrhoea, dysentery, typhoid and food poisoning. They also have been associated with the spread of numerous other diseases. As with other crawling insects, cockroaches spread pathogens mainly by dirt and infected food particles adhering to their bodies. Moreover, they also contaminate foodstuffs with their excreta and egg cases.

(ii) Control measures

Controls against cockroaches include:

- Gaps in skirtings, pipe ducts and dados etc., should be closed off. Voids to brick walls around disused fireplaces or kitchen ranges need to be properly sealed off and crevices around heating pipes sealed.

- Proper hygienic facilities for food storage and disposal of waste food should be provided.

- Heating and ventilation ducts should be so designed that they do not provide harbourage for cockroaches. Access points should be provided for disinfestation.

- Cockroaches are resistant to many insecticides, but dieldrin-based lacquers are often effective if applied at the base of walls where cockroaches must pass in search of food. Cockroach traps also are available, and cockroaches can be trapped in vessels containing beer, syrup or sweetened liquids.

(d) Bedbugs

Bedbugs can infest insanitary *and* hygienic housing but prefer warm conditions and feed only in darkness. Nevertheless, bedbugs thrive in dirty conditions at an optimum temperature of 25° C. Bedbugs feed readily on the blood of poultry, mice, rats and other animals, but humans are the preferred host. Adults, eggs and nymphs can be found in cracks and crevices on or around beds, together with the empty cast-off shells. A heavy infestation is characterized by an almond-like odour.

(i) Health effects

Bedbugs are not known to carry any communicable diseases and are mainly troublesome because of their nuisance value. Some people are also very sensitive and/or allergic to bedbug bites.

(ii) Control measures

Bedbugs can be controlled by:

- Normal hygiene measures, such as vacuuming of beds and mattresses will help control bedbug infestations. Cracks and crevices in walls and floors should be filled in.

- The eggs of bedbugs are unlikely to hatch at a temperature below 13° C, and their survival through the winter in unheated houses is unlikely. Conversely, a temperature of 45° C kills the eggs and adults in 1 hour.

- Fenitrothion or lindane should be sprayed on all surfaces where bedbugs are likely to be hiding. Bedding is preferably steam-treated.

(e) Fleas

The human flea can breed in dust in cracks of floors and wherever organic material has accumulated (e.g. hair, wool or flakes of skin). Fleas are able to lie dormant in the cocoon stage in empty houses and become activated by the vibrations of a person entering the house. Fleas are also carried by many domestic and wild animals, including dogs, cats, foxes and rats.

(i) Health effects

The rat flea conveys the bacillus of bubonic plague from rats to humans. It also transmits *Rickettsia mooseri*, the organism responsible for murine typhus. Rat fleas can remain infected with *Pasteurella pestis* for up to 43 days. Cat and dog fleas also feed on humans and cause considerable irritation through biting.

(ii) Control measures

- Rat fleas are best destroyed by extermination of rat populations through normal rodent control measures.

- Cat and dog fleas can be killed by periodic dousing of infested animals with a suitable insecticidal powder.

- Human fleas can be partly controlled through normal domestic cleaning activities, particularly vacuuming of floors, dusty crevices and other infected areas. Personal hygiene also plays an important role.

- Infested houses should be sprayed with an insecticide such as lindane and infested bedding treated with pyrethrin or pressurized steam.

(f) House mites

House mites and house-dust mites are common, endemic sources of allergens inside houses. Mites are extremely small in size (barely visible with the naked eye) and are easily distinguished from insects by having eight legs (rather than six) in the adult stage. The most common species of mite found in houses is the house-dust mite (*Dermatophagoides pteronyssinus*). This mite is nearly always found in bedding and mattress

Electronmicrograph showing house-dust mites (*Dermatophagoides pteronyssinus*) feeding on dead skin scales.

dust or in pillows, cushions (especially feather-filled), rugs and upholstered chairs, where it feeds on dead human skin cells. House mites and house-dust mites require a high relative humidity (RH) to survive and will die in very dry, very hot or very cold conditions. House-mite populations peak in late summer when the RH is high. At a minimum RH of less than 45%, mites die from desiccation. Optimum development of mites varies with the species: *D. pteronyssinus*, for example, prefers a RH of 80% at 25° C. Other mites found in housing include pests of stored food products. For example, *Glycyphagus domesticus* is a common pest of damp larders or walls where it feeds on mould spores. Other sources of mites in houses include infested bedding material for pets and other animals (e.g. hay and straw), floor coverings in cages and bird-nesting materials.

(i) Health effects

Many of these arachnids are parasitic and can produce a mild to severe dermatitis in some people. In addition, some mites are the causal agents of mange and scabies in humans and other animals.

Airborne mite faeces are the main source of allergens, but small airborne pieces of mites (<5 μm diameter) could be inhaled into the lungs and cause an allergic response. The symptoms of dust-mite allergy are similar to those of other airborne allergies (see section 2.7.1(h)), including irritation of the nose and throat and rhinitis. In some people breathlessness and asthma occur several hours after exposure.

(ii) Control measures

House-mite controls include:

- House mites and house-dust mite populations are best controlled by reducing the RH to below 45%. This is best achieved by controlling water vapour emissions from household activities, providing good ventilation to rooms and remedying housing dampness.

- Strong sunshine also kills house mites. Rooms, carpets, bedding and mattresses should, therefore, be regularly aired in strong sunshine. Furnishings should be vacuumed regularly to remove dust and house mites. Bird-nesting material should be removed from roof spaces.

- Steam treatment of mattresses and bedding will kill house mites, but insecticides are largely ineffective.

- In some cases, articles or furnishings giving rise to allergies should be replaced, but this may not always be practicable. In some cases, rehousing of sensitized persons may be necessary.

(g) Other insect pests

Other insect pests include beetles, weevils and ants (often found infesting food stored in damp, dirty and unhygienic food stores), earwigs, wasps, silverfish, house moths and woodworm. The former group are mainly of importance because of their nuisance value and can be treated by normal housing hygiene measures and suitable insecticides. However, wood-boring insects cause considerable damage to structural timbers, such as rafters and joists, and should be treated with suitable biocides. Pretreated timber should be used in areas particularly vulnerable to wood-borers. Alternatively, hardwood timbers, which are not as attractive as softwood to woodworm attack, should be used.

(h) Rats and mice

Rats, mice and other rodents play an important part in the spread of many diseases, either directly by contaminating human food with their urine or faeces, or indirectly through parasitic fleas and mites. They are common-place where housing hygiene is poor. In addition, numerous indirect effects on health need to be considered. These include aesthetic reactions to the presence of rodents, rodent damage to sewerage systems, and

Rats are a major threat to health.

losses of stored and growing food crops, which exacerbate problems of malnutrition and susceptibility to disease in local human populations. Rats also may cause fires by gnawing through the insulating material around electrical wiring.

(i) Health effects

The most serious rodent-borne disease is **bubonic plague**. It is spread by infected fleas of many rodents, the most significant of which is the rat. Like bubonic plague, **tularaemia** is a natural disease of rodents and lagomorphs (rabbits and hares) and may also be transmitted to humans by blood-sucking arthropods (e.g. mites, ticks), fleas and mosquitoes, contact with or ingestion of water, inhalation of dust contaminated by rodent faeces, or by contact with infected live mammals, their carcasses or insufficiently cooked meat.

Other diseases spread by rats and mice include rat-bite fever, leptospirosis, salmonellosis, trichinosis and murine typhus fever. Rickettsial pox is transmitted from the house mouse to humans by the bite of the house mite. Rat-bite fever is a public health problem associated with heavy urbanization, occurring primarily in lower economic areas with substandard housing, crowding and poor sanitation.

(ii) Control measures

- Good hygienic measures can eliminate harbourage for rats and mice. These include hygienically storing and disposing of house refuse, removing any accumulations of rubbish and destroying nesting material when disinfecting buildings.

- Rats and mice are attracted to houses with a plentiful food supply. Proper hygiene measures in the kitchen and other rooms of the house to ensure that food is not left uncovered and removal of waste debris together with routine cleaning measures will discourage rodent infestation.

- All reasonably practicable steps should be taken to ensure that houses and other buildings are so designed and repaired to make them rat-proof. Particular attention should be given to the spaces behind skirting boards, suspended ceilings, hollow partitions, ducts and conduits, holes in conduits and the drainage system.

- The whole building site should be covered with a concrete layer to prevent rats and mice from burrowing into houses.

- All bridges to buildings, such as cables, tree branches or objects leaning against walls, should be avoided.

- The eaves of roofs should be rat-proofed with expanded metal or wire mesh and wire balloons used at openings of all ventilation pipes connected to the drainage system.

- Access to roofs by vertical pipes close to walls can be prevented by 20-gauge metal pipeguards fitted tightly to pipes by an adjustable metal collar projecting out about 250 mm. Horizontal pipes and cables between buildings should be similarly protected.

- Junctions between wood floors and brick walls should be treated with fine wire mesh, and air-bricks, ventilators, doors, windows, etc., also need to be similarly proofed.

- Where necessary, buildings should not be erected with windows opening less than 1 m from the ground, and every opening should be protected by a heavy overhanging sill. Brickwork should be painted with high-gloss paint, up to 1 m from the ground to discourage climbing by rats.

- All possible points of entry below 1 m from the ground should be closed to prevent rats jumping up to openings.

- Gnawing at the bottom of doors can be prevented by fitting a 300-mm high, 20-gauge metal kick plate on the outside.

- All disused drain runs should be filled with compacted concrete. Drains in use should be fitted with intercepting traps where necessary to discourage rats from entering domestic drainage runs from main sewers.

- Drains, inspection chambers, fresh-air inlet grids and sanitary fitments should always be kept in good repair.

- Food storage facilities should be adequately proofed against the entry of rats and mice.

- Edible refuse and empty food containers should always be placed in bins with tightly fitting lids while awaiting collection.

- Rats and mice can be controlled by poisoning (including gassing) and trapping. Poisons can either be single dose (acute) or multiple dose (chronic) and can be incorporated into bait or used as contact poisons in the form of dust. Care must be taken that these rodenticides are not indiscriminately used and are properly stored in the home so they are not a source of danger to children and domestic animals.

- Rats in sewers should be controlled by regular baiting and/or trapping.

- Specifications for pesticides recommended for rodent control are published by the WHO. [62]

(i) Other animal pests

Other common animal disease vectors associated with insanitary housing include pigeons and other birds, which often infest lofts and dilapidated outbuildings and carry many parasitic insects and diseases, such as salmonellosis, from droppings. Therefore, roof coverings and eaves should be properly sealed and water storage tanks properly covered to keep out birds. Other animals that carry zoonotic diseases include foxes and other scavenging animals, which may find harbourage in poor housing. These animals are often infected with tuberculosis and carry a number of parasitic diseases in their faecal droppings. Where necessary, these animals should be controlled by shooting, poisoning, gassing or other methods.

2.4.8 Protection against intrusion by humans or dangerous animals

(a) Human intrusion

(i) Health effects

Human intrusion can be a major health and personal safety hazard in areas where burglaries and personal assaults are commonplace. This is a particular problem to people who live on their own, such as the elderly

Human intrusion can be reduced through security design measures.

who often live in continual fear of being attacked by intruders in or near to their homes and who often sustain serious injuries in such attacks. The problem is exacerbated where home security is inadequate, adding to feelings of insecurity and stress.

(ii) Control measures

- Housing developments should be designed so as to avoid hiding places for intruders by careful planning of open walkways and provision of approach roads that are well lit at night.

- Additional policing and security patrols may be necessary in housing developments with a consistent record of burglaries or personal assaults.

- Simple security devices, such as mortice deadlocks, draw-bolts, door chains, door spyglasses and window bolts, should be fitted to all entrance doors and accessible windows as appropriate. In some cases, more elaborate security devices, such as burglar alarms, close circuit TV and intercom-operated door entrance systems, may be appropriate to discourage human intrusion.

- Ground-floor front rooms should have adequately sized windows at eye level for effective surveillance. Bay windows and walk-in bays are better than windows flush with the frontage or high-level bays.

- Front doors should be recessed slightly so as not to impede the line of sight from windows. Front-facing doors are better than sideways-facing ones, providing they can be seen from front doors opposite.

- No high obstructions, such as walls, hedges, garages, meter compartments, pram sheds or dustbin kennels, should obstruct the view of the street from windows.

- Back gardens should not abut onto alleyways, paths or roads to maximize security for small children, prevent intruders from entering and to increase privacy. Layouts where the front of one row of houses faces the back of the next row are to be avoided. [63]

(b) Animal intrusion
(i) Health effects

Intrusion into housing by dangerous animals is a serious problem in many parts of the world. For example, bites by snakes and stings by insects that enter houses looking for food or shelter cause pain and discomfort to occupants, sometimes culminating in death. The psychological effects on occupants of this intrusion can be considerable.

(ii) Control measures
Housing should be adequately secured against intrusion by dangerous or poisonous animals. Cracks, crevices, gaps in roofs and other entry points or harbourages should be eliminated. In some cases, traps and poisonous baits can be used, but these may themselves create health hazards to young children unless proper safety precautions are taken.

2.5 DESIGN AND CONSTRUCTIONAL REQUIREMENTS

The detailed design and constructional requirements of housing hygiene encompass all of the technical factors relating to the shelter and the physical infrastructures serving it. For example, the adequacy of building construction is important not only in relation to stability, strength and durability of the structure but also in maintaining sanitary conditions, thermal comfort, reducing noise transmission, affording means of escape in case of fire, providing shelter against the external elements and security against intrusion.

These issues are described elsewhere in the guidelines as specific requirements. However, some common requirements relate to the performance of primary building components, such as foundations, walls, floors and roofs, and the toxicity of materials, which are briefly described in this section along with other matters specific to design and performance.

Methods of building construction, type of design and choice of materials will depend largely upon the desired requirements of the building, supplies of suitable building materials, manufacturing plant and availability of trained building construction workers, site conditions, climate, finance and consumer demands. Therefore, to comply with these requirements, each country must draw up detailed specifications relevant to its particular requirements and local conditions.

2.5.1 Provision of facilities which are designed to optimize performance of household tasks without causing undue physical or mental fatigue

This is an all-embracing parameter which in the main concerns environmental and housing facilities that meet general and individual physical and mental health requirements as well as comfort and aesthetic considerations. For example, sufficient but not excessive indoor space (including readily accessible storage space) will optimize the performance of household tasks. Floor, wall and other surfaces that are easy to keep clean will reduce time and physical effort spent on cleaning, and a good indoor thermal climate and indoor air quality will similarly optimize comfort while carrying out household tasks. Electrical household appliances such as vacuum cleaners, washing machines and spin driers, considerably reduce physical and mental fatigue. Provision of piped water and gas can reduce physical effort of collecting adequate supplies. Drainage and sanitation reduces time spent on sanitary tasks.

2.5.2 Provision of building components with sufficient strength, stability and durability to enable effective maintenance, repair and cleanliness

(a) General requirements

Good **healthy housing design** and construction is essential to enable cleaning and sanitary operations to be carried out effectively. In particular, floors, walls, ceilings, work surfaces and appliances should be constructed of smooth, impervious materials capable of being kept clean; all parts of housing should be accessible for cleaning; dust-traps in ducts or conduits especially should be avoided, and suitable hygienic facilities should be provided for storing domestic goods, personal belongings, etc.

The **building structure** should be sufficiently strong, in good repair and not likely to collapse. In particular, building materials, foundations and overall design should not facilitate subsidence, slipping or other movement, particularly in areas prone to soil movement or seismic activity. Remedial action should be taken to ensure that walls are not badly bulged or leaning dangerously (e.g. by shoring or underpinning walls).

- Loose roof tiles, slates or other coverings should be properly secured. Loose chimney pots should be taken down and rebedded into chimneys.

- Structural timbers, such as floor joists, wall-plates, floor-boards, lintels or roofing timbers, that are rotted or damaged because of fungal or insect attack should be replaced with new timbers impregnated with preservative.

- Ceilings that are loose, badly bulged or otherwise insecure should be replaced. Broken glass in windows can cause lacerations and should be replaced.

(b) Specific requirements
(i) Foundations

- Foundation design must take account of possible ground movement, the nature of the subsoil and the nature of the supporting structure so as to avoid differential building settlement. Therefore, it is important to know the nature of the subsoil both at the level of the foundations and for some depth below.

- Topsoil, which is composed of loose soil, plant life and decaying vegetation, is a very soft and unsatisfactory foundation for buildings and should be avoided.

- Fine-grained soil includes **clay** soils, which have high plasticity; it dries slowly and shrinks appreciably on drying. Under pressure of the load of foundations, clay soils compress as water is squeezed out and buildings may continue to settle for some years after completion.

- Foundations should be laid at a suitable distance below ground level to prevent the clay from shrinking on drying and expanding on wetting. In the UK, foundations are normally laid 1 m below the surface and up to 4 m or more deep below large trees. As a general guide, buildings on shallow foundations should not be closer to single trees than the height of the tree at maturity, and one-and-a-half times the height of groups of mature trees to reduce the risk of damage to buildings by shrinkage and swelling of clay soils. Special precautions need to be taken when rebuilding on clay soils after clearance of trees and shrubs from the site.

- **Rock** is normally a good substrate for building foundations, although the load-bearing capacity will depend on the type of rock. Unlike soils, rock does not compact under the weight of buildings.

- Ground that has been filled or made up with tipped soil, waste or refuse is unsuitable for building because of the difficulty in predicting the amount of compaction under load and the likelihood of uneven settlement. However, building on made-up ground is sometimes possible by using raft or deep-pile foundations. The construction of terraced housing on made-up ground, however, should be avoided because of the likelihood of differential settlement and cracking. Such sites also may be unsuitable for housing because of the possibility of toxic materials and chemicals from the ground being brought to the surface during excavation activities. Soils from made-up ground should be routinely tested for heavy metals and toxicity.

- Water-soluble sulphates, particularly in clay soils, can combine with the hardened cement in the concrete of foundations and cause expansion cracking and disintegration of concrete. In these situations, sulphate-resistant cements should be used. Dense, impermeable concrete is less susceptible to sulphate attack than poorly compacted forms.

- Frost heave is a particular problem where the water-table is near the surface. The water freezes and may expand when frozen, causing heave below foundations and causing them to move and possibly fracture. Frost heave is unlikely to occur in heated buildings.

- Building foundations should be designed to transmit the load of the building to the ground so that, at most, only a limited settling of the building occurs. It is especially important that foundation settlement is uniform and that movement is limited so as to avoid damage to service pipes and drains connected to the building.

- The width and depth of a concrete **strip foundation** depends on the bearing capacity of the subsoil and the imposed loads. The greater the bearing capacity of the subsoil, the less the width of the foundation for the same load. The minimum width of a strip foundation is 450 mm, which gives a reasonable bearing for most two-storey houses and provides space in the trench to lay any foundation brickwork. The minimum depth of concrete for a strip foundation is generally 150 mm, and the concrete should be at least as thick as the projection of the strip on each side of the wall. However, the thickness of the concrete should not be less than the projection of the strip on each side of the wall so that if a failure of the concrete by shear occurs, the 45° angle of shear would not reduce the bearing at the base of the subsoil. The minimum practical depth of a strip foundation is usually 450 mm of concrete.

- **Raft foundations** consist of a raft of reinforced concrete under the whole of the building so designed to transmit the load of the building to the subsoil. They are used for buildings on very loose or soft ground, such as very soft clay, or where soil is very compressible and where strip foundations would not provide a stable base.

- **Pile foundations** are used where the subsoil has poor or uncertain load-bearing capacity or where appreciable ground movement is likely, as with firm shrinkable clay.

- The foundations to walls on sloping sites can either be stepped or at one level depending on the degree of slope. Where foundations are stepped, the steps should be uniform in height and equal to the thickness of the foundation concrete and in no case less than 300 mm.

- Where the subsoil has poor bearing capacity for some depth below the surface (e.g. where ground has been made-up), a foundation of piers on **pad foundations** is often economical. The isolated concrete pad foundations are spread in the base of excavations, on which piers or columns of brick or concrete are raised to ground level to support reinforced concrete ground beams off which the walls are raised. The spread of the pad foundation is determined by the loads on it and the bearing capacity of the subsoil. The thickness of the concrete is either at least equal to the projection of the pad each side of the pier or the pad foundation can be reinforced.

(ii) Walls

The wall is either a load-bearing or non-load-bearing solid structure of bricks, stone, concrete, timber, metal or some other material enclosing and protecting a building or forming compartments and rooms internally. The functional requirements of a wall are to provide stability, strength, durability and fire resistance, to exclude rain and have adequate thermal properties and resistance to sound transmission. Internally, wall finishes need to be easily cleaned and sufficiently durable for household activities. No material or type of wall fulfils all these requirements with maximum efficiency, but choice of materials should take into account climatic factors, such as ambient temperature and rainfall, living patterns (e.g. degree of heating, occupancy) and density/design (e.g. noise insulation).

Other design factors to be considered are as follows:

- **Strength** A wall should be designed to safely support its own weight, and the load imposed by floors and roofs. Strength depends on the material characteristics of the wall and the wall thickness.

- **Stability** A wall should be able to resist foundation movement, irregular loads, wind forces and expansion/contraction due to temperature and moisture changes. This will be determined largely by thickness and stiffness of the walls and height of the building although buttresses or irregular profile walls can be used to give greater stability. Suitable lintels should be built over windows, doors and other openings.

- **Durability** Walls should be so constructed and designed to last the anticipated life of the building and require little if any maintenance and repair (excluding normal weathering). Again, the characteristics of the building materials and their suitability to the climate are the main factors determining durability.

- **Fire resistance** All walls should be able to provide adequate resistance to collapse, flame penetration and heat transmission during a fire, depending upon the period of resistance required. This in turn depends upon the size, occupancy and height of the building as well as the means of escape. In general terms, walls for traditional one- or two-storey buildings require less fire resistance than other types of development.

- **Protection against rain** The ability of walls to exclude rain depends largely upon the exposure of the wall to prevailing winds in terms of orientation, wind speed and rainfall. Other important factors include the proximity of the building to the coast and to other buildings, height of the building and its degree of elevation. A number of measures can be taken to exclude rain from penetrating a building such as cavity wall construction (where the inner wall is separated from the outer wet skin), increasing thickness, selecting impermeable building materials (these, however, may have poor thermal insulation properties), and by cladding wall surfaces with an outer skin of rendering, slates or tiles. In all cases, damp-proof openings to windows and doors as well as damp-proof course and flashings to any parapets are needed.

- **Protection against humidity** A wall should be able to absorb humidity produced from within the shelter and protect against interstitial condensation. This is particularly important in rooms such as bathrooms and kitchens where washing and cooking produce considerable moisture. It also is important in rooms such as living rooms and bedrooms where reduced ventilation rates coupled with intermittent heating, hard wall plasters and poor moisture-absorbent properties often cause severe condensation and mould growth.

- **Thermal insulation** Walls should be able to accommodate changes in thermal conditions originating from outside and inside the building in order to maintain reasonable and economical conditions of thermal comfort inside; that is, they should be able to provide adequate insulation against excessive loss or gain of heat, have adequate thermal storage capacity and be so designed so that internal wall faces are at a reasonable temperature. A balance between the need to heat or cool wall surfaces quickly in cold or hot conditions is essential. However, at the same time thermal storage capacity must be sufficient to prevent thermal discomfort when temperatures drop.

- **Noise transmission** Walls should be so designed that they do not transmit excessive noise and have sufficient sound insulation properties against impact sound.

A number of different materials can be used for walls, of which the most common are the following:

- **Clay bricks** provide good stability, durability and very good resistance against fire; they also have good thermal and sound insulation properties. Bricks are cheap to manufacture, providing that suitable supplies of clay are locally available. However, the varying nature of the clay and the methods of manufacture, firing etc., mean that the colour, texture, density and strength vary considerably. Therefore, bricks should be used for the purpose to which they are most suited and be bonded to maximize structural strength.

- **Concrete blocks** are used extensively for both load-bearing and non-load-bearing walls. Lightweight aggregate concrete blocks have good insulating properties, are cheap and quick to erect, and are often used for the inner skin of cavity walls. Their main disadvantage is that they suffer from moisture movement, which may cause plaster inside or rendering outside to crack.

- **Clay blocks** are made from special brick clays and are comparatively lightweight, do not suffer from moisture movement and have good resistance to damage by fire but are used mainly for internal non-load-bearing partitions since they have poor thermal insulation properties.

- **Concrete** is an extremely strong, durable building material with good protection against fire and is very resistant to the effects of weathering. However, it has a very drab appearance and is normally used only in non-traditional buildings over three storeys in height.

- **Asbestos** cement sheet is extremely durable and has good thermal insulation and fire-resistant qualities. However, it is relatively brittle and lacks structural strength. Although formerly used extensively in prefabricated housing construction, its use is decreasing because of the dangers to health associated with inhalation of asbestos fibres.

- **Corrugated iron** is not normally suitable for wall and roof construction because it has poor thermal insulation properties: it makes rooms excessively hot in warm climates and extremely cold in cold climates. It also needs to be regularly painted to prevent rusting and corrosion.

- **Timber** for wood-framed walls is a relatively cheap construction material, provided that it is in plentiful supply. A timber-framed wall has sufficient strength and stability to support the floors and roofs of small buildings and houses. Timber has good thermal insulation properties and is reasonably fire resistant if it is adequately covered with suitable non-inflammable wall and roof coverings. However, wood-boarded buildings require more maintenance. Provision also has to be made for timber movement and protection from insect attack, decay and the effects of weathering. Suitable insulation needs to be provided either between the wall studs or over the inside face of the wall, and measures taken to prevent moisture from the warm air side permeating into the insulation material.

(iii) Floors

The functional requirements of a floor are stability, strength, moisture resistance, durability, fire resistance, thermal properties, resistance to sound transmission and adequate sound absorption.

- For **stability**, vertical support for the floor structure should be adequate, and the floor should have sufficient stiffness against deflection when under load. A deflection of about 1/300 of the span is generally regarded as a maximum in the design of timber floors.

- For **strength**, a floor should be capable of adequately supporting people, furniture and household equipment, and be capable of supporting the dead load of the floor structure, partitions and other fixtures as well as anticipated imposed loads. Solid ground and basement floors are usually made of concrete (sometimes reinforced) and supported by a layer of compacted hardcore below.

- For **durability**, ground floors on a solid base or solidly supported suspended floors should last for the life of a properly constructed building.

- **Moisture penetration** through the floor is another hygiene consideration. The ground floor of a heated building tends to encourage moisture from the ground below to rise, making the floors damp, cold and uncomfortable under foot. This can aggravate respiratory illnesses of occupants. Dampness may cause wood rot and damage to timber floors and finishes, but the degree of moisture penetration depends upon the nature of the subsoil, water-table level, whether the site is level or sloping, and the adequacy of the floor itself including any damp-proof membrane to keep moisture out. For instance, on a gravel or coarse-grained sand base where the water table is usually well below the surface, little water penetration takes place, whereas on a clay base with the water-table close to the surface, the penetration of moisture from the ground will be appreciable. A slab of site concrete over the soil reinforced with a waterproof membrane will stop water penetration in all cases. However, earth floors are not satisfactory for housing hygiene because the continual penetration of water from the ground makes the floor damp and cold. Ground level, wooden, suspended floors can be adequately ventilated with air-bricks to prevent dry rot and dampness in timbers.

- **Fire-resistance** requirements depend mainly upon the height of the building. In high buildings, concrete floors, which have a higher resistance to fire, may have to be used.

- **Thermal properties** of floors must minimize transfer of heat from the building and prevent feet from feeling cold. The use of warm materials, such as timber, will meet these criteria, but ventilated, raised-timber ground floors need to be insulated against excessive transfer of heat.

- **Resistance to sound transmission and provision of sound absorption** are particularly important to upper floors. Concrete floors are better than low-mass timber floors for reducing transmission of airborne sound. Impact sound can be deadened by carpeting or other floor coverings.

- **Floor finishes** also need to be smooth, impervious to liquids, chemicals and grease, easy to keep clean and non-slip. Various finishes are suitable for floors, concrete and timber being the most common and appropriate especially if covered with suitable linoleum, rugs or carpets.

(iv) Roofs

The functional requirements of a roof are stability, strength, exclusion of rain and wind, durability, fire resistance and good thermal properties.

- A roof should be able to support the dead load of the **roof structure**, covering, snow loads, and resist pressure or suction caused by the wind. The stability of a **flat roof** depends on adequate support from walls or beams and the size of timber joists or concrete relative to spans and assumed levels. The stability of a **pitched roof** depends on the depth of the triangular framing at mid-span. The strength of both flat and pitched roofs depends on the materials used and the method of design and construction.

- A roof covering should be capable of **excluding wind and rain** from ·the building and keeping it sufficiently cool in hot weather and warm in cold weather. The degree of slope of the roof depends upon the size and type of roof covering.

- **Bitumen roofing felt** for covering flat roofs is cheap and easy to apply. Fibreglass-based felts are resistant to expansion and contraction, non-absorbent and rot-proof. The cheaper fibre-based felts are not suitable and in very hot or very cold climates easily tear, allowing water to penetrate. In all cases, adequate lap (50 mm at sides and 75 mm at ends) between each layer and sufficient fall (at least 18 mm) is important to encourage run-off of rainwater.

- A properly laid **asphalt roof covering** does not absorb water and does not have to be laid at a fall as any rainwater on it will eventually evaporate. Asphalt is comparatively cheap and durable, having a useful life of about twenty years.

- **Sheet metal coverings** such as copper, lead, zinc and aluminium are excellent roof coverings giving good protection against wind and rain; they also have good durability and are light in weight. Lead and copper have a useful life of up to 100 years, but zinc has only 20–40 years. All of them are more expensive than bitumen felt or mastic coverings and more difficult to apply.

- The **durability** of the roof is the main factor affecting water penetration that could rot timbers and cause decay to other structural elements.

- A roof and its coverings should have adequate **fire resistance** and resistance to flame spread to enable inhabitants to escape safely.

- In cold climates, roofing materials and structures need to provide adequate **insulation against transfer of heat** through insulation material in the roof space. In hot climates it is necessary to ensure that the roof does not become excessively hot (by using suitable covering materials) and ventilating the roof space. In all cases, a vapour barrier needs to be provided to ensure that moisture does not penetrate the insulation either through the roof covering or from humid air from inside the building. A ventilated roof space area between the roof covering and the upper ceilings is needed in all climates so that conditions of thermal comfort can be attained inside.

- A roof and its coverings must also **exclude animal intruders**, such as birds and rodents, that may damage structural elements of the roof. In vulnerable areas, roofing timbers should be treated against insect attack.

- **Clay or concrete roofing tiles** are extensively used for covering pitched roofs. Good quality tiles weather well, have good durability and are resistant to damage by rain, heat and industrial air pollutants. However, they are heavy in weight and need to be adequately supported and fixed to prevent movement and possible uplifting.

- **Stone slates** are hard and dense, do not readily absorb water, are not affected by frost damage and have a long useful life. The better quality slates do not absorb water and are practically indestructible. It is important that they are fixed adequately to roofing battens with copper nails as galvanized or iron nails rust in time, causing slates to slip.

2.5.3 Provision of non-toxic or injurious building materials, furnishings and consumer goods

A number of toxic chemicals and materials are used in buildings, furnishings and consumer goods. Some of these products contribute to indoor air pollution (e.g. asbestos and urea-formaldehyde products). Others are toxic through ingestion (e.g. lead). **Cleaning agents** and certain toxic varnishes may contain organic constituents that evaporate into the indoor air; hobbies or industrial processes within the home are additional pollutant sources (e.g. solvents, adhesives, paints, paint removers, soldering fluxes and welding materials).[5]

Other sources of potentially toxic materials include **polymers**, which have been widely used in housing for covering floors and walls, insulating pipes against heat and sound, waterproofing and sealing wall panels and partitions, and in the manufacture of prefabricated housing units. Plastics that have been used in buildings include polyethylene, polystyrene, polyvinyl alcohol, polyvinyl acetate, polyurethane, melamine, formaldehyde resins, polysiloxines, and the epoxy and coumarone resins. These polymers liberate volatile substances above $60°$ C, which may be harmful especially if burnt or heated. Polymers may also provide a substrate for the development of microflora, for example, in water pipes. Other polymers can promote allergies in susceptible persons. For these reasons, the use of polymers should be controlled strictly and balanced against the known hygienic benefits.

As regards consumer products generally used in building materials and products, a WHO Working Group on indoor air quality was unable to estimate the health risks because of the large numbers of constituents involved and the sometimes undetermined uses to which they are put. [5] Where there is any doubt, the WHO Working Group thought that the most appropriate control measures for toxic consumer goods were prohibition of toxic chemicals in certain applications, product substitution, or appropriate product labelling and other educational approaches.

(a) Asbestos

Three types of asbestos fibre have been used in the home and environment: chrysotile (white), amosite (brown) and to a lesser extent crocidolite (blue). These fibres have been used widely in building materials, such as asbestos cement products, insulation boards, water pipes, lagging to boilers and pipes, sprayed decorative/fire-protective coatings to ceilings, and as a constituent of roofing materials. Asbestos also is used to make textiles, brake linings and consumer goods such as oven gloves, ironing board pads, and seals and gaskets to ovens, boilers and flues.

The main properties giving asbestos its commercial value as a building material are incombustibility, strength and effectiveness as a reinforcing or binding agent when combined with other materials such as cement or plastic. The different fibre types also are resistant in different degrees to high temperatures, electrical current and alkalies, and at absorbing sound.

Asbestos fibres tend to split into finer fibres when subjected to suitable treatment. Fibres tend to break not only into shorter fibres but also, because of their crystalline structure, to split lengthwise into finer fibres (or fibrils) invisible to the naked eye (two million can sit on a pinhead). These fibres can penetrate the lung.

The main risk of exposure to asbestos fibres in the home arises through do-it-yourself or maintenance operations; damage to asbestos panels and other products through abrasion; mechanical vibration or deliberate disruption of asbestos surfaces, and indiscriminate removal. For instance, sanding, drilling, cutting or breaking asbestos panels releases substantial amounts of asbestos fibres (e.g. sanding asbestos insulation board will release 6–20 fibres/ml, and power-sawing asbestos cement sheets produces 10–20 fibres/ml in air. [64] Concentrations are highest at the point of initial impact and vicinity of immediate exposure. The softer, more friable forms of asbestos products with a high asbestos content (e.g. boiler lagging or sprayed coatings) are more likely to release large numbers of asbestos fibres to indoor air, compared with compact, hard formulation products with a low asbestos content such as asbestos cement sheeting.

(i) Health effects

Release of asbestos fibres to indoor air poses a potential health risk as reflected in epidemiological, technical and experimental findings linked to asbestos exposure (i.e. direct occupational exposure, para-occupational exposure and true environmental exposure). Asbestos fibres, especially >5 μm in length and <1 μm in diameter and having a length-to-diameter ratio of >10 are biologically the most active and have been shown to cause asbestosis, bronchogenic carcinoma and mesothelioma. All types of asbestos fibre (crocidolite, amosite and chrysotile) have been implicated in causing disease, but crocidolite (blue) has been shown to be the most dangerous form and is more likely to appear in the lung area, whereas chrysolite is found largely in the pleura. This has been linked with fibre dimensions rather than chemical type. At present, asbestos-related disease has been associated mainly with occupational exposure. It has not been possible to come to a reliable quantitative assessment of the risk of malignancies for the general public since present evidence does not point to a threshold level of dust exposure below which tumours will never occur. [65]

All asbestos-related diseases have a long latency period to onset of symptoms – often 10, 20 or in the case of mesothelioma 15–40 years after first exposure. They are nearly always fatal (often resulting in a long, painful death), and despite improvements in medical technology, none of the diseases are curable.

(ii) Control measures

A WHO Working Group on indoor air pollutants concluded that the emission of asbestos from building materials has sufficiently serious short-term and long-term consequences to warrant taking action to limit the problem by whatever measures feasible, in both new and existing buildings. [66]

- The Working Group concluded that the use of asbestos materials that can release fibres to the indoor atmosphere should be avoided in new construction. Existing buildings should be surveyed for such materials, and measures taken to eliminate or prevent them from releasing further fibres.

- Whenever possible, suitable non-asbestos alternatives should be used in new housing and public buildings. The choice of substitutes will depend on the specific performance required of the material (e.g. fire resistance) and the overriding need to ensure that alternatives do not themselves create a health hazard.

- The mere presence of asbestos-containing materials in the home does not necessarily constitute a hazard, and removing undamaged material may create more hazard from dust and fibre release than would leaving it in place. The course of action for dealing with asbestos in existing buildings will therefore depend upon a number of factors:

  - **Condition** of asbestos (i.e. whether damaged or not).

  - **Friability** of material: fibres released from asbestos contained within hard materials such as concrete or plastics are negligible compared to soft asbestos boards containing little else apart from asbestos fibres and adhesive.

  - **Treatment of surface** (e.g. painted or papered asbestos provides some protection from fibre release).

  - **Position**: asbestos is more hazardous inside a dwelling compared with outside (externally, fibres quickly disperse and are heavily diluted). Air currents passing over asbestos surfaces (e.g. heating duct linings) increase the chances of release.

  - **Accessibility**: the more accessible the materials, the greater the risk of damage, particularly during maintenance operations or by accidental or non-accidental damage to asbestos products.

  - **Content**: the concentration of asbestos fibres in the material.

The relative importance of each of these factors can be weighted on a points-scale basis for determining whether to remove, seal or leave the asbestos undisturbed. This procedure would enable some removal priority to be established as part of an overall asbestos policy. Local health administrations should keep a register of the location of asbestos in their districts and keep details of persons exposed.

- In certain cases, it may be possible to seal in asbestos by painting or spraying with paint, bitumen or other suitable sealants.

- Health education programmes need to be drawn up to inform housing residents, members of the public and maintenance workers of the dangers of asbestos in the home and environment and the preventive measures available to control exposure.

(b) Non-asbestos mineral fibres

The numerous non-asbestos mineral fibres have various uses and characteristics. The most common mineral fibres are 'man-made' (MMMF), glass fibres made from molten slag, rock or glass. Manufacturers characterize MMMF products by their nominal diameter. In occupational health, fibres are arbitrarily defined as elongated particles with a length-to-diameter ratio of 3 to 1. For example, a particle of 3.5 μm diameter must be at least 10.5 μm long to qualify as a fibre. [67]

Slagwool and rockwool fibres are used mainly to make insulation wools, which are then compressed into blankets, boards, sheets or used as loose wool for loft and building insulation and as a reinforcing material in cements and mortars. Other mineral fibres include special purpose glass fibres with very small diameters and ceramic fibres used in high-temperature conditions.

(i) Health effects

MMMF can cause skin irritation but have not otherwise been demonstrated convincingly as hazardous to health (i.e. through inhalation). A conference on the biological effects of man-made mineral fibres, convened jonitly by WHO and IARC, concluded that 'there is no clear epidemiological evidence of increased cancer death or other diseases associated with MMMF exposure'. [67] However, animal studies show that inhalation of long, thin fibres can cause cancer (e.g. fibres with a diameter <0.25 μm and a length of >20 μm showed the maximum carcinogenic potential). Increasing the fibre length increases the proportion of fibres deposited in the lung. At present, MMMF represents a much safer alternative to asbestos in thermal insulation and fireproofing applications.

(ii) Control measures

There is little need to control the uses and applications of MMMF in the home and environment. Indeed, MMMF should be encouraged as an acceptable alternative to asbestos. However, it would be prudent to reduce exposure to the lowest possible point permitted by available technology. [68]

- Direct handling of these materials should be avoided by use of protective clothing and some form of respiratory face mask during installation or maintenance operations.

- Whenever possible, long, thin MMMF within the respirable range should be specified for applications within the home.

(c) Lead

Lead has been widely used in housing for water pipes, fittings and soldered joints. Lead oxides also have been used as a paint additive, particularly in lead primers. In normal circumstances, the most important sources of exposure are lead from food as a result of weathering of lead-rich ores and minerals in the soil, contamination of canned food by lead solder used in making cans, contamination of tap water used in cooking by lead in the plumbing system, and contamination of soil, crops and food by lead in air and dust. [69] Adventitious sources include eye cosmetics, medicinal products and lead-glazed food utensils.

(i) Health effects

The intake of lead in food, air and water is a major public health concern, particularly because of the pervasive toxic nature of lead exposure of the general population. In terms of acute lead poisoning, old lead paintwork has been identified as the most serious source. For example, Sachs [70] reported that 80% of patients seen because of evidence of lead absorption had a history of eating paint or plaster and another 10% revealed lead in the abdomen. A small paint flake 2–3 mm in diameter may contain over 1000 μg of lead, or over ten times the daily intake from all other sources. [71] A child who habitually ingests this amount can suffer severe lead poisoning in 3–4 months. In the UK, as in many other countries, old lead paintwork in the home is the single most common cause of severe lead poisoning and accounts for about one third of all known cases and about a quarter of all poisoning deaths from non-medicinal substances other than carbon monoxide. [69]

Lead is an important neurotoxin, and young children are more susceptible to lead poisoning than adults because a child's lower body weight means that it cannot tolerate the same dosage as an adult; the effects of low-lead intoxication disproportionally reduce a child's concentration, intelligence and educational attainment; children absorb more lead into their bodies (particularly bones) as part of their normal physical development; and children are more exposed to lead than adults because of their tendency to lick or chew old lead paintwork or eat or lick dirt or dust containing lead.

The symptoms of early lead intoxication include apathy, loss of appetite, anaemia and abdominal pain. In some cases, this leads to convulsions, ataxia, persistent vomiting and coma, which denote the onset of encephalopathy sometimes culminating in death. However, these cases of lead poisoning should be distinguished from subclinical effects characterized by behavioural disorders, learning difficulties, hyperactivity and other disorders which have been claimed to be associated with elevated blood-lead levels in young children.

(ii) Control measures

- Each country should investigate the sources and distribution of lead in its housing stock with a view to formulating a policy that incorporates technical, legal and educational objectives aimed at minimizing lead intake from all sources. Such a programme could incorporate a routine blood-lead or preferably tooth-lead screening programme for pre-school children and other high-risk groups and routine monitoring of lead in paint, soil, air, water and food.

- Childhood lead poisoning can be minimized by ensuring that lead-free paint is specified for all interior wood surfaces in new housing projects (especially in children's bedrooms, toys, nursery furniture and outdoor playground equipment).

- A number of control measures should be taken in existing housing to minimize the effect of high-leaded paint on walls, woodwork or other sources: loose or flaking lead paint to walls, woodwork or other sources should be carefully scraped off or removed with paint stripper, heat guns or wet sanders. (Dry power sanders should **not** be used as they release very large amounts of lead dust into the room.) Window sills, balustrades, cot furniture and door architraves need special attention as these are likely places where a child might chew. In all cases, old paintwork should be repainted with a lead-free paint.

- Replacement of lead piping and lead-lined water tanks should be considered in areas where chemical attack from water is a problem ($<$pH 7). Water authorities should take all possible steps to reduce levels of lead in tap water by adjusting acidity of water and by using non-lead alternatives for water supply pipes and fittings. When lead pipes are replaced by copper, lead-soldered joints or brass fittings containing lead should not be used.

- Lead-glazed earthenware intended for storing or cooking food should be tested to ensure that lead does not leach out onto food.

Badly chewed lead paintwork to window ledge can result in lead poisoning.

2.6 SANITATION REQUIREMENTS

The importance of sanitation as a healthy housing requirement has long been recognized by the WHO. As long ago as 1949, a WHO Expert Committee defined environmental sanitation as 'the control of those factors in man's physical environment which exercise or may exercise a deleterious effect on his physical development, health and survival'. In particular, it refers to 'the **control of housing** to ensure that it is of a character likely to: (i) provide as few opportunities as possible for the direct transmission of disease . . . and (ii) encourage healthful habits in the occupants'. Provision of basic sanitation in human settlements has remained a primary objective of the WHO and other United Nations programmes for developing countries, but over half the people in the Third World still do not have safe water to drink and three quarters have no sanitation. [24]

In practical terms, housing sanitation necessitates a clean supply of water (either piped into the dwelling or readily accessible to it) for drinking, preparation of food, domestic washing activities and personal hygiene; a sanitary means for disposing of solid and liquid household wastes; and controlling insect, parasitic and other animal vectors of disease. The principal objective of sanitation is thus to minimize the

95

spread of food and waterborne enteric infections as well as other diseases. This objective can be achieved through improvements in sanitation, provision of infrastructural and hygienic practices and health education programmes.

2.6.1 Provision of sufficient, clean water supply reasonably accessible to the dwelling and protected against pollution from outside and within the dwelling

The provision of potable and non-potable water supplies for drinking and washing purposes, respectively, is a basic housing hygiene measure still denied to millions of people around the world, particularly in rural areas of developing countries. Surveys by the WHO indicate that an estimated 1800 million people are without clean water and 2400 million are without satisfactory sanitation out of the total world population of approximately 3200 million. [72] In addressing this problem, the United Nations Conference at Mar del Plata, Argentina, decreed 1981 to 1990 as the International Drinking-Water Supply and Sanitation Decade. The decade's objective was to provide the entire global population with safe water supplies and hygienic waste disposal systems.

In the European Region, water supply provision varies considerably, but as expected, the developing countries and in particular rural areas are most deprived. For instance, a WHO rapid assessment exercise in 1981 showed that in one group of countries (Albania, Bulgaria, Czechoslovakia, Greece, Hungary, Ireland, Italy, Poland, Rumania, San Marino, Spain and Yugoslavia), 90–97% of the urban population were connected to a good quality water supply but only 40% were connected to a sewerage system, whereas in the rural areas most of the population was served only by private wells and only 15% were connected to a sewer. [73] European countries with an industrially based economy also have deficiencies, with an estimated 40–95% served by a community water supply system and 0–30% connected to a sewerage system. However, in urban areas 95–99% were connected to a satisfactory water supply system and 70–75% to a sewerage system. [73]

(a) Health effects
Historically, the location and eventual growth of human settlements have always been related to some extent to the availability of adequate water supplies from rivers, wells, springs and other sources. Without water, the human body dehydrates and physiological processes become severely impaired, leading in a few days to death. Humans also need water for growing food crops, preparing food, cleaning and washing. Water is thus important for long-term economic growth, prosperity and

community development. Health problems can occur when the demand for water outstrips supply because of natural consequences, such as drought or adverse hydrological conditions, unmatched population growth, excessive water demands related to industrialization or increased water consumption.

The qualitative aspects of water supplies are also important. Human or animal excreta and toxic industrial effluent can **pollute** water supplies, making it unfit to drink or be used for other domestic operations. Contamination can occur either at source or during carriage from source to consumer. Some of the diseases caused by waterborne pathogens, viruses, parasites, chemicals and heavy metals are listed in Table 2.8. Of these waterborne diseases, diarrhoea is the major cause of morbidity and mortality in young infants and children, who are particularly susceptible to the effects of enteric diseases: a minimum of 1000 children under the age of 5 years die every hour in developing countries from diarrhoeal diseases, amounting to 8 million children a year. In the countries of the developing world, 30–50% of all deaths of children under 5 years are attributable to diarrhoeal diseases. [74]

In addition, polio can be transmitted through chlorinated surface water, filtered water or untreated well water. The hepatitis virus can survive normal chlorination, and coagulation and sedimentation methods of treatment must be used to eliminate these viruses from water supplies. All these diseases are caused by pathogens from **untreated sewage** (principally human excreta) which can contaminate water supplies. Epidemiological studies have shown that the rate of *Shigella* dysentery in children up to 10 years of age living in housing without an inside water supply was about twice that of a corresponding group whose homes had a pressurized inside water supply. [74] Other American studies have shown that the prevalence rate for shigellosis, the incidence of *Ascaris* infections and the morbidity from diarrhoeal diseases were inversely related to the availability of water, [75, 76] that is, the further away the premises are from the water source, the greater the number of diarrhoeal diseases. [77] Other diseases, such as schistosomiasis, may be related to the absence of a piped water supply to houses, necessitating the collection of water for domestic use from a natural source and thereby exposing people to the disease.

Another infectious agent causing periodic outbreaks of disease is *Legionella pneumophila*, the cause of **Legionnaire's disease**. This bacteria has been isolated from water in air-conditioned cooling towers and evaporative condensers, hot and cold water taps and showers, and from creeks, ponds and the soil from their banks. *Legionella* spread through water-contaminated air has become a major problem in some hospitals and major public buildings. However, it has very rarely been found in domestic premises.

Table 2.8 Typical diseases associated with water supplies

Bacteria		
	Vibrio cholerae	Cholera
	Salmonella typhi	Typhoid fever
	Salmonella paratyphi	Paratyphoid fever
	Other *Salmonella* spp.	Gastroenteritis
	Other *Salmonella* spp.	Salmonellosis
	Shigella	Bacillary dysentery
	Legionella pneumophila	Legionellosis
Viruses		
		Enterovirus infections, including poliomyelitis and Coxsackie virus
		Echovirus and rhinovirus infections
	Hepatitis A	Epidemic hepatitis
Parasites		
	Roundworm	Ascariasis
	Nematodes	Oxyuriasis
	Whipworm	Trichuriasis
	Hookworm	Ancylostomiasis
	Guinea worm	Dracontiasis
	Flukes	Fascioliasis
	Flukes	Fasciolopsiasis
	Lung fluke	Paragonimiasis
	Flukes	Schistosomiasis
Chemicals		
	Iodine deficiency	Goitre
	Fluoride deficiency	Caries
	Excess fluoride	Fluorosis
	Excess inorganic salts	Diarrhoea
	Excess inorganic salts	Gastric upsets
	Sulphates	Nephrolithiasis
	Cadmium	Hypertension
	Sodium	Methaemoglobinaemia
	Nitrates and nitrites	Cyanosis
Heavy metals		
	Lead	Lead poisoning
	Arsenic	Black foot disease
	Arsenic	Skin and lung cancer
	Cadmium	Nephropathia
	Cadmium	Itai-Itai disease
	Mercury	Minimata disease
	Mercury	Nephropathia

Chemical contamination of water supplies for drinking and cooking can also adversely affect health. For example, excessive amounts of **nitrates and nitrites** from agricultural fertilizers can seriously contaminate water sources in some areas and may be responsible for causing methaemoglobinaemia in infants. Also, certain forms of cancer (e.g. bladder or gastric cancer) may be associated with very high levels of nitrate/nitrite in water through in vivo formation of nitrosamines and secondary or tertiary amines. The bacteria and optimum pH levels needed for the nitrosamine formation are available in the living organism. However, the link between nitrosamines and cancer has not been confirmed epidemiologically and it could be associated with food as well as with water.

Contamination of water from **lead** used in water supply pipes and fittings also can significantly contribute to blood-lead levels in children and adults, particularly in areas where plumbo-solvency is a problem. Other chemical contaminants of water include **copper, iron and zinc** from water pipes and fittings, but their adverse health effects under normal circumstances have not been proven. Nevertheless, large concentrations of copper and zinc can act as an emetic, and evidence from some Scandinavian countries suggests that copper in water is one cause of infantile diarrhoea, which has been fatal in these countries when water containing copper at levels of over 6000 μg is used to prepare an infant's bottle feed. [78]

Other heavy metals which can adversely affect health include cadmium, mercury and arsenic. A more insidious concern is the presence in water of many organic compounds, often in very small concentrations and frequently unidentifiable with present techniques. Little is known about the health effects of these chemicals. For instance, at a WHO conference in 1975, toxicological data were available only for 45% of the 289 compounds occurring in water.

(b) Control measures

Wholesome supplies of drinking water and sanitary disposal of liquid waste products are of paramount importance to public health and housing hygiene, particularly in controlling enteric disease. A safe water supply is estimated to reduce the cases of all diarrhoeal diseases by 50%, with a similar reduction in bacillary dysentery, amoebic dysentery and gastroenteritis, while reductions in cases of typhoid could be expected to be as high as 80% and cholera 90%. [72] In rural areas of developing countries, no single measure can do more to improve health and well-being than an ample supply of safe water, providing that adequate facilities are made for the sanitary removal of waste water and excreta disposal.

- In general terms, potable water supplies should be wholesome, which means that its physical appearance, taste and odour are acceptable to the consumer and that it does not contain anything deleterious to the health of the consumer. Developing countries should carry out a countrywide survey of human settlements to ascertain which populations have reasonable access to clean water supplies and to identify those not served. Following the survey, short-term and long-term water supply plans should be drawn up to take account of the degree of scarcity of drinking water; number and location of settlements where enteric disease is endemic; total population of settlements to be served; per capita cost of each project and available capital; and the practical considerations of terrain and feasibility of providing disposal/treatment facilities for waste water.

- In new developments, water supply, water distribution, waste water disposal, drainage and sewerage should form an integral part of a master development plan.

- An institutional framework should be established for setting up an organization with the necessary manpower resources for planning, installing, operating and maintaining water supply and sanitation systems. Administrative, technical and managerial staff should be trained where necessary to enable personnel to plan, design, construct, operate and maintain the various water supply installations. Where possible, a single ministry, department or agency should be made responsible for water supply and waste water/sewage disposal administration.

- All reasonable steps should be taken to ensure that water supplies are quantitatively and qualitatively adequate at source. In particular, wells, streams, springs, reservoirs and other water supplies should not be polluted by human or animal excreta, toxic waste or other chemical contaminants such as nitrates and fertilizers.

- Where possible, water supplies should meet the standards specified in the International Standards for Drinking Water recommended by the WHO [79] and EC directives in countries belonging to the European Common Market. Water supplies need to be sampled and tested regularly to ensure compliance with these standards.

- Piped water supplies need to be protected against cross-contamination from harmful bacteria or chemicals in the ground. In urban areas, water supplies are normally chlorinated or otherwise treated at source, but this is rarely undertaken in rural areas. In these cases water supplies should be adequately protected from excreta or chemical contamination (e.g. through separation of water supplies from excreta disposal points).

- Water supplies in urban areas should be continuous, adequate, safe and supplied under sufficient pressure: interruption of service, intermittent supply or continued low pressure in the distribution system leads to the introduction of pollutants, such as sewage, into the water system. Also, a high water table can cause back pressure in water pipes if the water pressure is low. Vacuuming can occur in peak hours due to increased demand over supplies (particularly in furthermost areas). This can be a major source of entry for soil pollutants, causing outbreaks of enteric disease. When this occurs, pipes should be flushed with a high chlorine concentrate. The minimum water pressure for piped supplies is 1 kg/cm for each 10 m run.

- Potable and non-potable water supplies should be separated to avoid the possibility of cross-connection between the two systems.

- In principle, adequate supplies of safe water should be provided for the domestic use of every inhabitant. Preferably, this should be by a piped supply of chlorinated water into the home but this may not be possible in some rural areas or in temporary, shanty-town or slum housing. In these cases, deep-bore wells should be used, preferably pumped by electric pump and totally enclosed by a concrete surround. Deep springs can also be used for water supplies, providing they are protected from surface and faecal pollution. If water supplies are at risk of being polluted, double jar disinfection with a mixture of sand, chlorine and sodium phosphate should be used.

- As an alternative to piped supplies, standpipes or public hydrants should be provided as near as possible to dwellings. Hygienic facilities should be provided for drainage of water from standpipes, including a surround. However, these measures should be regarded as short-term options in permanent human settlements.

- Water storage tanks either inside or outside the home should always be kept covered to discourage algae growth following exposure to sunlight, and to prevent the entry of mosquitoes, rats, mice, squirrels and birds that could contaminate supplies. Storage tanks also need to be regularly cleaned to remove grit, dirt and other debris. They should also be secured from children.

- Materials used for water services should not provide a source of bacterial or chemical contamination to supplies. In areas where plumbo-solvency is a problem, lead should not be used in service supplies or tanks.

- In view of the importance of safe water supplies, individual countries should formulate legislation to control the design and construction requirements of all new and existing water installations and services from source to supply. The disposal of sewage and other wastes also should be similarly regulated to prevent water supplies from becoming polluted.

- Local codes, ordinances and regulations should prescribe, in detail, construction materials and sanitary design of all water services, fittings and appliances. Provision should be made for enforcing the legislation at district level. Surveillance procedures for monitoring raw water quality and the quality of drinking water throughout the distribution system need to be implemented.

2.6.2 Provision of sanitary means of waste- and surface-water disposal

The construction of new water-supply systems increases the need for the sanitary collection and disposal of domestic waste water, yet such systems are either non-existent or grossly inadequate in many communities throughout the world. The collection, treatment and disposal of waste is often delayed until long after water supplies have been provided, despite the fact that community water supplies, a water-carriage waste-disposal system and sanitary disposal of excreta are all basic inter-related requirements for controlling enteric and other diseases. Thus, the provision of piped water supplies to an area commonly causes a deterioration in existing health conditions until adequate waste disposal facilities have been installed. [80]

Non-industrial countries are hampered by limited financial resources, skilled labour and lack of a manufacturing base for materials and plant; more priority and money thus need to be given to provision of drainage and sewage disposal schemes when installing community water supplies if waterborne diseases are to be controlled effectively.

(a) Health effects
Inadequate drainage arrangements for waste and surface water may result in pools and puddles of muddy and marshy areas that provide breeding places for mosquitoes, flies and other insect disease vectors. Similarly, water run-off from standpipes, latrines and food preparation areas can provide a major source of biological contamination, particularly when mixed with animal excreta and solid waste.

Inadequate surface-water drainage also can cause periodic flooding of roads, wells and housing, creating further hazards to health and safety.

Waste-water disposal to an internal trapped gully.

(b) Control measures

- Waste-water collection/carriage systems should be installed at the same time as new piped water-supply systems wherever practicable. However, each waste-water treatment problem is unique and the solution must be adapted to local resources, including water availability, labour and materials, rather than blindly adopting waste-water treatment processes appropriate to other countries.

- A piped water-carriage system connected to a main sewer is the preferred method for removing foul water and sewage. However, it is important that the design and construction of drainage systems conform with sanitary principles and that drainage effluent does not leak out into surrounding ground, contaminating water supplies or otherwise causing a public health hazard. In particular, improperly made joints and sewer connections are responsible for many leakage

103

problems associated with a piped disposal system. Uneven settling of pipes resulting from poor installation or soil movement is the main cause of pipe fracture and leakage to the surrounding ground.

- Rainwater can be disposed of by individual soak-aways situated at a minimum distance of 4 m from a building. Water must be able to permeate from soak-aways into the surrounding subsoil, which is not possible where the surface material is impervious (e.g. in heavy clay soils) to water. In these cases, a soak-away should be carried down into permeable soil below.

- To prevent waterlogging, soak-aways should be carried above the highest natural level of the water-table.

- Rainwater and surface water can also be drained directly to a stream or other watercourse without treatment. Open rainwater-drainage channels frequently become blocked with rubbish, leaves and other debris, creating a public health hazard. Enclosed pipes with access points for maintenance and appropriately protected from traffic etc., are preferred.

- Access to drains and sewers should be provided by inspection chambers so that every length of drain is accessible for maintenance (>90 m between access points). This is particularly important at all changes of drain direction and gradient (except where change is not too great for cleaning), at all drain junctions where cleaning is not otherwise possible and at the head of each length of drain. (A rodding eye may suffice for a shallow branch drain.) Inspection chambers need to be watertight and large enough to enable them to be cleaned from the surface. Suitable materials include brickwork, cast iron and precast concrete.

- The flow in a waste-water collection system is normally at atmospheric pressure, with the direction of flow being from a higher to a lower elevation. To enable self-cleansing and flushing, a waste-water plumbing system should make use of the smallest pipes that will conduct waste water away rapidly without clogging or siphonage of traps. Plumbing should be easily accessible for ease of maintenance and should be designed to avoid back pressure that might lead to contamination of the water-supply system.

- The plumbing system should normally be vented to prevent siphonage and loss of water seals. Venting also provides circulation of air in the drainage system, ensuring gravity flow and minimizing smells. Alternatively, unvented, single-stack systems constructed to proper sanitary design should be used.

- Venting stacks should not generally be of less than 32 mm diameter, should extend vertically through the roof and discharge so that foul air does not cause nuisance.

- Traps should be used on all plumbing fixtures to provide a liquid seal preventing passage of air without interfering with waste-water flow.

- To prevent back siphonage of waste water from a plumbing fixture or vessel into water-supply pipes due to negative pressure (particularly in plumbing fixtures or tanks with inlets below the level of the top rim), potable and contaminated waters should be separated by an air gap.

- Cleaning access points must be readily accessible at each major change of direction of plumbing pipes.

- Materials for the plumbing systems should be selected for strength, durability and ability to resist the corrosive action of wastes discharged into them. Cast-iron pipes with lead-caulked joints have long been the standard material for main indoor plumbing, galvanized steel being commonly used for vent pipes. Plastic is replacing metal for plumbing because of ease of construction and cheapness.

- Underground drains and sewers should be of sufficient size to accommodate the number of properties serving them, including any future demands arising from new development. Separate sewers for foul and surface waste water are often advantageous. Although initially more expensive than a combined sewerage system, this system reduces scale and cost of sewage treatment in the long term.

- House drainage pipes should be a minimum 100–150 mm in diameter with a smooth, even internal bore, and be constructed of strong, durable materials impervious and resistant to chemical or acid attack. Suitable materials for underground drainage pipes include cast iron, vitrified clay, concrete, asbestos cement or in some cases pitch-fibre or unplasticized polyvinyl chloride. Choice of materials depends mainly upon loading, thermal movement and ground conditions, particularly ground movement. Where separate sewage and storm water sewerage systems are used, adequate provision must be made to prevent cross-connections.

- House drains should be laid straight and at a sufficient gradient of not less than 2% to enable a self-cleaning velocity to be maintained.

- Drainage pipes are joined by either rigid or flexible joints. In general terms, flexible joints are preferred where ground movement or thermal expansion of pipes is likely. In these cases, pipes need to be adequately supported by readily compacted granular material. Pipes with rigid joints should be encased in concrete to ensure water tightness, prevent root penetration and maintain structural strength. The depth of cover over a drain or sewer beneath a paved surface should be not less than 450 mm and beneath an unpaved surface not less than 600 mm.

- Gullies with a minimum water seal of 50 mm should be provided to drains carrying waste water and surface water. Intercepting traps are sometimes used to disconnect the passage of air from a sewer or cesspool into a drain. However, these often block up and need frequent inspection and maintenance.

- All parts of the house drainage/sewerage systems should have a free passage of air through each part of the system. Permanent openings are required at the lowest and highest points with due regard to preventing odour nuisance.

- All old drain pipes should be removed or properly sealed off to prevent them being used as rat runs.

- Adequate drainage needs to be provided for rainwater run-off to courts, yards or paved areas.

- A number of technical, legal and educational measures need to be taken to ensure that all parts of the drainage system do not get damaged, become blocked up, cause nuisance or create conditions prejudicial to health. The drainge and plumbing system must be regularly inspected and maintained.

- Building codes and ordinances should specify design and construction requirements for all new drainage. Owners should be legally required to submit plans and proposals for all new drainage works or alterations of the existing system to the local health administration for approval. Agencies need to be established for inspecting and testing drainage works as necessary and enforcing codes and ordinances.

- Wherever practicable, owners of new and existing buildings should be encouraged or legally made to connect with a sanitary sewerage system when provided. Financial assistance may need to be given in some cases to pay for connection costs.

- Owners of existing buildings should be legally required to make satisfactory provision for drainage and to repair, alter or unblock insanitary appliances, fittings or pipework. This should include filling up, removing or otherwise treating a disused cesspool, drain or sewer.

- Drainage legislation should also make a legal offence the putting of any matter into a sewer or drain that is likely to impede the flow or affect the treatment and disposal. This would include controlling disposal of chemical waste, steam, petroleum products and foreign objects.

2.6.3 Provision of toilet facilities of such a nature as to minimize the danger of transmitting disease

(a) Health effects

Numerous epidemiological studies have shown that insanitary toilet facilities encourage the spread of enteric diseases. These diseases are usually transmitted through the faecal–oral route by contaminated

Insanitary WC accommodation can contribute to the spread of enteric infections.

hands or disease vectors such as flies and crawling insects. Open-air defaecation or bucket privies are still commonplace in many underdeveloped and developing countries, and satisfactory toilet facilities are still deficient, particularly in villages and shanty-towns. Communal or shared toilet accommodation is often extremely insanitary and provides a route for cross-infection of enteric diseases.

Research in Nottingham, England, over a 10-year period showed that typhoid fever had an incidence of 1 in 137 for persons residing in dwellings served by a privy compared with a case incidence of 1 in 558 for persons residing in dwellings with indoor flush toilets. [81] An American study showed that the incidence of diarrhoeal disease was about twice as high in dwellings with privies for excreta disposal compared with persons living in houses with inside flush toilets. [82]

A national health survey in 1935 and 1936 in the USA showed an excessive incidence of typhoid and paratyphoid fevers, diarrhoea, enteritis and colitis among persons living in housing without private inside flush toilets as compared with families having them. [83]

Studies of diarrhoeal disease in Guatemala during the 1950s showed that *Shigella* infection was approximately three times greater among families living in areas where inside toilets were available in less than one half of the dwellings than among those families living in areas where more than one half of the houses had such facilities. [84]

(b) Control measures

- Every dwelling unit should be provided with its own separate inside **sanitary accommodation**. However, this may not be possible in housing shared by more than one family or in some multiple housing schemes where sanitary accommodation has to be shared. In these cases, special care has to be taken that sanitary arrangements are adequate and regularly cleaned to reduce the risk of spreading infection.

- To prevent odour nuisance, sanitary accommodation should preferably be so sited that it does not open directly into a habitable room or kitchen (i.e. there should be an intervening ventilated lobby between rooms and sanitary apartments). Where possible, a compartment containing a WC, urinal or slop sink should be situated on an external wall.

- Outside toilet accommodation is rarely convenient to users, especially at night. However, where provided, it should be within reasonable distance of the dwelling unit and easily accessible to all members of the household. Alternatively, in some cases, it may be practicable to provide covered access to it.

- Every sanitary compartment should be constructed with smooth, impervious surfaces to floors and walls that enables easy cleaning. In particular, floors should be coved at their junction with walls to enable effective cleaning operations.

- Sanitary compartments should be suitably lighted and ventilated by means of a window opening directly to the outside. Where mechanical ventilation has to be used, the apartment should have an exhaust system. Both natural and artificial ventilation systems should provide at least three air changes per hour.

- Adequate sound insulation should be provided between WCs and adjoining rooms. Silencer tubes should preferably be fitted to water supply pipes.

- WCs rely entirely on the wash-down action of the flow and are the preferred method for the sanitary disposal of excreta. The closet receptacle should have a smooth and readily cleansed non-absorbent surface, so constructed and fitted as to discharge through an effective trap to a drainage pipe or sewer. Both the wash-down closet and siphonic closet are self-cleansing and are suitable fixtures for normal use, providing that the flushing apparatus can effectively cleanse the toilet bowl. Enamelled fireclay and glazed earthenware (porcelain) are strong, durable materials suitable for heavier types of fitting such as toilet closets.

- Siphonic units are more expensive than wash-down types but are neat, generally quieter and more hygienic because the flushing action does not create such an aerosol. However, they are more liable to blockage within the siphon.

- Toilets with timber inserts of the rim are useful where hard, rough usage is anticipated but are not as hygienic as those fitted with drop-down seats and covers.

- Where blockage might be a problem, toilet pans with an integral clearing eye should be provided. Toilets should be so arranged that drain pipes are directly connected to a soil-vent pipe, or in the case of ground floors, to the underground drain.

- **Eastern closets** are a typical feature in many developing countries. They are particularly popular in communities where cultural traditions discourage bodily contact with a toilet seat as in traditional WCs. This separation overcomes the risk of cross-infection by this route. However, eastern closets frequently become badly soiled and insanitary, particularly in the bowl area. It is therefore important that satisfactory flushing equipment for cleansing the closet bowl is provided and regular arrangements made for routine cleaning and maintenance. This is best achieved by a flushing cistern permanently connected to a piped water supply. Where this is not possible, manual pour-flush cleaning can be used.

- To prevent nuisance from odours, eastern closets must be properly disconnected from the sewerage system by a trapped interceptor, particularly when connected to a cesspool, pit latrine or septic tank.

- The **earth closet** uses the well-known power of dry earth to neutralize faecal matter deposited in a storage receptacle. The earth chosen should be clean, dry, fertile topsoil sifted through a 6-mm mesh (sand and ashes are not suitable). This is deposited in a stout galvanized receptacle of not more than 55-litre capacity held in position by a suitable guide and fitted closely into a suitable enclosure.

- Earth closets are not, strictly speaking, sanitary fixtures but are still commonly used in many rural areas lacking piped water supplies or a water-carriage sewerage system. Earth closets are not recommended for collecting and storing excreta as the need to regularly empty and dispose of contents in a sanitary manner often creates public health problems.

- Earth closets should be so situated that they do not pollute any spring, stream, well or other source of water which is used for drinking or domestic purposes. In particular, the storage receptacle should be of non-absorbent material and be watertight.

- **Chemical closets** use a deodorizing, liquefying or sterilizing liquid that neutralizes faecal waste. The closets are usually constructed of fibreglass and range from an enclosed bucket to semi-permanent, recirculating units. As with earth closets, adequate collection and disposal arrangements must be made with this sytem.

- **Slop sinks** are hopper-shaped sinks with a flushing outlet similar to a toilet pan. They are used for receiving and discharging excreta and are particularly common in communal systems. They should be provided with siphonic flushing cisterns or flushing valves in the same way as WCs and properly connected to the drainage system.

2.6.4 Provision of sanitary arrangements for excreta disposal

Sanitary facilities for excreta disposal are still inadequate in many developing countries. This has always been a problem in villages and rural areas, which are rarely connected to main sewerage schemes and where dry systems for excreta disposal are commonplace. For instance, a survey of community water supply and sewage disposal conditions conducted by the WHO in 1971 and 1972 in 91 developing countries showed that in urban areas, only 28% of the population were served by a public sewerage system, while 29% (114 million people at 1970 figures) had no sanitary system whatsoever. In rural areas, 92% of the population (or 962 million people at 1970 figures) were without sanitary facilities at all. In the European Region alone, less than 10% of the rural population in developing countries have adequate facilities for excreta disposal at the present time. [8]

(a) Health effects

A significant number of epidemiological studies have been conducted on the significance of correct drainage and excreta disposal in preventing enteric and other diseases. In the main, these are related to cross-contamination of water supplies through leaking drainage pipes or direct contamination of water sources by untreated sewage. Water pollution from disposal of domestic sewage, liquid wastes and industrial effluents also can directly contaminate food crops. Overflow from latrines, cesspools or septic tanks can contaminate well water or underground water courses as well as create insanitary surface conditions that expose

Insanitary disposal of excreta onto vegetable plot from shanty house.

people directly to helminthic and protozoal parasites and other pathogenic organisms, and encourage fly infestations.

Table 2.9 summarizes the principal viral, bacterial and protozoan pathogens found in human excreta. In carriers, 1 g of faeces can contain about 10^{10} bacteria, of which 10^8 are coliform; moreover, 10^8 salmonella organisms have been found. These bacterial and viral diseases may be spread to humans by polluted water supplies, contaminated food, house flies, crawling insects and other disease vectors. These pathogens are a major source of enteric disease (particularly in children) in developing countries.

Human faeces may also contain eggs of cestodes (tapeworms), such as *Taenia saginata* and *Taenia solium*, or of nematodes, such as *Trichinella spiralis*, from human hosts who have eaten infected meat.

Table 2.9 Viral bacterial and protozoan pathogens found in excreta [85]

Group/Organism	Disease*	Reservoir
Viruses		
Polio virus	Poliomyelitis	Humans
Echovirus	Various	Humans
Cocksackie virus	Various	Humans
Hepatitis A virus	Infectious hepatitis	Humans
Rotavirus	Gastroenteritis in children	
Bacteria		
Salmonella typhi	Typhoid fever	Humans
S. paratyphi	Paratyphoid fever	Humans
Other *Salmonella* spp.	Food poisoning	Humans and other animals
Shigella spp.	Bacillary dysentery	Humans
Vibrio cholerae	Cholera	Humans
Other *Vibrio* spp.	Diarrhoea	Humans
Pathogenic *E. coli*	Gastroenteritis	Humans
Yersinia spp.	Yersiniosis	Humans and other animals
Campylobacter spp.	Diarrhoea in children	Humans and other animals
Protozoa		
Entamoeba histolytica	Amoebic dysentery and liver abscess	Humans
Giarida lamblia	Diarrhoea and malabsorption	Humans
Balantidium coli	Mild diarrhoea	Humans and other animals

*All diseases listed have a symptomless human carrier.

Up to 90% of the rural population in Mediterranean countries shed worms in excreta, the most common being roundworms, hookworms and ringworm. These parasitic diseases may be perpetuated by human excreta on land used for grazing by cattle, pigs and other intermediary hosts, indiscriminate excretion or insanitary sewage disposal methods. Concerning pathways for human contact, edible animal tissues or products might be contaminated through primary and secondary impact, possible bio-accumulation processes and transfer from soil to animal tissues.

In addition, inadequate disposal of sewage effluents or sludges onto land can seriously raise the levels of metals normally present in sewage, such as copper, lead, zinc, cadmium, chromium or mercury. Finally, the inadequate drainage of standing water from a neighbourhood also carries the risk of widespread epidemics of filariasis in some tropical cities by providing breeding sites for mosquitoes which spread the disease. Insanitary domestic drainage and sewage disposal arrangements may also cause considerable nuisance from odours and attract flies as well as possibly interfere with the local ecology of watercourses used as open sewers.

(b) Control measures

- In urban settlements, a piped water-carriage system is preferred for effluent removal, which can then be treated at a suitable sewage treatment plant serving the whole area. The aim of such treatment is to remove pollutants from the waste water to the extent necessary to achieve the desired quality in the plant effluent.

- Communities lacking sanitary excreta and waste water disposal facilities have to rely on ditches, streams, open conduits or direct disposal to the ground. Where water supplies are inadequate, dry systems for excreta disposal may be used. As has been pointed out, these unhygienic methods are an obvious source of nuisance and threat to health: their removal should therefore be a main priority of any housing hygiene policy. In the interim period, arrangements need to be made for the proper collection and disposal of excreta to suitable disposal points.

- **Large-scale sewage treatment schemes** are appropriate only in large urban settlements, providing that water is served by piped water supplies and a piped drainage system. The quality of treatment effluent must meet international standards for sewage effluent before discharge to land, watercourses or the sea.

- In rural or remote areas, **septic tank** installations enable waste to be treated biologically and ensure that polluting factors are removed from the liquid or otherwise rendered harmless before discharge over the site or into an adjacent stream. The plant comprises of settling tanks where anaerobic bacteria break down the solids into liquid form and contact or filter beds where aerobic bacteria remove the solids left in suspension before final disposal of the liquid waste. Sludge settling in the bottom of septic tanks has to be removed occasionally by a tanker or spread over the site and dried. This can then be composted. Septic tanks are particularly suitable for small groups of buildings not accessible to a main drainage system, but which have facilities for disposal of the treated effluent.

- The principal criteria for septic tank installations and other disposal schemes is that they must be automatic, require a minimum of attention and not cause nuisance, either from odour or leakage to surroundings.

- Purified sewage effluents may be disposed of by surface or subsoil irrigation or sometimes by discharge into a stream. The siting of the tank and the outfall should be carefully considered so that it does not cause nuisance or pollute water supplies.

- The type of soil on-site must permit septic tanks to dispose effluent evenly and harmlessly when other outlets such as streams are unavailable. For example, a septic tank installation would be unsuitable in heavy clay soil (unless the required standard of purification could be obtained without the need for land filtration and it could be fed direct to a stream) or if the water-table is likely to be within 1.5 m of ground level for periods lasting several weeks.

- A settlement tank or septic tank should be of suitable depth, of adequate size and capacity for its use and be covered or fenced in. In addition, it should be properly ventilated and constructed with access for inspection, emptying and cleansing.

- Septic tanks should be situated away from trees and protected from falling leaves with wire mesh or other means.

- **Cesspools** are the cheapest and therefore the commonest means of hygienic storage of sewage outside a sewered area, providing they are designed and located in accordance with sanitary principles.

- Cesspool tanks should be constructed and designed to be impervious to surface water and rainwater (i.e. they should be watertight and not have any outlet for overflow or discharge other than the outlet provided for emptying or cleansing). This is of particular importance if cesspools are situated near watercourses or other water supplies.

114

- Cesspools should have sufficient capacity. Ideally, they should not be less than $18 \, m^3$ and be so situated that they can be emptied easily and hygienically (usually three or four times a year). In developing areas, the drainage system to the cesspool should be so positioned that it is capable of being easily connected to a new sewerage system at a later date.

- Cesspools should be adequately ventilated and fitted with a suitable manhole cover to permit inspection, emptying and cleansing, and be of a suitable depth for complete emptying.

- Cesspools should be used only for storing excreta and foul water; surface drainage should be discharged into soakaways.

- **Pit latrines** are more common in developing countries where, because of cheapness, they are the only economically appropriate method for excreta disposal. Several different designs in use rely on either a single- or double-leeching pit that may or may not be watertight.

- The location of pit latrines and their watertightness should depend upon the positioning of underground water supplies and available resources for emptying of pits. Double pits permit excreta to decompose into a harmless and organically rich fertilizer. Provision has to be made for a water seal to be installed between the latrine pit and the fittings.

- Numerous international standards for drainage and sewerage construction materials exist, including several relevant to EC countries. Also, several WHO publications detail the various drainage and sewage disposal options [86] and design and construction of septic tank installations. [87]

2.6.5 Provision of sanitary arrangements for domestic washing and drying of clothes

Domestic washing facilities include those relating to food preparation, washing of food utensils, domestic cleaning, and the washing and drying of clothes and other household items.

(a) Health effects

The washing and cleaning of vegetables, fruit, salads, fish, meats and other food products with clean water is important in removing dirt, bacteria and surface contamination from food, thus minimizing food poisoning. Similarly, hygienic washing facilities enable removal of grease and food debris from cooking and eating utensils ensuring that they do not provide harbourage for harmful bacteria. Hot and cold water facilities are needed for domestic cleaning operations (removal of dirt and germs on walls, floors and other surfaces).

Hot water, with a suitable detergent or cleaning agent, is essential for cleaning food utensils and for washing clothes, bed linen and other textiles. Clothes washing is important not only for personal self-esteem but also for removing dirt, grease, bacteria, dead skin, unpleasant body secretions and sometimes vermin such as fleas, bedbugs and lice, which often infect clothes and bed linen, and which may adversely affect health and well-being.

(b) Control measures

- Each dwelling should be provided with a suitably sized deep sink and draining board with hot and cold supplies of clean water for preparing food, washing utensils, filling buckets and carrying out other domestic cleaning chores.

- Sinks may have single or twin bowls and single or double draining-boards. Units with combined draining-boards are much more hygienic than those with detached draining-boards. Drainage of waste water should be adequate. Overflows moulded into the sink itself are more easily cleansed than other types.

- Glare from white-enamelled or mirror-finished stainless steel draining-boards located under sunny windows can be avoided by using non-reflecting finishes.

- Hardwood timber draining-boards are quieter and less prone to cause breakages than other materials but are less hygienic and need to be treated periodically to extend their life.

- In cold and temperate climates, facilities for drying clothes and household washing should be adequate. This can best be accomplished by a drying room, airing cupboard or ceiling airer. Ventilation should be adequate to enable water vapour to be expelled to the outside air.

- In hot climates, wet clothes and washing are best dried by the sun's rays, which have a strong bactericidal effect on any pathogens present.

2.6.6 Provision of sanitary arrangements for personal washing and bathing

Personal washing facilities are essential for effective personal hygiene as well as for personal self-esteem. They encompass a clean supply of water to a fixture such as a wash basin, wash tub, bath or shower.

These facilities are necessary for all persons regardless of age, sex or state of health. However, individual requirements do differ slightly. For instance, babies, incontinent persons, food handlers and persons engaged in dirty operations need to wash more frequently than others.

(a) Health effects

Regular washing of the skin and hair is necessary to remove dirt, grease, dead skin and sweat products. The armpits, feet and genital area need special attention. Also, if washing is not performed regularly, the body will begin to smell, and sticky waste products on the skin attract more dirt and bacteria, which sometimes leads to skin infections or encourages formation of spots, blackheads, etc. Regular washing of the body and hair also stimulates blood flow to the skin, giving a feeling of freshness, warmth and well-being.

People also need to wash their hands after using the WC compartment: American studies have shown that the availability of water for hand washing was an important factor in reducing the incidence of *Shigella* infections. [78] Hands and fingernails are main vehicles for transmitting salmonellae and other pathogenic organisms to food, often causing food poisoning and other enteric diseases by the faecal–oral route. Examples of these diseases include salmonellosis, typhoid, dysentery and enteritis. Cross-contamination of food and cooking utensils may occur if hand washing is carried out in sinks used for food preparation and washing-up, as can occur in housing without separate hand-washing facilities. Similarly, infected hands contaminate domestic surfaces, articles, appliances and other persons (particularly children during play) with pathogenic organisms, thus facilitating the spread of disease (particularly dysentery). Washing with soap and hot water is extremely effective in removing grease, dirt and bacteria from the skin, and thus reducing a source of infection.

The genital area is another part of the body requiring frequent washing because pathogenic organisms from the bowel, such as *Escherichia coli*, are a frequent cause of cystitis and similar infections, particularly in women. Other bacterial and parasitic infections of the genital area can be spread by sexual contact (e.g. herpes). Facilities for cleansing the genital area before intercourse or other sexual activities may reduce the spread of infection although this is unlikely to reduce transmission of venereal diseases, such as syphillis or gonorrhea.

Women need frequent access to personal washing facilities during menstruation to remove sweat and dried blood, which is an ideal medium for bacterial infection.

Washing facilities are also particularly important for babies. Babies' buttocks soon get soiled from nappies and get very sore if not kept clean; some babies tend to be a little sick after feeding and will smell rather unpleasant if not washed regularly. Also, as the tear glands of babies' eyes are not functional for several weeks after birth, they easily become infected unless the eyes are washed regularly.

Personal washing is also important for discouraging vermin, such as body lice, head lice, crab lice, fleas, bedbugs and scabies mites, which can infect both the human body and clothing. These parasites cause skin irritation and in some cases transmit disease to the host. For instance, the body louse *Pediculus humanis* transmits typhoid fever and louse-borne relapsing fever.

Facilities are needed for the regular washing of the teeth, which is essential for removing food deposits, thus discouraging dental caries and plaque.

(b) Control measures

- An abundant, readily available supply of clean water for personal washing of the body is an essential basic housing hygiene requirement.

- Ideally, running supplies of water under pressure should be piped direct to personal washing appliances within the dwelling unit. Alternatively, suitable water supplies should be available from a tap inside the dwelling or by other supplies readily accessible to it outside.

- Personal washing appliances should preferably be supplied with piped hot water from a geyser, boiler or other source. In the short term, every dwelling should be adequately provided with some facilities for heating water for personal washing, cleaning and cooking purposes (e.g. use of a stove, range or open fire).

- Each dwelling unit should be provided with a wash basin (separate from the sink) situated as near to the WC compartment as possible. If space does not permit both a hand-wash basin and a sink to be provided then the latter should be provided.

- There is little hygienic difference between wall-hung basins and pedestal wash basins, but all basins should have a slight slope towards the bowl so that waste water can drain away.

- Each dwelling should have a suitable fixed bath, wash tub or shower to enable body washing. This should preferably be placed in a separate bathroom and not combined with the WC compartment which restricts the use of toilet facilities.

- Choice of bath fixtures largely depends upon shape, finish, location and weight. It is important that baths are positioned at right angles to joist runs of timber floors in order to accommodate the weight. Bath panels should be fixed so that they can be easily removed for maintenance.

- Showers are particularly useful where there is insufficient room to install a fixed bath. They are also much more economical in water usage. Sometimes a shower unit is incorporated into a bath although because a shower unit takes up less room than a bath it can often be placed into the corner of another room without difficulty. Packaged shower units, including the tray, screen walls and sometimes the service pipes and fittings, can be conveniently used in existing housing schemes. The shower trap should be a minimum 900 × 900 mm in size.

- In situ showers consist of a concrete slab laid to fall towards a floor channel which discharges into a trapped gulley. The walls and floor are usually finished with glazed tiles, or other easily cleaned, hard-wearing impervious material, such as concrete.

- There should be a minimum 1 m head above the highest position of the shower head or otherwise the flow will need to be pump-assisted.

- An impervious membrane should be laid below the shower unit to prevent penetration of water.

- Traps to showers can easily become blocked. Therefore, access facilities are needed should blockages occur. A maximum 4 m waste run with a gradient of not less than 1 in 50 is necessary for pipework to be self-cleansing.

- All personal washing appliances should provide for the sanitary removal of waste water from the household.

- Where separate personal washing facilities inside each dwelling are not possible, communal bathing facilities should be provided. In these cases, hygiene and washing arrangements need to be adequate to prevent cross-contamination and spread of communicable diseases.

- The design of washing facilities in terms of size, type, use and finish varies considerably but should take account of the number of people using them, location in relation to room layout and plumbing systems, and compliance with sanitary principles. Whenever possible, sanitary appliances should be positioned so that they can be conveniently connected to the drainage system.

- A good sanitary appliance should be made of hard, smooth, impermeable material designed and constructed to be self-cleansing as well as to assist the flushing of the drainage system itself.

- Vitreous china is strong, rustless, non-fading and acid-resistant and is particularly suitable for lighter types of fittings such as basins.

- Stainless steel is now widely used for sinks, wash basins and urinals. It is particularly useful where vandalism or other damage might be expected.

- Pressed steel, fibreglass or cast iron are suitable materials for bath construction.

- Plastics are now widely used for sanitary fittings such as baths, basins and shower trays. However, plastics are usually not structurally strong and, being a relatively soft material, can be easily burnt or scratched. Plastic also has greater thermal movement than traditional materials, and a good sealed joint between fixed surfaces, such as partitions and the fitting itself, is important to prevent water entry and bacterial growth.

2.6.7 Provision of hygienic arrangements for the storage, preparation and cooking of food

Food poisoning is a major problem in many countries and is usually associated with poor personal hygiene of food handlers (particularly faecal–food infection) or food contaminated with food-poisoning organisms such as salmonellae, staphylococcae or clostridium bacteria, or more rarely by chemical contamination and animal (including insect) transmission (e.g. rats and mice carry food-poisoning organisms in their lower gut, flies and cockroaches carry germs on their bodies). Other causes of food poisoning directly arising from poor housing hygiene include unhygienic food storage facilities, poor temperature control for food storage, cross-contamination between cooked and uncooked foods, contaminated water for cooking, washing and food preparation, lack of personal and other washing facilities, and contaminated food preparation areas.

(a) Health effects
Hygienic facilities for storing, preparing and cooking food play a major part in reducing food contamination and food poisoning cases in domestic housing. For example, in England, 2719 domestic cases of food poisoning were reported in 1981, representing approximately 22% of all cases of food poisoning identified. In developing countries, the figure is probably very much higher.

The symptoms of illness vary with causal organism but include severe nausea, vomiting, diarrhoea, stomach pains, fever and malaise, sometimes resulting in death, particularly in infants and the elderly.

Unhygienic facilities for food preparation pose a major threat to health and safety.

(b) Control measures

- All walls, floors, ceilings, work surfaces and food preparation areas should be kept in good repair and constructed of materials which do not provide harbourage for dirt, grease and bacteria and that are capable of being kept clean. Suitable materials for floors include concrete (preferably covered with non-slip tiles) or alternatively, heavy-duty vinyl coverings. Walls are best tiled or covered with a similar washable and durable material.

- A suitably sized work surface should be provided, preferably adjacent to the cooker for preparation of food. Ideally, formica or other laminated coverings should be used, as wooden surfaces are difficult to keep clean and require frequent maintenance.

- Kitchens should be properly lighted and ventilated to enable effective and hygienic cleaning and food preparation.

- Adequate facilities are needed to keep rooms cool and to remove water vapour to the outside, thereby discouraging bacterial growth on food and room surfaces.

- Adequate facilities should be provided for the hygienic storage of fresh food products such as meat, milk, dairy products and fish. Particular care needs to be taken to prevent cross-contamination of cooked and uncooked foods. These requirements can normally be met by a refrigerator that keeps food below 10° C. Alternatively (or in addition), a food cupboard or larder with permanent ventilation should be provided in the coolest part of the room. Any ventilation openings should be covered with fine mesh to keep out flies and insects.

Basic facilities for preparation and cooking of food.

- Suitable dry, clean, hygienic storage arrangements also need to be provided for packed, canned and other food products such as cereals, pulses and flour. These also should be proofed against vermin and insect infestation. Similar storage facilities are needed for cooking utensils, crockery and kitchen equipment.

- Kitchens need to be suitably protected against infestation of vermin, insects and other food-poisoning vectors. Pest control measures should be taken to eradicate infestations.

- A suitably sized deep sink with a drainage board should be provided with hot and cold water supplies for preparing food, washing utensils and performing other cleaning operations. Waste-water disposal should be sanitary.

- Facilities for cooking and heating food should be adequate. In most cases, this means providing a cooker or stove with at least two heater rings, an oven and a grill.

- Food handlers should have adequate personal washing facilities (including hot water) and sanitary toilet arrangements.

- Easy-to-keep-clean rubbish bins (with tight-fitting lids) or a garbage grinder (suitably designed for safety) can adequately store and dispose of waste food and rubbish respectively.

2.6.8 Provision of sanitary facilities for the storage, collection and disposal of solid and household waste

Facilities for the hygienic storage, collection and disposal of domestic refuse are essential housing hygiene requirements as well as being aesthetically and environmentally desirable. How this is achieved will depend partly upon the volume and composition of the waste. Waste is gradually changing: it is becoming lighter and more bulky and now contains a high proportion of paper, vegetable and putrescible matter and disposable glass or plastic. However, refuse composition varies considerably with consumer usage. In poorer countries, very little material is thrown away.

Refuse storage arrangements depend mainly upon the type of housing development, with bin or sack containers being more commonly used in traditional housing and chute-feed bulk storage systems for multiple-housing schemes. Choice of disposal methods depends largely upon the availability of suitable sites, cost of transport, socioeconomic factors and local conditions. However, far too often refuse is dumped without consideration for hygienic methods of disposal, thus creating a potential health hazard and spoiling the amenities of the neighbourhood.

(a) Health effects

A WHO Expert Committee on solid waste disposal and control concluded that harm from waste products could arise from

> inflammability because of paper content or by spontaneous combustion when in heaps; production of smoke; disgusting or nauseating smells and liquids during exposed fermentation in the open; the scattering of paper, plastic and dust by the wind; and the breeding of flies and rodents, the role of which is still of great importance in the spread of disease. There are also some long-term problems of man's food chain that have to be examined. [88]

Poor refuse storage and disposal arrangements attract insects, particularly flies of which the housefly and blowfly are the most significant. Flies feed on and breed in waste food products and are a major cause of spread of enteritis and other diseases. Similarly, rats and mice will infest uncontrolled deposits of domestic refuse and could quickly pose a serious health problem as these vermin are reservoirs of a number of communicable diseases. Domestic and other animals frequently scavenge and scatter improperly stored solid waste throughout the neighbourhood. In these situations, gastrointestinal infections and mortality are high, particularly in children. Accidental injuries from broken glass, tins, etc., also escalate. Secondary infections can occur if cuts and sores become septic by handling solid waste products. Accidents and falls caused by tripping over piles of improperly stored rubbish are another safety hazard.

Refuse chute systems in multiple dwellings could be a source of noise nuisance, thus interfering with sleep unless proper design and noise insulation measures are taken. Finally, on-site refuse incinerators may cause public health or nuisance problems from dispersal of dust suspended in flue gases and of unpleasant fumes, and toxic gas emissions from the burning of plastics, particularly polyvinyl chloride but also other undesirable pollutants, including particulate matter, sulphur dioxide, nitrogen oxides, various hydrocarbons and other noxious gases that may have deleterious effects on the health of those who inhale them.

(b) Control measures

- Local health or government administrations should take responsibility for refuse collection and disposal services, including those in peripheral and shanty-town areas. If this is not possible, community self-help schemes should be organized.

124

- Building codes and ordinances should provide for the hygienic storage, collection and disposal of solid waste in new and existing housing schemes.

- Facilities for handling waste should provide adequate storage and, where appropriate, space for on-site treatment, combined with the maximum convenience for the occupier and waste collector and the highest practical standards of hygiene, amenity, safety from fire risk and smoke, and sound insulation.

- Suitable individual storage containers for each dwelling are the best means of storing and collecting waste in houses and low-rise dwellings. The containers should be located in the open air and away from windows and ventilators and, if possible, in shade or in a shelter.

- The waste collector should be able to access all containers easily and should not be required to pass through dwellings.

- Suitable materials for refuse receptacles include galvanized steel, high-density polythene bins and paper or plastic sacks.

- Paper sacks and plastic sacks should be attached to holders specially designed for the purpose and suitably guarded, or used as liners in individual storage containers. Disposable sacks should be sufficiently strong to contain the waste without breaking between collections.

- All refuse containers should have tight-fitting lids to keep out flies and vermin, prevent nuisance from odours, and to keep refuse dry. Rubber lids should be fitted to prevent noise nuisance. Damaged or defective bins should be replaced regularly.

- Refuse containers should be placed on a hard, impervious, free-draining surface in a position with convenient access to the kitchen door.

- A refuse shelter that is an integral part of the building or outbuilding should be open to the air. It also should be of sufficient size to take two containers and of adequate height to permit the container lid to be removed or fully opened, without withdrawing the container.

- Waste storage containers for communal use with chutes are suitable for dwellings in low-rise blocks. Chutes should be spaced at not more than 60 m intervals, on the assumption that an occupier should not be required to carry refuse a distance of more than 30 m.

- Where chutes are not installed, communal waste storage containers are preferable to individual containers. The former should preferably be housed in chambers with doors and provided with a platform to give ready access to the top of the container. Free ventilation is essential.

- Communal chutes can be used for dwellings in blocks with more than four storeys, providing they are properly designed to carry waste without blocking up. This is a particular problem where refuse is not bagged prior to disposal. In many cases, it may be better for a porter to collect bagged refuse each day outside the dwelling. This method is practicable only where a lift is provided.

- The number and siting of chutes will depend upon the layout of the building, the volume of waste, the systems of storage, and the collection and means of access for the collecting vehicles. Chutes should preferably be not less than 450 mm in diameter.

- The chute should preferably be continued full bore and set open to the external air. Where this is impracticable, the chute should be connected above the level of the top hopper to a ventilating pipe continuing to such a height and so positioned that foul air is carried away from the building and any windows or ventilation inlets.

- To avoid noise nuisance (which can be considerable), chutes should not be situated adjacent to habitable rooms.

- Hoppers should not normally be situated within a stairway enclosure, enclosed staircase lobby or enclosed corridor. In no case should hoppers be situated within a dwelling, habitable room or place where food is stored or prepared.

- Each hopper should be contained in compartments constructed of material having a fire resistance of half an hour, be fitted with a self-closing access door and be freely ventilated to the external air to give at least six air changes each hour, by mechanical means if necessary.

- Hoppers should be accessible to the occupants of each dwelling on or near their own floor level. To maintain hygienic conditions and to prevent exceptional wear and tear of the waste disposal facilities, no more than six dwellings should share one hopper. Hoppers should be fixed at a height of 750 mm measured from floor level to the lower edge of the inlet opening.

- The hopper should be designed and constructed such that no dust or fumes can be emitted, and excessive noise is prevented when the hopper is in the closed or open position; no part of the hopper or frame should obstruct the free passage of waste.

- The surface of the wall around the hopper should have a surround

126

of at least 300 mm in width made with glazed tiling or other impervious material that can be easily cleaned.

- A hard impervious material with a smooth, finished surface should be used for paving the floor adjacent to each hopper.

- Whenever the design of a building permits, hoppers should be in freely ventilated positions in the open air (e.g. sheltered balconies).

- Waste storage chambers should be located at vehicle access level (essential in the case of bulk containers), preferably away from the main entrance to the building. They should be constructed such that containers can be removed directly to the outside air, without passing through any part of the building served by the chamber except by way of a passage.

- The walls and roofs of the chambers should be formed of non-combustible and impervious material, and have a fire resistance of at least half an hour.

- The walls should be constructed of or lined with hard impervious material with a smooth finish suitable for washing down. The floor should be not less than 100 mm thick and formed of hard impervious material with a smooth finish, and there should not be steps and projections at the entrance. The junctions of the walls with the floors should be coved, and the coving so formed to prevent damage to walls by containers. The distance between the floor of the chamber and the bottom of the chute should be such that, with the container in position, no waste is discharged onto the chamber floor.

- To vent any dense flammable gases that may escape from portable gas or aerosol containers in the waste, permanent ventilation should be provided. The ventilators should be protected against flies and vermin and located as near the ceiling and the floor of the chamber as possible but away from windows of dwellings.

- Arrangements should be made for washing out the chamber compartment. Drainage should be via a trapped gully connected to the sewer. The floor of the chamber should have a suitable fall towards the drainage point. Gullies should be so positioned as not to be in the track of container trolley wheels. Rainfall or other surface water should not be allowed to flow into the chamber.

- Where communal waste storage accommodation or chutes and container chambers are installed, separate enclosed accommodation at ground level in an accessible position should be provided for storing large and bulky articles or salvageable materials or both, so that the collection authority can make special collection arrangements.

- The layout of roads should ensure reasonable convenience for the collecting vehicle and the collectors. Roads should have a minimum width of 5 m and be so arranged that collecting vehicles can continue mainly in a forward direction.

- Turning places, if required, should provide for the largest vehicle likely to be used. The collection authority should be consulted about turning places and vehicle weights.

- All refuse receptacles, dustbin areas, chutes, hoppers and ventilation shafts etc., should be cleaned and maintained regularly. Hoppers of chute systems can rapidly become fouled and need to be cleaned as part of a routine maintenance programme. Special care needs to be taken that collection areas do not cause nuisance from odours, flies, rats and other vermin.

- All refuse should be properly disposed of off-site by the refuse disposal authority through controlled tipping, sanitary landfill, incineration, composting or some other hygienic disposal method. Particular attention needs to be given to ensuring that disposal sites are situated so they do not give rise to nuisance from odours, flies, rats and other vermin.

- Many countries have detailed standards for collecting and disposing of solid waste. Detailed guidelines for disposing of solid waste are described in a number of WHO publications, including one on solid waste disposal and control. [88]

2.6.9 Provision of separate sanitary arrangements for housing of pets and other domestic animals

In many developing countries, people still share their homes with domestic animals, including horses, sheep, pigs, cattle and poultry. Animal diseases may be transmitted to humans either through direct contact or via soil and dust. Examples of diseases transmitted from farm and other domestic animals to humans include anthrax, tetanus, brucellosis, tuberculosis, listeriosis, salmonellosis, rabies, psittacosis, larva migrans, histoplasmosis and mycotic dermatophytosis.

In most urban environments, dogs and cats are normally well integrated into the house as pets. They represent a considerable emotional asset to their owners and provide companionship and security to a large number of people, particularly the elderly and others who live alone. However, dogs and cats may breed indiscriminately outside human dwellings and are potential vectors of disease.

(a) Health effects

Dogs, cats and other pets transmit numerous diseases to humans. For example, rabies is virtually always fatal in humans and is characterized by nervous derangement often followed by a change in temperament and paralysis in the final stages. It is spread to humans via the bite of rabid dogs, cats, foxes, wolves, badgers, stoats, rodents etc. Dogs and cats not only can contract **tuberculosis** from humans but may also be dangerous sources of infection to humans, especially children through droplet infection.

Salmonellosis can be spread by infected dogs, and a dog can become a symptomless carrier of *S. typhimurium* which can infect humans. Cats may carry *Salmonella* transmitted by caught infected rats and mice. Infected animals can directly contaminate food products, equipment or food preparation areas.

Toxocariasis is caused by a roundworm parasite of the genus *Toxocara* found mainly in the dog and fox, although worm larvae have been found in rodents, which may infect hunting cats. *Toxocara* is of public health importance because larvae have been found in human tissues, giving rise to visceral larva migrans, which in rare instances has caused death and occasionally blindness, especially in children playing in areas where dogs have defaecated. Eggs enter the body through mouthing activities, and are often found in the animal's fur, box and blankets.

Leptospirosis is a bacterial disease commonly found in dogs. For instance, a survey in Glasgow showed that 40% of dogs had at some time been infected with *Leptospira canicula*.

Ringworm is a contagious skin disease caused by the growth of certain fungi living either on the surface of the skin or in the hairs of affected areas. A number of domestic animals are affected, including cats, dogs and horses, and the disease is spread to humans through contact with infected animals.

Leishmaniasis is a disease of humans and dogs caused by minute protozoan parasites. Visceral leishmaniasis occurs in dogs in the coastal countries of Mediterranean countries.

Toxoplasmosis is a coccidian parasitic disease thought to be spread to humans by the domestic cat. It is a systematic, protozoal disease harboured in the cat's intestinal tract; rodents, swine, cattle, sheep, goats, chickens and other mammals and birds are intermediate hosts of the protozoan. Postnatal infections may be acquired by eating raw or under-cooked infected meat or more commonly by ingestion of infective oocysts. Drinking water contaminated with cat faeces has been incriminated. **Cat scratch fever** is a human disease probably caused by a virus carried by cats.

In addition, other diseases that can be transferred from domestic pets to humans include echinococcosis, trichinosis, strongyloidiasis, campylobacteria-caused diarrhoea, lymphocytic choriomeningitis and schistosomiasis. Dogs and cats also carry fleas, which then infest humans. Cat and dog hairs may give rise to allergic reactions in susceptible persons. Caged birds may cause respiratory allergies, and bird faeces provide conditions for fungi and arthropods which can cause allergic symptoms in humans.

(b) Control measures

- The control of communicable diseases from pets to humans depends largely upon hygienic measures for the animals themselves, including veterinary care where necessary, suitable animal housing and health education of animal handlers.

- Domestic animals should be provided with housing separate from the dwelling.

- In some cases, animals may need to be housed outside the dwelling unit and infected animals should be isolated from the home altogether. Special hygiene and cleaning arrangements need to be taken to ensure that animal faeces are removed from areas frequented by young children. Play areas should be enclosed to exclude entry of animals.

2.7 INDOOR AIR QUALITY REQUIREMENTS

Indoor air quality is determined by the air quality outside the building, pollutant emissions within the building and the ventilation rate. More than eighty indoor air pollutants have varying adverse health effects, depending on toxicity, concentration and occurrence inside rooms. In housing, the most common pollutants include carbon and nitrogen oxides, odours, formaldehyde, tobacco smoke, water vapour, airborne allergens, asbestos and other mineral fibres, airborne pathogens and toxic emissions from polymers and consumer goods. Many of these are byproducts of construction materials and furnishings etc. (see section 2.5.3), while others are products of household activities and combustion processes. Epidemiological information on specific causal relationships is limited, but analysis of the literature indicates that buildings do not necessarily protect people from outside air pollution and that the combination of internal atmospheric pollutants entering from outside can increase the chemical toxicity level in humans beyond that imposed by pollution outside.[89] Generally, pollutants entering a building will be at lower concentrations than those outside. [48] Exceptions to this rule will depend on the proximity of housing to industrial plant and major roads.

(a) Health effects

In essence, the whole complex of factors of the indoor environment influences the general condition of the organism by increasing or reducing the degree of tension of the mechanisms regulating homeostasis and changing the adaptation/protective forces of the organism. [20] However, more studies are needed to examine the precise relationships between the various indoor air pollutants at moderately high or low levels and their effects on health. Also, more needs to be known about interactive or possible synergistic effects. The need for this information is particularly important as additional and new sources of contaminants are introduced into the home, and because increased concern for conservation has produced a tendency to reduce ventilation and infiltration, resulting in a build-up of indoor air pollutants.

The WHO Working Group on Assessment and Monitoring of Exposure to Indoor Air Pollutants concluded that field studies of exposure to indoor air pollutants and the adverse health effects associated with them should be carried out, preferably on sample populations. The Working Group also concluded that building and housing codes be reviewed to ensure that indoor air quality is achieved. In addition, existing data concerning construction materials, heating methods and room sizes could be used to study the effects of building characteristics on the health of the occupants. [48] In view of the uncertainty about the delayed health effects of chronic exposure to indoor pollutants at concentrations moderately above background levels and the inadequate knowledge about population exposure, a Steering Committee has been set up by the WHO Regional Office for Europe to examine the health effects and the physical, chemical and biological characteristics of indoor air pollutants.

(b) General control measures

Three main methods are used to control indoor air pollutants: removing the source of the pollutant from the dwelling, controlling pollutant emissions at source and expelling the pollutants from the dwelling through ventilation measures. However, a combination of control measures is often used to reduce indoor air pollutant concentrations. The CIBS Guide gives recommended maximum allowable concentrations for a wide range of gases and vapours and international acceptance for reference standards. [90]

2.7.1 Provision of an indoor atmosphere which is free from excessive chemicals, toxic and/or noxious odours, water vapour, pathogens and other contaminants or pollutants

(a) Carbon monoxide

Carbon monoxide (CO) is a colourless, odourless, tasteless gas produced by incomplete combustion of carbon-containing fuels and is also a byproduct of some industrial processes. Open coal, wood, coke or gas fires routinely release CO indoors, as do unvented gas appliances, especially when the flame is in contact with metal surfaces.

(i) Health effects

Each winter in many colder countries, accidental deaths from asphyxia occur due to faulty heating systems. For instance, in Portugal in 1983, 18 people died of CO poisoning caused by faulty gas water heaters. The elderly are particularly vulnerable to CO poisoning. Its health significance as an air pollutant is due largely to its affinity to form a strong bond with the iron atom of the protohaem complex in haemoglobin, forming carboxy-haemoglobin (HbCO), thus impairing the oxygen capacity of the blood as well as restricting oxygen supply to tissues.

Exposure to high concentrations of CO will damage organs, including the brain and the heart, and may cause death. The effects of exposure to CO concentrations resulting in carboxy-haemoglobin levels of 10% or less are not so obvious. However, experiments on laboratory animals and also humans would suggest that low-level exposure to CO may impair vigilance, perception and the peformance of fine tasks without producing clinical signs or symptoms, but results are inconclusive because other factors could produce the same result. Of much greater importance is the effect of CO on the ischaemic myocardium, which is especially vulnerable to additional hypoxia. Evidence has been reported of changes in cardiac function and the onset of angina pectoris on exercise when carboxy-haemoglobin levels exceed 2.5%. A WHO task group on environmental health criteria for CO concluded that patients with heart or lung diseases, anaemic persons, the elderly, postoperative patients or those with cerebrovascular arteriosclerosis may be at special risk, as well as people living at high altitude. [91]

(ii) Control measures

In view of the toxicity of even low concentrations of CO to humans, the presence of this gas in inhabited rooms must be regarded as inadmissible. As most cases of CO poisoning are caused through incomplete combustion of heating and cooking fuels, appliances, service pipes and flues should be kept properly serviced and in good repair (see section 2.9.6) and ventilation requirements must be sufficient (see section

2.7.2). The use of electric cooking and heating appliances might be appropriate in cases where CO poisoning is thought to be a special danger (e.g. in housing for the elderly or chronically sick). The American EPA standard for CO is 9 ppm for 8 hours of exposure per year. The CIBS Guide recommends a maximum allowable concentration of $55\,mg/m^3$ (threshold limit values). [90] Also, as **carbon dioxide** (CO_2) in the supply air for combustion can affect burner performance, CO_2 concentration should be limited to 0.5%.

(b) Nitrogen oxides

The major source of man-made emissions of nitrogen oxides is the combustion of fossil fuels (heating, power generation, internal combustion engines). Indoor sources include gas appliances, such as cooking stoves, water heaters, gas lamps, fires; heating appliances which burn oil or coal; faulty flues and vents; and cigarette smoke. The NO_2 level increases significantly with a forced-air heating system. Other oxides of nitrogen also exist in the atmosphere and in indoor air but are not known to have any biological significance to humans.

(i) Health effects

Most health effects associated with nitrogen oxides have been attributed to NO_2. High levels of NO_2 can be lethal (i.e. above $282\,mg/m^3$) while concentrations in the range of $94-282\,mg/m^3$ can produce chronic lung disease. [92] Studies on humans show that the earliest response to NO_2 occurs in the sense organs. Odour can be detected at $0.23\,mg/m^3$ and dark adaptation is impaired at $1.40\,\mu g/m^3$. [93] Exposure to higher levels can affect respiratory and expiratory flow resistance. Animal studies show that NO_2 can reduce resistance to respiratory diseases; they also suggest a link with bronchitis and emphysema.

This link is particularly relevant to small children: studies have shown a small but apparently significant incidence of respiratory symptoms and disease for children living in houses with gas stoves compared with those in houses with electric stoves. [94, 95] Nitrogen dioxide levels in kitchens and bedrooms are between 1.5 and 6.0 times higher in gas homes than in electric homes after adjusting for tobacco smoking habits, social class and outdoor levels. These effects have not been observed in adults living in similar environments. However, results are somewhat inconclusive and at this stage a definite answer as to whether nitrogen dioxide is harmful or not in homes where gas is used for heating or cooking is not possible.

(ii) Control measures

- Flueless gas appliances should be vented to the outside air or alternatively replaced by electric cookers or heaters.

- Vents and flues to fires and cookers should be checked and maintained regularly to ensure they are gas-tight.

- Increasing the draught settings to certain types of stove can reduce NO_2 emission from the appliances.

- Eliminating or reducing cigarette smoking inside buildings will reduce ambient NO_2 levels.

- Good ventilation will help dilute nitrogen oxides indoors.

- A WHO indoor air quality steering group reported concentrations of NO_2 of 0.05–1.0 mg/m^3 in indoor air and suggested that a concentration of <0.19 mg/m^3 is of limited or no concern. A WHO task group on environmental health criteria for nitrogen oxides proposed 0.32 mg/m^3 as the maximum exposure for 1 hour, consistent with protection of public health.

(c) Formaldehyde

Formaldehyde can be released in dwellings by various building materials, such as wood shavings, particle boards (especially those treated with urea formaldehyde or phenol formaldehyde binder), synthetic floor coatings, glued wood products, varnishes, paints, textiles and foam (UF) insulation. Formaldehyde concentrations are higher indoors compared with outside, but the degree of ventilation, air temperature and age of the material all affect emissions. [97] To a lesser extent, formaldehyde is produced by incomplete combustion of tobacco and also is an intermediate of photochemical oxidation of hydrocarbons in the atmosphere.

(i) Health effects

At low concentrations, formaldehyde irritates the eyes and the upper respiratory tract; it also is the subject of numerous complaints, such as nausea, headache, rash, tiredness and thirst, the tolerance of which varies with different persons. [98] People with some degree of airway hyperactivity are thought to be especially vulnerable, and others may be allergic to formaldehyde. Allergies are usually genetically acquired, but sensitization also occurs through frequent contact with the compound [99] and may appear in skin or bronchial form. Formaldehyde has been shown to be mutagenic [100] and is suspected to be carcinogenic. [101] It can also affect the menstrual cycle, cause difficulties during pregnancy and result in a lower birth weight. Table 2.10 indicates adverse health effects found at various formaldehyde concentrations.

(ii) Control measures

- A WHO Working Group on Indoor Air Quality concluded in 1979 that the emission of formaldehyde has sufficiently serious short-term

Table 2.10 Adverse health effects from formaldehyde [102, 103]

Effect	Concentration (ppm)
Neurophysiological (e.g. tiredness, nausea, infant vomiting)	0.05–1.5
Odour threshold	0.05–1.0
Eye irritation, menstrual irregularities	0.01–2.0
Upper airway irritation	0.01–25.0
Lower airway and pulmonary	5–30
Pulmonary oedema, pneumonia	50–100
Death	100 +

and long-term problem consequences to warrant taking action to limit the problem by whatever feasible means in both new and existing buildings. [48]

- The Working Group also concluded that the use of materials with high rates of formaldehyde emission should be minimized.

- Formaldehyde emissions in new buildings can be minimized by using specially coated resin-based chipboard or alternative materials for construction.

- The use of urea-formaldehyde foam for cavity wall insulation has been banned in some countries (e.g. Canada) despite its excellent thermal insulation properties. In the UK, some local authorities have also banned its use but mainly because of rain penetration problems rather than fume complaints. The ban on its use in the USA was lifted in July 1983. Formaldehyde emissions from urea-formaldehyde cavity wall insulation can be reduced by ensuring that the cavity and the internal brickwork are properly sealed (i.e. gas-tight). Gas can escape in timber-framed homes along several pathways, and its use is not normally recommended in these cases.

- Restricting cigarette smoking inside the home will reduce formaldehyde levels.

- Indoor formaldehyde gas concentrations can be reduced by increasing room ventilation through dilution.

- Formaldehyde emissions from indoor sources should be controlled through enforcement of maximum allowable emissions from furniture or other consumer goods used indoors.

- Germany and the Netherlands have set a recommended air quality limit for formaldehyde of 120 $\mu g/m^3$ for continuous exposure. These standards are very strict: sidestream smoke from one cigarette, for example, produces 130 μg of formaldehyde alone. In the USA, an indoor standard in the range of 240–600 μg/m³ has been proposed.

- WHO has proposed that concentrations of <0.06 mg/m³ are of limited or no concern and that a concentration of 0.12 mg/m³ during both long- and short-term exposure is a measure of concern. [67]

(d) Odours

Some substances in the indoor environment, generally arising from humans, domestic animals or their activities, evoke unpleasant odour sensations. The sources of malodours include the expired air of persons with decaying teeth, foul mouths or certain disorders of the digestive system, and is due in part to volatile fatty acids given off from skin excretions and soiled clothing. Tobacco smoke, cooking odours and odours from toilet areas are other unpleasant sources of odour emissions. Odours are also given off from odourizers in cleaning agents and furnishings.

(i) Health effects

Disagreeable odours can be a considerable cause of annoyance or nuisance, and high concentrations can lead to stress and behavioural change, and adversely affect social well-being. Some individuals are particularly sensitive to odours and become nauseous on exposure. Odours may be a first warning sign of inadequacies in the ventilation system.

(ii) Control measures

- Good housekeeping and prevention at source, together with elimination of odours by ventilation, are the most practical control measures for odours. In some cases, activated carbon filters can be used to absorb odours (e.g. in cooker extract fans), but these are expensive and need to be changed regularly.

- Body odour is best controlled by regular washing and personal hygiene measures. Suitable washing facilities, including hot and cold water supplies, are essential housing hygiene requirements. Health education may be effective in encouraging personal hygiene practices and minimizing unpleasant odour emissions.

- The fresh air supply necessary to maintain body odour at a satisfactory level depends upon standards of personal hygiene and differs between adults and children. The air supply rate per person for odour removal is inversely related to occupational density (i.e. a lower air supply rate per person is needed as occupational density (m^3/person) increases).

(e) Tobacco smoke

Tobacco smoke contains many specific pollutants, most of which are in the respirable range of 1 μg (e.g. nicotine, carbon monoxide, acrolein and polycyclic aromatic hydrocarbons). Other components include phenols, naphthalenes, trace metals, hydrogen cyanide, ammonia and radioactive polonium-210. [104] Many of these pollutants will be filtered out in the smoker's lung (e.g. 70% of particulate matter). [105] However, residual pollutants from exhalation and sidestream smoke (unfiltered smoke from an idling cigarette) can be a major source of contaminants in indoor air.

(i) Health effects

The adverse health effects on the smoker are obviously more serious than for the non-smoker and are well documented. [106] However, non-smokers may become involuntary passive smokers in rooms polluted with tobacco smoke and are subject to the short-term effects of high carbon monoxide levels (which are of particular consequence for cardiorespiratory invalids) and also of possible carcinogenic substances released to the atmosphere with tobacco smoke. Specific dose–effect relationships between tobacco smoke and health have not yet been developed, but circumstantial evidence suggests an association between involuntary smoking and adverse health conditions. For instance, children living in housing where parents smoke have been found to have adverse pulmonary effects compared to those from non-smoking households. [107] Parental smoking also appears to be a cause of increased respiratory disease in the first year of life, and a study of non-smoking Japanese women indicated that wives of heavy smokers have a higher risk of developing lung cancer than those married to light or non-smokers. [108]

Eye irritation, coughing and possible nausea from inhalation of aldehydes, NO$_2$ and small particulates are typical adverse health effects, and are particularly serious for respiratory invalids. [109-11]

The odour of the smoke also produces complaints of nuisance and irritation among non-smokers, but the long-term effects of passive smoking, particularly in vulnerable groups such as the young, elderly and pregnant women, need to be researched more fully before concluding a definite cause and effect relationship. However, an American study shows that each smoker in a home contributes approximately 20 μg/m^3 to the indoor respirable particle concentration. [112]

(ii) Control measures

Controls against tobacco smoke include:

- Restriction of smoking in public places and occupied rooms together with good extract ventilation will help minimize tobacco smoke pollution. However, to be effective this approach needs to be linked with a long-term public education programme.

- The WHO Working Group on Indoor Air Pollutants concluded that because of the complex nature of tobacco smoke, meaningful maximum concentrations could not be given. The Japanese standard for tobacco smoke is $0.15\,mg/m^3$. [67]

(f) Water vapour and condensation dampness

Water vapour (H_2O) is a normal byproduct of metabolic, respiratory and thermoregulatory responses in humans and other animals. Water vapour can also penetrate a building because of poor building design and construction. More commonly, it is produced by indoor combustion and indoor domestic activities such as cleaning, washing and laundry operations (Table 2.11). The main deleterious effect of water vapour as an indoor air pollutant is in causing condensation. Conversely, damp parts of the building structure can in certain circumstances add to water vapour levels.

Table 2.11 Activities producing moisture inside a house [113]

Source	Moisture (kg)	Comment
4 people × 12 h indoors	2.5	Breathing out water vapour. Much of this will be overnight in bedrooms, which may have very low ventilation rates
Gas cooking		
Breakfast	0.4	Normal kitchen activities
Lunch	0.5	total 3.7
Dinner	1.2	
Dish washing		
Breakfast	0.1	Kitchen doors often are kept open and
Lunch	0.1	moisture can disperse to other parts of
Dinner	0.3	the house
Floor mopping	1.1	
Clothes		Amount of washing not specified
Washing	2.0	
Drying	12.0	
Bathing		Number not specified
Shower	0.2	
Bath	0.1	

Condensation dampness occurs when air saturated with water vapour condenses onto surfaces as soon as the temperature drops — the warmer the air, the more moisture it can hold. Condensation is a common problem in rooms where a lot of water is produced (e.g. kitchens and bathrooms), but it is also frequently found in unheated rooms where ventilation and movement of air is poor. Condensation has a number of causes, usually brought about by poor building design and frequently by a combination of poor heating, poor insulation and poor ventilation.

Condensation is normally considered a problem only when it does not disappear quickly, that is, when it starts to affect living rooms, bedrooms or the structure or leads to mould and fungal growth on walls or clothing. In serious cases, condensation is found on the surface of walls, floors and ceilings, damaging the plaster and decorations or rotting woodwork. It can also occur inside the actual building structure, damaging concrete and brickwork, and rusting metals. This is caused by interstitial condensation produced by warm moist air from inside the house coming in contact with cold air from outside.

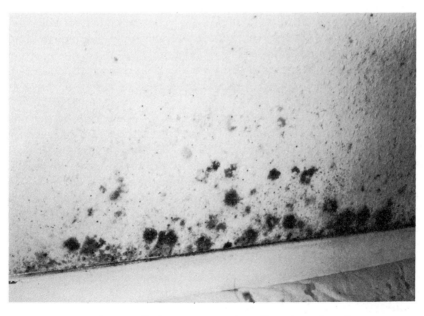

Mould growth on walls is a common sign of condensation dampness.

Condensation is a major housing problem in colder countries during the winter months. The usual situation is that air coming through windows from outside is so cold it cannot hold much moisture. On entering a building, it is warmed and can take up more water vapour. Some of this water vapour escapes through ordinary ventilation but enough may remain to cause condensation either on the surface or inside the structure. It is frequently associated with poverty, because the poorer members of communities frequently live in poorly heated, poorly insulated and poorly designed housing which is commonly affected by serious structural condensation.

(i) Health effects

The concentration of water vapour in air can have a marked effect upon health. For instance, lowering of the water vapour content of air to <30% relative humidity (RH) at room temperature may make bacteria and suspended moulds less viable. However, it has been hypothesized that very low RHs can dry the eyes, skin and the mucous membranes of the nose and throat, which serve to trap foreign substances (including micro-organisms) before they reach the lungs. Generally, RHs near the 50% range of values tend to be more lethal to airborne micro-organisms than RHs of lesser or greater values. [114]

Where water vapour levels are high, condensation can encourage mould, fungi and other micro-organisms to grow on moist surfaces (see section 2.7.1h). Some of these are known to be associated with elevated rates of respiratory illnesses and certain allergies: many moulds in damp houses are allergenic and provide a food supply for house mites, which also are potential allergens. People with impaired heart function tend to be very sensitive to high RH and react with extrasystolia or other kinds of dysfunction.

Mould growth occurs when the RH exceeds 70% for long periods, or about 12 hours per day. House-dust mites (*Dermatophagoides pteronyssinus*) require a RH between 75 and 80% for population growth, while storage mites, such as *Glycyphagus domesticus*, prefer a lower RH of around 73%. However, fungi may reduce the number of house-dust mites in cellars or rooms with moist walls and RH above 80%.

Within the range of comfortable temperatures (18–24° C), variations in humidity have little effect on evaporation of sweat or feelings of discomfort. For example, at 22% RH, profuse sweating does not occur until a temperature of 30° C is reached, but at 60% RH, sweating begins at 20–25° C, increasing thermal discomfort and strain and posing a health risk to vulnerable individuals. [115] Also, the combination of high humidity with either warm or cold air adversely influences a person's thermal condition as well as his sense of well-being. Moist air feels cooler than dry air at the same temperature because of increased heat loss from the body due to higher heat conductivity and thermal capacity of moist air and increased absorption by moisture of radiant heat from the body.

(ii) Control measures

- In general terms, water vapour emissions can be controlled through good housing design, building maintenance programmes and health education, removal of excessive water vapour from buildings by proper ventilation and maintenance of a suitable hygrothermal indoor climate which prevents water vapour from condensing onto cold surfaces.

- Constructional measures should be undertaken to ensure that the shelter is protected from penetration dampness (e.g. through provision of vapour barriers) as this can seriously add to RH levels inside.

- Good ventilation should be provided to kitchens and other rooms used for washing, clothes drying or cooking. This can be achieved by opening windows and keeping room doors closed when water vapour is being produced. An extract fan of 150 mm diameter should be effective in removing water vapour from kitchens, etc. and preventing permeation into other rooms. Ventilation hoods over cooking stoves facilitate the removal of steam to the outside air.

- Some degree of permanent ventilation should be provided inside rooms and to void spaces within the dwelling (e.g. cavity walls should be ventilated to prevent moisture from accumulating inside). Joisted flat roof spaces should be cross-ventilated to provide $300 \, mm^2$ openings per 300 mm run of structure at each end of the roof cavity space.

- Airing cupboards should preferably be ventilated to the outside and heated to enable clothes drying.

- Portable paraffin or flueless gas heaters should be avoided inside housing where possible, as each litre of oil burnt produces the equivalent of about 1 litre of water in the form of water vapour. Rooms must be well ventilated if these heaters are used.

- A water-vapour barrier on the room side of an external structure will prevent entry of water vapour from outside where it could potentially condense onto cold surfaces.

Exhaust ventilation in kitchens and bathrooms is extremely effective
for reducing condensation.

- Wherever possible, all rooms should be partially heated in cold
weather. Condensation most often occurs in unheated bedrooms and
as a cold building takes a long time to warm up, a small amount of
heat should be provided for a long period rather than a lot of heat
for a short time. This is particularly important in houses and flats
left unoccupied and unheated during the day.

- Heating methods should be selected which low-income groups can
afford to run.

- Thermal insulation to walls, floors, ceilings etc., should be sufficient
to prevent excess heat loss from rooms and to prevent water
condensating onto cold surfaces.

- Insulation of cold walls can sometimes be improved by external
cladding with insulation, or by internal dry-lining of walls with a

suitable insulation material which has a water-vapour backing (e.g aluminium foil).

- Cold bridging of external walls should be avoided at the design stage to prevent condensation occurring at local cold spots (e.g. on or below cold roof members or dense concrete/steel beams).

- If a cold bridge at the junction of the external wall and solid ground floor slab is at all likely, perimeter insulation for a width of 600 mm should be provided.

- Cold, impermeable surfaces to walls, floors and ceilings (especially to flat roofs or low pitched roofs) should be avoided.

- Condensation to windows can be remedied by providing 5 mm diameter condensation channels in sills at 300 mm centres. These should be lined with copper or plastic tube. Strip ventilators or pivot shutter vents to windows provide draught-free ventilation over windows.

- Cold-water tanks and pipes located in warm, humid situations, such as airing cupboards, should be insulated with at least 12.5 mm thickness of insulation material to prevent condensation formation.

- In developed countries, electrically operated dehumidifiers are sometimes used to remove moisture from the air. They can be effective in reducing water vapour levels inside buildings (e.g. in helping to 'dry out' new buildings), but they are costly to purchase, incur additional running costs and do nothing to cure the original cause of the dampness. They also agitate movement of dust and other particles which could cause an allergic response in sensitive persons.

- From the standpoint of health, the RH should not exceed 60% or be lower than 30% at room temperatures between 18 and 20° C and not more than 50% at higher temperatures.

- Structural condensation should not occur if the building has a 'U' value (insulation value) of not greater than $1.7 \text{ W/m}^2 \,^\circ\text{C}$, and reasonable ventilation and heating is provided. In general terms, this means providing one to two air changes per hour and a room temperature at least 5° C above outside temperature in cold climates, especially at night. Normally, an indoor temperature of at least 18° C should be maintained.

(g) Airborne pathogens

Airborne pathogens are responsible for a number of communicable respiratory diseases which are often associated with overcrowding and poor indoor air quality and climate. Airborne pathogens spread through dust particles in air and droplet spray, which may be related to poor housing, are identified in Table 2.12. The main epidemiological factors connected with housing and infectious diseases were reviewed at a WHO meeting in 1983. [28]

Table 2.12 Main respiratory diseases possibly related to poor housing

Group	Species	Disease	Transmission
Bacteria	*Corynebacterium diptheriae*	Diphtheria	Respiratory
	Streptococcus haemolyticus	Scarlet fever	Respiratory, contact
	Mycobacterium tuberculosis	Tuberculosis	Respiratory
	Diplococcus pneumoniae	Pneumonia	Respiratory
	Neisseria meningitidis	Meningitis	Respiratory
	Bordetella pertussis	Whooping cough	Respiratory
	Legionella pneumophila	Pneumonia	Respiratory
Viruses	Virus of rubella	Rubella	Respiratory
	Virus of measles	Measles	Respiratory
	Myxovirus parotitidis	Mumps	Respiratory
	Adenoviruses	Respiratory infections	Respiratory
	Chlamydia psittaci	Psittacosis	Respiratory
Yeast, fungi	Various species	Mycoses	Contact, respiratory
Mites	Various species	Infectious allergies	Respiratory

(i) Health effects

Pathogens in air Micro-organisms in suspension can survive for seconds, hours or several months. Small particles remain airborne for up to 2 hours. The main risk of infection from them is within the room of origin. The chance of spread to other rooms in the same building is usually slight, though this can occur if ventilation or conventional air currents move in the appropriate direction. Retention of particles in the respiratory tract depends on the size of particles inhaled and the depth of their penetration. The smaller the particle, the greater the chance that it will be inhaled into the pulmonary spaces. Particles larger than 10 μm diameter are almost completely removed in the nose and upper respiratory tract. Particles in the range of 1–2 μm have a 50% chance of reaching the alveolar spaces. Agents such as *Mycobacterium tuberculosis, Chlamydia psittaci*, A-fever rickettsiae and some fungal agents must be dispersed in very small particles if they are to penetrate alveolar spaces.

Such small particles are produced by coughing and even more effectively by 'singing', which fragments the larger particles by vibration. **Pathogens in droplet spray** Sneezing, coughing and speaking expel a spray of droplets (mostly saliva) but also a small number of microbes from the nose, throat and lungs. Sneezing is the most active spreader of droplets; it can expel up to a million small droplets <100 μm and thousands of larger ones. The large droplets (>0.1 mm) fly forward and downward from the mouth to a distance of a few feet, reach the floor or bespatter surfaces or persons within a few seconds. The small droplets (<0.1 mm) evaporate immediately to become minute solid residues or droplet nuclei (1–10 μm diameter) that remain airborne like minute dust particles, and may then be inhaled (e.g. measles, varicella). Dust is reactivated by air currents or domestic manipulation (e.g. bed-making) or by walking. The latter, however, is limited to about 50 cm above the floor. The spread of sedimentation of particles depends on their size; for example, particles of 0.1 μm settle at 0.29 cm/h, particles of 1 μm settle at 12.8 cm/h and particles of 4 μm settle at 173.7 cm/h. [116] *Mycobacterium tuberculosis*, *Corynebacterium diphtheria*, staphylococci and streptococci survive for days, weeks or months in room dust at room temperature, in contaminated clothing, and in bed clothes, particularly if protected from daylight. Although *C. diphtheria* can resist drying and will survive under these conditions for up to 20 years, it is killed, however, in a few weeks in rooms with sunlight. Meningococcus is destroyed by light or drying but could survive 25 days. The highest dust spread in air occurs in connection with making up beds.

Airborne droplets of water and waste water may contain enteroviruses that may cause infection when inhaled. Droplets containing viruses may be formed by the flushing of a toilet, spray irrigation or by any occurrence in which bubbles rise through contaminated waters and burst at the surface.

The use of the WC produces an aerosol that persists for up to 4 hours and disseminates enterobacteria and enteroviruses. The aerosolized, excreted viruses most encountered by people in developed countries are those produced by the flush toilets in their houses. [67] These organisms can remain airborne long enough to settle in large numbers on surfaces throughout the bathroom and presumably also to be inhaled by people in the bathroom.

(ii) Control measures

- Adequate natural ventilation to rooms will help dilute airborne micro-organism concentrations. (In some cases, artificial ventilation will assist the spread of micro-organisms from one room to another.)

- Direct sunlight (spectrum of 250–200 nm) should be able to enter all rooms. In normal circumstances, this will be achieved by a glazed or unglazed window, which will allow ultraviolet radiation to penetrate and destroy many micro-organisms inside buidings. This is especially important in toilets.

- Sufficient natural and artificial lighting needs to be provided to enable inspection and cleaning of rooms.

- Measures to control RH inside rooms to about 50% will help reduce numbers of airborne pathogens.

- Domestic hygiene measures, such as washing, cleaning and disinfection of surfaces contaminated by dust and airborne pathogens, should be encouraged to reduce numbers of micro-organisms in rooms — especially toilet areas.

- Personal hygiene measures to control spread of infection caused by coughing, sneezing or unnecessary dust-raising during domestic operations should be included in health education programmes.

- Sufferers of respiratory diseases should be isolated in a separate room if possible to contain infection.

- Eliminating overcrowding will reduce the potential for transmission of many infectious agents.

(h) Allergens

Allergens are foreign substances that provoke a harmful, abnormal or exaggerated immune response in individuals hypersensitive to them. Once hypersensitivity has developed, a very small amount of allergen can provoke an allergic reaction.

Housing hygiene conditions can substantially increase allergen concentrations. For instance, high RH and housing dampness favour the development of allergenic mould spores and house-mite populations (see section 2.7.1f). Similarly, dust-raising activities, including repair work, substantially increase the number of airborne spores, mites and other allergens in indoor air.

In daily life, the human body is exposed to numerous substances with the potential to produce allergic responses. In the home environment, these include food, drugs, chemicals, animal hair and faeces (from domestic animals or pets), moulds and fungi, bird faeces (especially from parakeets), rat urine, insect emanations from cockroaches, houseflies, bedbugs and carpet beetles, fauna in house dust (e.g. dust mites), mattress fillings and building materials (e.g. chromium or nickel metals, plastics, paints, varnishes and formaldehyde).

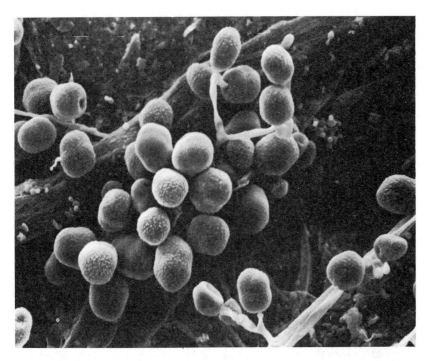

Electronmicrograph of damp wallpaper showing fruiting bodies of moulds.

Many moulds and fungi typically found inside houses are allergenic. The commonest fungal spore allergens are *Alternaria, Cladosporium* spp., *Penicillium* and *Aspergillus* spp. (especially *A. fumigatus*). Also important are the dry rot fungi *Merulius lachrymans* which commonly affect damp timber inside houses. Spore concentrations indoors are typically one fifth of those outdoors, but damp houses have about the same concentrations of spores as outside.

Each mould favours different indoor climate conditions (e.g. *A. repens* will grow at around 68% RH when a suitable food supply is available). Much of this food supply is provided by cellulose-based wallpaper and wallpaper pastes containing starch. Moulds also will grow on many other materials, including woodwork, textiles and clothing, or paintwork. Temperature considerations also are important to fungal growth, but moderate temperatures of 13–15° C will favour the growth of mould allergens such as *Penicillium* or *Aspergillus* species.

The requirements of air spores to qualify as allergens include buoyancy, abundance and allergic toxicity, that is, a sufficient concentration of air spores in the range of 1–5 μm. 'Abundance' in air implies an abundant source and an efficient spore-launching mechanism.

(i) Health effects

Allergic syndromes and diseases are a prime cause of disability and disruption of life in children and adults, probably affecting about 10% of the population. This frequency usually appears during the first two years of life but is sometimes delayed to late childhood, adolescence or adulthood. The family usually has a history of allergies.

The clinical features of allergies depend upon the site where allergens are deposited, the nature of the allergen and the immunologic reactivity of the host. Allergic diseases include bronchial asthma, allergic extrinsic alveolitis, rhinitis, urticaria, eczema, gastrointestinal allergy and acute allergic conjunctivitis of the eyes.

Typical allergic symptoms include irritation in the nose and throat, rhinitis and in the 'type III reaction', asthma several hours after exposure. Larger particles are trapped in the nose, causing sneezing and eye-watering; smaller particles are deposited mostly in the windpipe and lung where they may cause asthma (e.g. mite asthma). Highly sensitive persons may develop urticaria or flares of allergic eczema from direct physical contact with an implicated species of allergen.

Extrinsic allergic alveolitis (hypersensitivity pneumonitis) may be caused by inhaling the proteins of faeces from pigeons and parakeets, but an increasing number of organic materials have been implicated. Ventilation pneumonitis is due to a reaction to thermophilic actinomycetes spores growing in offices and houses with contaminated ventilation systems.

Allergic bronchopulmonary aspergillosis is a specific reaction in the airways to inhaled *A. fumigatus*, a widely distributed fungus with spores about 3 μm in diameter; when inhaled, they grow at body temperature, stimulating specific IgE antibody production. This disease is characterized by recurrent attacks of pulmonary eosinophilia and is usually associated with asthma.

Humidifier fever is another allergic condition found in housing where the atmosphere is humidified, often as part of an air-conditioning process. Flu-like symptoms and fever with associated breathlessness develop 4–6 hours after onset of exposure. The causal precipitins of this disease have not been identified but are thought to originate from bacterial sludge contamination in humidifier tanks.

(ii) Control measures

- The most effective method for controlling allergens in the home is to remove the primary source or remedy the causal factors that give rise to sensitivity.

- Mould spore allergens can also be controlled by reducing moisture levels in indoor air. Special attention should be given to remedying condensation (see section 2.7.1f). Anti-fungicidal paint or agents to control moulds in buildings are highly toxic and should not be used in family housing. Diluted bleach is an effective fungicide for killing mould on walls and other surfaces. Dry rot fungi should be treated at source and causes of allergens rectified (i.e. curing dampness and providing adequate ventilation to flooring and other timbers).

- Sensitive persons should avoid contact with pets, birds and domestic animal allergens.

- Insects, rodents and other allergen infestations should be treated with suitable insecticides and rodenticides. Buildings should be adequately protected against vermin attack.

2.7.2 Provision of sufficient ventilation to maintain health, comfort, air quality and hygrothermal requirements

The object of ventilation is to provide a pure supply of air to occupied rooms, continually remove odorous, vitiated or polluted air and to preserve an indoor climate that is dust free, at the correct temperature and humidity, and with adequate air movement conducive to health and comfort of occupants. In its most general sense, ventilation refers to the total exchange of internal and external air through specific openings such as openable windows, air-bricks and through infiltration openings such as cracks around windows, door frames and skirting boards. Natural ventilation is caused by pressure differences across openings in the fabric of the dwelling as a result of wind movement around or over the structure and differences between internal and external temperatures. The level of ventilation depends on two factors: size of the pressure differences and size and characteristics of the openings. [117]

Ventilation may be naturally or mechanically induced, but in both cases there is an implicit assumption that cleaner and/or cooler air will replace the air being removed. The importance of adequate ventilation in maintaining good indoor air quality is becoming more widely recognized not least because of the tendency towards lower ventilation levels in dwellings, either as a result of changing construction styles and techniques or deliberate action to reduce heat losses. In fact, ventilation requirements depend greatly upon climate and energy costs: in cold or temperate countries, for example, an adequate thermal environment is often achieved by reducing ventilation. For instance, in the USA approximately half of the energy used to achieve a comfortable or 'acceptable' thermal quality in human habitations is consumed by infiltration and ventilation. [9] In these cases, the benefit of any energy saving achieved by reducing ventilation may have to be set against a deterioration in indoor air quality. In hot climates, however, thermal insulation is not so important as the overriding objective to keep buildings cool. Since window openings in hot climates tend to overheat buildings by insolation, the tendency has been to build housing without windows or to restrict their size, thereby increasing levels of indoor air pollutants. Alternatively, air-conditioning or mechanical ventilation is sometimes provided but its expense makes it impractical in low-cost housing, which usually has to rely on natural methods of ventilation.

(a) Health effects

Good ventilation promotes physiological and psychological functioning of the human body, engendering a sense of well-being and comfort. By contrast, deterioration in the physiochemical properties of the indoor atmosphere adversely affects the comfort and health of the occupants. For instance, some people experience a feeling of oppression and fatigue in insufficiently ventilated rooms. Ventilation is also the primary method of controlling build-up of internal sources of pollution that include the products of human activity (anthropotoxins) and of incomplete combustion of fossil fuels, volatiles from building materials, airborne bacteria, viruses, moulds and allergens, excess moisture and heat from domestic activities. The adverse effects of these pollutants are discussed in detail in other sections of these guidelines (sections 2.7.1 and 2.8).

In very hot countries, air-conditioning systems provide an optimum microclimate and therefore reduce the strain on the thermoregulatory system. However, the air in air-conditioned buildings undergoes certain changes in physiochemical properties. Complaints of 'stuffy air sensation', undue fatigue, frequent headaches and a sensation of insufficient fresh air and oxygen have been made in relation to air-conditioned buildings. Objective studies have detected hypertension, vegetative dystonia, and asthenic state in many cases. Respiratory illnesses also are higher in office workers in buildings with air-conditioning than those in rooms with natural ventilation. [118] It is not known whether similar effects can be expected in houses. Fungi, actinomycetes spores and contaminated dust in air-conditioning conduits and water reservoirs can cause such diseases as chronic bronchitis, pneumonia, asthma, allergic reactions, Legionnaire's disease and humidifier fever. Air-conditioning also has an unfavourable effect on beneficial ion composition and ozone concentrations.

Window openings provide an effective means of ventilation.

(b) Control methods

- All habitable rooms, halls, common stairways, kitchens, bathrooms and WC compartments should have adequate ventilation either by openable windows or other devices.

- All dwellings with openable windows support ventilation rates that are way beyond those normally required for the control of indoor air contaminants. Openable windows permit a wider range of ventilation rates than would be achieved, for example, by a mechanical ventilation system. Therefore, where possible, natural ventilation systems are preferred to mechanical systems, which are costly to install, maintain and run.

- Where practicable, rooms should be designed with through ventilation except in extremely cold climatic zones, as rooms having windows in opposite walls increase the air renewal rate by up to 100% more than rooms having windows in only one wall. Back-to-back housing

151

development with no provision for through ventilation should therefore be discouraged.

- Natural non-organized ventilation (infiltration) can provide an invaluable form of permanent ventilation to rooms particularly if it 'trickles' into rooms at low velocity. Its main disadvantage is that being non-controllable, it can give rise to uncomfortable draughts when wind direction is unfavourable and may be the cause of excessive heat loss.

- Air filtration alone may in some dwellings provide an acceptable average level of air exchange, i.e. 0.5–1.0 air changes per hour. [119] However, all dwellings should ideally have the facility for additional controlled ventilation, designed to be effective and easy to use. In particular, control of moisture at source is recommended in kitchens and bathrooms by use of humidistat-controlled extract fans.

- Openable windows, such as side-hung casement windows, which open in opposite directions, normally provide adequate ventilation in houses and are preferred to double-hung sash windows. A top-hung sash and/or a hopper window is suitable for general use.

- The window design should also incorporate 'trickle ventilation' features such as two-position casement fasteners, and in all cases the design should allow easily operated and controllable ventilation.

- Glass louvres, hit-and-miss ventilators and sash windows that open at the centre while closed at the top and bottom also assist natural ventilation.

- A flue to an open fireplace assisted by exhaust ventilators or cowls fitted to the roof is extremely effective in providing natural ventilation and may represent 2–5 air changes per hour in rooms up to 57 m^3. Ventilation can be regulated by flue-throating settings.

- Another form of inlet ventilator relies upon the window to propel air down a pipe and discharging inside to a point near the floor level. Combined with exhaust ventilators, this system can provide a cheap, automatic and highly efficient form of ventilation in single-storey buildings.

- Permanent ventilation to rooms can be provided by an air-brick (which is usually placed high up in the corner of a room) or by ventilation slits or holes bored through walls at strategic points, but the effectiveness of these methods relies entirely on wind direction and orientation of buildings.

- Mechanical extract ventilation fans are usually of the propeller type and are placed high up in external walls or in the roof. Sometimes these are connected to rooms by ducting. In all cases, air inlets should be so situated that no stagnant air pockets remain and should be large enough to ensure that incoming air travels at a low velocity so as to avoid draught.

- Extractor inlets must be placed as near as possible to points of fume or water-vapour emission and discharged at a point so as not to cause nuisance to adjoining properties. Inlet ventilation supplies a controlled amount of air that is usually heated, cleaned and discharged at a convenient point outside a room by large centrifugal fans. Great care is necessary to prevent draughts. Suitable extract points (such as windows and doors) must be available at all times.

- A combination of inlet and outlet ducting connected to fans with air heaters and cleaners on the input side provides a surplus of input air over extract air.

- **Air-conditioning** is an elaborate form of balanced ventilation and cleans, heats, cools, humidifies and dehumidifies the air. Recirculated air is usually supplied at points high in rooms and vitiated air extracted at or near floor level.

- Air-conditioning systems are costly to install and maintain, and are recommended only in very hot climates where ambient room air temperature is at least 26° C. Even in these cases, centralized air-conditioning systems are not preferred, and air-conditioners should be used only during the hottest hours of the day. A WHO report on health aspects of indoor climate concluded that 'unwarranted widespread use of air conditioning in regions with moderate climate when there are no serious reasons for it is inexpedient'. [30]

- Ventilation requirements for new housing should be subject to building approval by the local health administration and incorporated into building codes and ordinances.

- Minimum statutory ventilation requirements for habitable rooms are often expressed by the proportion of openable window area to floor area. A ratio of 1:20 is typically used as a legal standard, with the proviso that at least a part of the openable ventilation area shall be provided at a distance of 1.75 m above the floor. In addition, modern housing hygiene practice includes detailed reference to open space requirements outside windows to ensure that natural ventilation and lighting to rooms are unimpeded by existing obstructions. Future building development extending into these zones could be expressly prohibited by building regulations.

153

- The first report of the WHO Expert Committee on housing proposed that approximately $0.3\,m^3$ of air changes per minute per person be provided within the occupied space in temperate climates (i.e. $18\,m^3/hour$). [12]

- Table 2.13 shows minimum ventilation rates with known density of occupation.

Table 2.13 Minimum ventilation rates with known occupancy density [119]

Air space per person (m^2)	Outdoor air supply per person (litres/s)		
	Minimum	Recommended minima	
		Smoking not permitted	Smoking permitted
3	11.3	17.0	22.6
6	7.1	10.7	14.2
9	5.2	7.8	10.4
12	4.0	6.0	8.0

- Research based on physiological observations of volunteers indicates that when the volume of air per person corresponds to an air cube of $25-30\,m^2$, the air must be renewed at least once per hour.

- The minimum standards for the rate of air extraction in rooms in the USSR are $25-30\,m^3/h$ per person, $60\,m^3/h$ in kitchens (150–$300\,m^3/h$ when gas cookers are in use) and $25\,m^3/h$ in the bathroom and toilet.

- Ventilation requirements in the USA are indicated by ASHRAE standards and minimum property standards (MPS). Both sets of standards are voluntary but may become mandatory under specific conditions, namely:

  Minimum ventilation rates $0.14-0.56/m^3/min/person$
  Recommended ventilation rates $0.19-1.41\,m^3/min/person$
  Intermittent exhaust rates (kitchens) 15 air changes/h
  Intermittent exhaust rates (bathrooms) 8 air changes/h.

2.8 INDOOR CLIMATE REQUIREMENTS

The environmental conditions in dwellings, or indoor climate as it is more commonly known, was defined by McIntyre [120] as covering 'those aspects of the thermal environment and air quality that affect comfort, health and safety'. The significance of indoor air pollution and ventilation to housing hygiene is described elsewhere in these guidelines, but both are inter-related with thermal comfort and relative humidity. Good indoor climate also has a relationship with home safety because accidents are less likely in well-lit, properly ventilated surroundings. The interaction of these various components means that each should be considered in relation to the other, particularly when devising standards. For example, increasing window area to improve natural lighting will cause excessive overheating from the sun's rays in hot climates. Conversely, this will increase heat loss in cold climates. Noise insulation also could be adversely affected. Similarly, thermal insulation measures, such as draught-proofing, reduces ventilation. These contradictions are not always easy to resolve. Inevitably a 'trade-off' has to be made between any competing demands when setting comfort standards.

2.8.1 Maintenance of a thermal environment which will not impose any significant strain on the thermoregulatory mechanisms of the body

Thermal comfort is defined as the state in which no significant strain is imposed on the thermoregulatory mechanisms of the body so enabling optimal conditions of all functional systems of the organism and a high level of working capacity to be achieved. [121]

Except when engaged in strenuous exercise or work, an individual will normally liberate from 418.68 to 437.36 kJ of heat per hour, depending upon the extent of physical exertion. In temperate zones and cold climates, some of this thermal energy is used to maintain normal body temperature. In warmer climates, some heat from body metabolism must be dissipated by ventilation and some must be used to cool the body by perspiration. [121]

Maintaining an external thermal equilibrium should therefore prevent undue raising or lowering of body temperature, while at the same time assisting physiological functions to proceed at a level most favourable to rest, psychological comfort and the recovery of strength after previous exertions.

(a) Health effects
The conditions under which thermal comfort requirements are satisfied depend upon the state of the thermal environment and the fundamental physiological health needs of the human body. The basal metabolic rate decreases progressively with ageing, as does evaporative heat loss [122] (i.e. the two changes seem to offset each other). However, the elderly spend more time in sedentary occupations and in cold conditions

seem to have a narrower temperature range over which they can increase their thermal resistance. [18] Young children and people with cardiovascular diseases also have decreased thermoregulatory functions.

Conditions that lead to discomfort and disturb the body's heat-regulating mechanism and equilibrium may lead to a number of conditions, such as pharyngitis and neuralgia, through cooling or overheating of the body. [121] However, the common belief that chilling the body creates greater susceptibility to upper respiratory infections has not been scientifically proven, [123] although many observations have been made that upper respiratory infection often follows an episode of chilling. [30] The human body easily compensates for changes in temperature from about 15 to 25° C. [123] Outside this range, the body has to expend a lot of energy to compensate for temperature changes and even within, it will react very sensitively to comparatively small changes in atmospheric conditions.

(i) Physiological criteria for thermoregulatory control
All birds and mammals (including humans) have evolved an internal temperature-regulating mechanism to ensure that body temperature is maintained at a constant level independently of climatic conditions and environmental conditions.

Thermoregulation is therefore concerned with dissipating or conserving body heat, depending upon various environmental conditions. The body temperature of a healthy person varies within very narrow limits. The rectal temperature is usually $37 \pm 0.5°$ C, and the armpit temperature is $36.6 \pm 0.5°$ C. However, **skin temperature ('shell' temperature)** can vary over quite wide limits ($28 \pm 15°$ C) without being noticed by a healthy person. When the environmental temperature falls, the temperature of the shell also decreases with the result that heat loss is slowed. Conversely if the environmental temperature rises, heat loss correspondingly increases. The body also compensates for changes in skin temperature by either reducing or increasing blood supply to tissues by dilating or constricting blood vessels. This mechanism ensures that insulation remains approximately constant despite changes in mean skin temperature. However, this compensatory mechanism is not very effective in extremes of cold and in these circumstances, physical thermoregulation of the environment is particularly important.

When the skin temperature exceeds 35° C, the body becomes covered with sweat, which increases heat loss by rapid evaporation of this moisture. The effectiveness of this mode of heat loss is often reduced by environmental conditions, particularly high relative humidity of the air and poor air movement (i.e. instead of evaporating, sweat will drip off the body so reducing its cooling effects).

The **deep body temperature** or **core temperature** remains more or less constant and responds to external temperature changes by increasing or decreasing heat production. If heating or cooling is continued or increased beyond the capacity of the compensatory mechanisms, the temperature of the core may fall or rise respectively and if prolonged will adversely affect health.

Under conditions of extreme cold, the body reacts chiefly by increasing its heat production, a process encouraged by shivering. However, prolonged cooling of the body can cause cold injury such as frost bite and hypothermia (lowering of body core temperature to below 35° C). This condition is characterized by a slowing down of heart and respiratory rates and, depending upon age and other factors, by mental confusion. Hypothermia, especially among the elderly, is often associated with the following conditions:

- low air temperatures in living rooms and bedrooms
- poverty and social isolation
- general deterioration in total body functions. [124]

Many elderly people are killed by hypothermia during cold periods of the year, and early diagnosis of the disease is often difficult since sufferers usually fail to recognize hypothermia symptoms.

If the deep body temperature exceeds 39° C, a state of hyperthermia is said to exist. High temperatures are a potential problem in some regions, particularly during persistent high atmospheric air temperatures that place extreme demands upon thermoregulatory mechanisms of susceptible persons. This reduces heat production and blood pressure while increasing the respiration and blood circulation rates, together with secretion of sweat and changes in general metabolism. In advanced stages, heat stroke, cramp, exhaustion and eventually complete breakdown of sweating mechanisms may occur, often with fatal results.

(ii) Physiological effects of heat exchange by convection and radiation

Humans are very sensitive to small differences in the temperature of walls and surrounding objects and ambient air (negative radiation). The body will feel cold even when the heat loss to walls or other surfaces is only 0.007–0.01 J/s, this effect becoming pronounced at a heat loss of 0.02–0.05 J/s. Heat loss by radiation increases rapidly when the temperature of the surroundings decreases, causing a sensation of being cold and a drop in skin temperature, regardless of air temperature.

If surroundings are at a low temperature, heat is lost not just from the skin surface (as in the case of convection heat loss) but also directly from the deeper tissues, particularly the muscles and blood vessels. The greater the proportion of heat exchange by radiation, the greater the physiological effect. As the body is less able to compensate for heat loss by radiation (compared with convection), a delayed thermal equilibrium may result.

Where radiant heating is used, the human body loses considerably less heat to the environment. For instance, under conditions of radiant heating, 10% less energy is required for the performance of a given task than with convection heating. This is because radiant heat not only acts on the body surface but also penetrates it and influences the deeper lying tissues, stimulating enzyme processes, internal organs and the central nervous system [125] as well as imparting a feeling of freshness and vigour. As a result, comfortable thermal conditions can exist with radiant heating at a lower air temperature than with convection heating.

(iii) Air movement

Movement of air in rooms is important for providing a constant supply of fresh air and removing indoor pollutants by ventilation. However, too rapid movement of air causes cooling of skin temperature and a loss of thermal comfort.

Air movement facilitates the heat loss by evaporation and, depending upon air temperature, generally has a cooling effect on the body. Still air unfavourably influences the general metabolism and thermal state of the body, often causing a sensation of oppression, heat discomfort, excessive fatigue and sometimes an adverse effect on respiratory organs. However, excessive air velocities of 0.03–0.05 m/s can cause a perceptible change in temperature of an unclothed person, and is experienced as 'draught' by skin chilling.

(iv) Diurnal and seasonal variations in thermal comfort

Seasonal changes in the thermoregulatory reactions of the body lead to changes in the conditions necessary for thermal comfort (i.e. the human body becomes acclimatized to higher temperatures during the summer season compared with the winter). For example, research in the USSR has shown that in winter the range of acceptable temperatures in the home is 21–22° C in cold climates and 17–18° C in warm climates; in summer the temperature range is 23–35° C. This phenomenon may be explained by the effects of sharp body cooling experienced outdoors in cold climates, necessitating a higher indoor temperature to restore thermoregulatory balance – a requirement that does not apply in warm and hot regions. Also, in cold climates, houses are likely to have different radiant conditions inside rooms compared with hot climates where there is usually little difference between mean wall temperatures and room air temperature thereby facilitating a lower operative temperature. However, radiant balance also is affected by other factors, including orientation and insolation of building, wind temperature, and direction and insulation properties of walls, floors and surrounding surfaces, all of which are especially important factors in maintaining thermal comfort in cold climates.

(v) Thermal comfort during sleep

Thermoregulation is markedly inhibited during sleep. Even with only slight overheating, sleep is uneasy, whereas if the skin is adequately insulated, a moderate reduction in the temperature of the inspired air facilitates the deep inhibition of thermoregulation associated with sound sleep. A slightly lower night-time temperature is therefore generally acceptable for maintaining thermal comfort.

(b) Control measures

The four principal factors controlling heat loss from the human body involve air temperature, mean radiant temperature of surrounding surfaces (e.g. walls, windows, floors, ceilings, furnishings, radiators), air movement and relative humidity. Of these, air temperature and mean radiant temperature are the most significant. Their combined effect is defined as the 'operative temperature', which is approximately the mean between air temperature and wall temperature and is often used as a basis for heating standards. Other factors that determine optimal temperature requirements for housing include clothing, state of health, habits and activities of the dwellers. Considerable differences in thermal environment also exist between hot and cold climates and in countries where opposite extremes of temperature are normal at different times of the year. In these cases, housing has to perform a dual role of keeping people warm during cold winter months and cool during hot weather. Thus, housing design, heating methods, ventilation and thermal insulation standards should be adequate to meet varying thermal comfort requirements of average healthy individuals, as well as children, sick people and the elderly, in all climates and seasons.

(i) Air temperature

Optimum air temperatures for rooms depend largely upon climatic region and whether convection heating or panel radiant heating is used. The optimum air temperatures for residential rooms should be 20–22° C. [30]

- A report by a WHO Working Group on the effects of housing indoor climate on the health of the elderly concluded that: 'Thermal comfort for 80% of the elderly has been reported to occur when the range of the indoor ambient air temperature is between 18° C and 30° C or the range of the indoor operative temperature is between 16° C and 32° C. At lower temperature values, to obtain thermal comfort, individuals usually require additional or warmer clothing and at higher temperature values, less or cooler clothing is often needed'. [9] The lower values are not likely to provide thermal comfort for children.

- Operative temperature standards assume that occupants are normally clothed and at rest. In all regularly occupied rooms, this temperature should be maintained at knee height (i.e. 0.5 m from the ground) to prevent chilling of the legs and feet and to provide thermal comfort for children. Air temperatures should be increased or decreased to compensate for changes in mean radiant temperature above or below air temperature. However, mean radiant temperature should not be less than 3° C below an assumed optimum indoor temperature of 20° C.

- The temperature of rooms occupied by persons of subnormal vitality should be increased to provide a minimum operative temperature of 22° C at knee height. Family housing should therefore have sufficient heating and thermal insulation capacity to meet this standard.

- A report published by the Institute of Housing and The Royal Institute of British Architects [126] recommends that the heating system be capable of raising internal temperatures to the following levels when the outside temperature is 0° C:

Living areas	21° C
Kitchen and circulation areas	16° C
Bathrooms	21° C
Bedrooms	18° C

- Optimum mean air temperatures must also take into account the distribution of heat within a room if thermal comfort is to be achieved (i.e. there should not be excessive horizontal and vertical differences in air temperature). For example, a 3° C drop in the vertical temperature can cause the feet and lower limbs to feel cold and cause reflex changes in the temperature of the upper respiratory tracts. Considerable vertical differentials of air temperatures also are undesirable because they waste fuel and increase convection currents. In poorly heated and insulated houses, differentials of 18° C or more have been observed. The horizontal difference in air temperature should not exceed 1–2° C, and the difference between floor temperature and the temperature at a height of 1.5 m from the floor should not exceed 2–3° C. Under these conditions, a normally clothed person should not be aware of any unevenness in temperature. This is particularly important for children who move in cooler surroundings near the floor.

- Bathrooms need to be 2–3° C higher than other rooms to prevent chilling of the body, and at night, room temperatures should be 2–3° C lower than during daytime. In all cases the interdependency of air temperature with radiant temperature means that optimum air temperature norms are valid only if wall temperatures are not more than 2–3° C below room air temperature.

(ii) Mean radiant temperatures

Maintaining optimum temperatures to walls, floors, ceilings and other surfaces is important in preventing cooling of the body by radiation and in some cases chilling by physical contact with cold surfaces. Ideally, surface temperatures should be about the same as optimum air temperatures, but this depends on thermal insulation properties of materials, outside temperature and type of indoor heating system. 'Negative radiation' can be prevented by ensuring that temperatures of interior wall surfaces are not lower than 3° C of the optimum indoor air temperature. Wall temperatures that are more than 6° C below air temperature will encourage water precipitation from the air to the wall, causing condensation dampness. Table 2.14 summarizes temperature requirements for typical room surfaces.

Table 2.14 Temperature requirements for typical room surfaces

Surface	°C	Reference	Notes
Floor (wood)	25.5	127	Optimum temperature
Floor (concrete)	27	127	Optimum temperature
Ceiling	26	30	Minimum temperature
Glass	10–12	128	Maximum difference between air and glass temperature

(iii) Air movement

Optimum air mobility norms in rooms during cold periods of the year should be between 0.1 and 0.15 m/s. During the summer, 0.3 m/s is acceptable. [31]

If the air speed is at least 0.2 m/s, a higher room temperature is required to produce the same degree of warmth for the occupants (Table 2.15). High air speeds may occur if a poorly designed heating system generates draughts by natural or forced convection: for example, if the room is of great height (when natural convection may generate substantial vertical air currents) and is close to open windows or other openings.

(iv) Humidity

The combination of high humidity with either warm or cold air adversely influences a person's thermal condition as well as sense of well-being.

Table 2.15 Comfortable room temperatures ($^\circ$ C) in still air with corrections for air movement [129]

Clothing	Sleeping	Sitting	Standing	Active
Nude	31	29	25	23*
Light	29	26	21	18*
Normal	27	23	17	13*
Air movement (m/s)		Correction to be added		
0.2	0.5	1	1	1.5
0.4	1	1.5	2	3
0.7	1.5	2	3	4
1.0	1.5	2.5	3.5	5

*Estimates subject to some uncertainty.
Note The values above have been calculated by considering the heat exchanges taking place between a person, his clothing and his environment. The temperatures are globe temperatures.
Example For a person in normal clothing, sometimes sitting and sometimes standing, the top half of the table gives 20° C (average of 23° C and 17° C) as the comfortable temperature. For an air speed of 1 m/s, the lower half of the table gives 3° C (average of 2.5° C and 3.5° C) as the correction to be added, and thus 23° C as the comfortable temperature.

In particular, a high relative humidity (RH) reduces sweat evaporation and lowers heat loss in hot conditions. The significance of water vapour as an indoor pollutant is discussed more fully in section 2.7.1f, but from a standpoint of health the RH should not exceed 60% or be lower than 30%. [121]

(c) Detailed control measures
In **hot** countries or during hot seasons of the year, it is important to prevent overheating of housing by raising indoor air temperatures to an uncomfortable level. A suitable indoor temperature can be provided in hot climates by a combination of macro-design measures to reduce insolation and constructional design measures within the dwelling to remove excess heat. These requirements are dealt with specifically in section 2.4.2.

Thermal comfort in **cold** countries or winter periods of hot countries can usually be achieved by good indoor heating and thermal insulation. To a lesser extent, orientation can assist by maximizing insolation and protecting principal living room areas from cold winds.
(i) Heating methods

- Radiant heating is preferred to heating by convected warm air wherever possible. Where warm air systems are used, outlets must be correctly positioned for efficient circulation of heat without

Central heating is the preferred choice for maintaining thermal comfort.

causing uncomfortable differences in temperature gradient. Convection systems also must be so designed and maintained as not to give rise to noise nuisance or distribute dust and bacteria around a building.

- Central heating by thermostatically controlled radiators is the optimum choice of heating in cold climates. This system also provides domestic hot water supply, and in large multiple-housing schemes, water can be supplied to each apartment from a central source.

- Low-temperature electric radiant panels to walls and ceilings are an acceptable alternative to central heating in many cases. Ordinary electric radiant fires also are useful for providing a point source of heat for 'topping up' in cold periods.

- Flueless gas and oil stoves are not recommended as a main form of heating because they contribute to indoor air pollution. However, modern gas fires connected to a flue are an efficient and easily regulated method of heating in single rooms.

- The ordinary open-fire burning of coal or wood is not an ideal choice for space heating for the following reasons:

    - open fires are inefficient and waste fuel — less than 30% of the heat value of fuel is used

    - the heat emitted is poorly distributed, particularly in outer areas of large rooms

    - induced draughts are often excessive, difficult to regulate and cause further heat loss

    - open fires are a major source of dust, soot and air pollutants inside rooms.

These objections are partly (but not entirely) overcome by use of smokeless fuels and specially designed fireplaces which increase combustion efficiency.

- Solid fuel or wood-burning closed stoves with a back boiler for hot water provide a cheap and efficient alternative to full central-heating systems. Closed stoves provide much better control of combustion air than open fires and give out heat mainly in the form of convected warm air at about 70% efficiency. Three or four radiators can often be run from a stove with a back boiler to provide background heating to other rooms at relatively low cost. In other cases, they also provide heat for cooking and hot water supply.

- Underfloor electric heating cables or heated ceilings provide an effective form of radiant heating but are expensive to run and difficult to regulate. Electric storage heaters that run on off-peak electricity are a better choice, but a prerequisite of all electric heating systems is an efficient supply of electricity at a price that low-income consumers can afford to pay.

- District heating may be economically viable in any new medium-sized human settlement of 25 000–100 000 population, particularly if waste heat from nearby power stations can be used. [130] Economies also might be achieved by using solar, wind and geothermal energy and heat pumps, or heat from cooling water of thermal power stations and industrial plants. [8]

- In all cases, heating systems should be simple to control and use. Provision should be made for an alternative form of heating if the primary source fails.

• Consideration should be given to assistance with heating allowances to people with limited financial means or to occupiers of housing which is expensive to heat. Several European countries directly subsidize domestic heating costs or pay heating payments through income maintenance allowances.

(ii) Thermal insulation
An important factor in housing hygiene in cold climates is the thermal insulation qualities of construction materials. Effective thermal insulation assists not only warming in winter but also cooling in summer, and is an important safeguard against condensation dampness. Thermal insulation is also important in reducing consumer's heating costs, maximizing the possibilities for comfortable air temperature of low-income groups, and conserving a nation's energy resources and thus its overall energy bill. For instance, in temperate climates, a drop of 1 °C in indoor temperature requirements leads to savings in heating costs of 7%. [8]

A number of factors influence the rate of heat loss, including thermal transmittance through exterior walls and roof, the air change rate, difference in temperature between inside and outside air, external area of dwelling, window size and type of heating system in use. These factors need to be accommodated within the building design.

• The external parts of a dwelling, such as the ground floor, external walls, roof and uppermost ceilings, are the most significant areas of heat loss from a dwelling.

• Typical methods of improving insulation to exterior walls include use of materials with low thermal conductivity, such as lightweight thermal blocks. These are best used in inner cavity walls with a brick or concrete outer facing. The cavity should be at least 50 mm wide and preferably filled with insulation material such as expanded polystyrene granules. Other construction designs, such as timber-framed buildings with an insulating infill, often have a good heat insulation capacity. Thick walls of brick or mud with an insulation space provide reasonable insulation to external elements and are often preferable to cold concrete materials.

• For a building of any given floor area and construction, the rate of heat loss is greater for the area of the external surfaces. For instance, in temperate and cold climates, terraced houses insulate each other better against heat loss than a similarly sized detached house that needs up to 40% more energy for heating purposes. [8]

- Heat loss is higher if large windows are installed although good building orientation and curtaining of windows can, to some extent, compensate for this.

- Single-glazed windows account for about 20% of the total heat loss from a dwelling. In general terms, double-glazed windows with an air space of 12 mm will halve thermal transmittance and cut overall heat loss of an average house by 10%. They also tend to improve comfort levels by reducing down-draughts from windows and increasing the area of acceptable comfort in the room.

- Measures to improve thermal insulation of floors largely depend upon design and construction details. Compressed strawboard or similar materials are often used to insulate suspended wooden floors, but coverings such as rugs and carpets also help reduce heat loss and air infiltration from sub-floors. Warm floor coverings are particularly useful on stone or concrete floors to stop chilling of feet.

- About 20% of heat loss from a dwelling occurs through non-insulated roof spaces and upper ceilings. This can be considerably reduced by laying glassfibre quilt, vermiculite granules or other insulating materials between ceiling joists to a depth of at least 10 cm. Thermal insulation of roofs, ceilings and floors is particularly effective for reducing vertical differences in air temperature: customary differentials ranging from 6 to 12° C between floor and ceiling in a non-insulated house are significantly reduced when insulation is installed. However, roofs must be adequately ventilated at the eaves to stop condensation. Also, cold water tanks and pipes should be insulated to prevent freezing.

- External doors (including letter boxes, keyholes) should be tight-fitting and adequately draught-proofed with weather stripping. However, in all cases care must be taken that ventilation requirements are not reduced to an unhygienic level; the rate of air change depends on the magnitude of wind and temperature difference between inside and outside air. This is directly affected by draught-proofing measures and size of external openings.

- Appreciable heat losses can occur from flued appliances, the influencing factors being the restriction of air flow provided by the appliance and the cross-sectional area of the flue throat. For example, the volume of air passing up the flue of an open fire with a normal-sized throat may be about 170 m^3 but if the throat is not greater than 130 cm^2 in area or if the appliance is a flued gas heater, the air flow is likely to be less than half this volume. [130a]

2.8.2 Provision of adequate daylight, artificial illumination and avoidance of glare

Adequate natural lighting by daylight and artificial illumination within houses and public buildings are essential healthy housing requirements. The penetration of direct sunlight into living accommodation has favourable psychophysiological effects on both thermal comfort and biological activity of the body. It also has a bactericidal effect. Daylight gives housing occupants a feeling of direct contact with the outside world, an important factor for mental and social well-being.

Natural illumination varies widely within the course of a day. At sunrise and at sunset, the intensity of natural illumination is only a few hundred lux rising to about 100 000 lux at noon on a sunny day. After sunset, it may fall to a fraction of a lux. The intensity of natural light also varies with latitude, season and climatic conditions such as cloud cover. The altitude to which the sun rises also is an important factor in sunlighting rooms or in determining the spacing of houses and governing the height of buildings and the width of streets. This is particularly important where high buildings surround rooms which then cannot receive the full benefit of daylight, since light entering through ordinary glazing merely falls onto the floor immediately below windows without lighting the remainder of the room. In congested districts, buildings obstruct sunlight to themselves and to buildings facing them.

The extent to which a room is lit by daylight, therefore, depends upon the amount of floor and wall area in direct line with the open sky (i.e. the angle of aperture, which in turn depends upon the amount of available sunlight, site arrangement, orientation of buildings, size, shape and room layout, degree of obstruction to windows, window size and the use to which the room is put). Differences can also be expected among groups such as infants and elderly persons who often need higher lighting requirements to compensate for poorer eyesight. Natural lighting is thus usually insufficient to provide adequate illumination inside houses at all times and has to be supplemented by artificial sources which quantitatively and qualitatively offset any deficiencies in natural lighting (e.g. by including long-wave ultraviolet radiation of measured quality and compensation in the lighting source). In general terms, however, natural lighting is more beneficial than artificial lighting for health and performing normal household activities.

(a) Health effects

Under natural conditions, humans are exposed to all components of solar radiation, including ultraviolet, visible and infrared radiation, all of which have a differing and contributory effect on biological activity, health and well-being. **Ultraviolet radiation** plays an important part in stimulating the nervous system, endocrine glands and enzyme systems. Prolonged deprivation of ultraviolet radiation leads to decreased formation of vitamin D, which regulates phosphorus and calcium metabolism. Disorders in bone formation, rickets and osteomalacia, and increased caries are typical adverse effects of vitamin D deficiency. Ultraviolet radiation diminishes the number of colds and enhances body growth and development. [131] The incidence of influenza, tonsillitis and other infectious diseases also is reduced by disinfecting the air by ultraviolet radiation (particularly at wavelengths between 254 and 258 mμ). Ordinary window glass will absorb most ultraviolet radiation with wavelengths shorter than 320 mμ and therefore reduce the biological and hygienic effects of sunlight entering the room.

The eye is able to perceive extremely small changes in **light intensity**, and will quickly modify its sensitivity depending on degree of brightness and the conditions of illumination within the environment. Visual comfort depends upon the degree of illumination provided and the lighting requirements for carrying out particular tasks. For instance, dark objects can be better discerned when bright light is falling upon a white background, and in poor lighting the eye is unable to perceive differences in colour. The speed of visual perception and the ability to discern details within a certain time also diminish in poor lighting conditions.

The visual function also is adversely affected when light quality is poor, i.e. when light reflections are suppressed or uneven over the surface of an object and its surroundings (walls, ceilings, etc.) or poorly contrasted between object and background. The direction, degree of diffuseness and spectoral composition of the light are also important to light quality: too sharp a difference between the brightness of an object and surroundings decreases visibility and capacity of visual function. [121]

If lighting conditions preclude clear perception, the eyes become tired and this is often followed by eye-strain, pain and headache. Visual fatigue and eye-strain will also occur when the eye is exposed to qualitatively poor lighting. For example, out of three colours of equal brightness (red, green and blue-violet), green produces the lowest and blue-violet the highest degree of fatigue.

The biological effect of **infrared radiation** varies according to its wavelength and duration of exposure. In excess, infrared radiation can cause heat stroke and heat prostration. Infrared radiation of wavelengths between 0.7 and 1.4 μ can penetrate human tissues, whereas infrared radiation with a wavelength exceeding 1.5 μ is absorbed mainly by the skin, thus increasing skin temperature. The effects of low intensity infrared radiation at wavelengths of 8–20 μ are inconclusive, but infrared rays may stimulate or inhibit the central nervous system, influence the rate of intercellular metabolism and cause perceptible changes in skin pigmentation that can lead to burns following excessive exposure.

With regard to **artificial lighting**, inadequate illumination adversely affects working capacity and productivity. However, the colour effect produced by **fluorescent** daylight lamps is very similar to that of natural daylight and has a more beneficial physiological effect than light from incandescent lamps. [132] Careful consideration needs to be given to the positions of the light sources and visual tasks to avoid glare, which can impair vision (disability glare) or cause visual discomfort (discomfort glare). This effect is often cumulative and can result in excessive tiredness towards the end of the day.

(b) Control measures

The aim of good lighting practice should be to ensure the most favourable conditions for the general and working capacity of the occupants by providing lighting that is both quantitatively and qualitatively adequate. In general terms, this can be achieved through good design of the housing environment and individual shelter. However, in hot countries, strong sunlight can cause thermal discomfort in housing unless steps are taken to keep the dwelling cool. For this reason, natural lighting tends to be restricted. A balance thus needs to be maintained between natural lighting requirements and those concerned with thermal comfort.

- Macro-design measures should be taken to ensure that buildings receive adequate natural lighting but without being overlooked (e.g. narrow streets with tall buildings on either side are often inadequately lit (particularly on lower storeys) as are buildings facing a central courtyard. Such designs should be avoided at the planning stage since remedial action is usually impracticable.

- Good orientation of buildings and correct spacing between building blocks will assist natural lighting of the apartments.

- To ensure an even distribution of daylight, the sky must be visible, not only from near the window but also from most places within the room. Whether this is possible depends upon the size and position of the windows and the presence or absence of obstacles such as other buildings and trees outside them. The usual rule of thumb is that no obstacle should increase the angle at which sunlight enters the room to more than 15–18° from the level of the window sill.

- Sunlight falling upon the sides of buildings or entering between them is particularly valuable, since it enters the windows at a low angle and reaches the remotest corners of rooms. Where it is impossible to plan an angle of less than 18° for sunlight, open-patterned streets with spaces between the buildings are to be preferred to continuous lines of buildings. [30]

- Natural lighting should be provided to WC compartments wherever possible as it is a good bactericide. Special glass which transmits a higher proportion of ultraviolet rays should be used in these rooms. If ordinary glass is used, windows should be left open in warm weather for at least 3 hours to allow shorter wavelength ultraviolet radiation to enter and assist in bactericidal action.

- Goromosov [121] described six criteria for domestic illumination that satisfy physiological and health requirements:

  - optimum intensity of illumination in all workplaces and in their surroundings within the field of vision

  - avoidance of great variations in brightness within the field of vision, thus avoiding interference with the normal adaptation of the eye

  - protection of the eye against glare from direct or reflected light

  - avoidance of sharp shadows on work surfaces

  - adequate contrast in brightness and in colour between details and background

  - optimal biological activity of the light.

- The aim of establishing standards for artificial illumination should be to produce conditions of visual comfort by ensuring that the spectrum of artificial light resembles that of sunlight. If necessary, such light should be enriched with biologically active ultraviolet rays of relatively long wavelengths.

- The health recommendations for fluorescent indoor lighting can be summed up as follows:

  - improvement of the spectrum of light emitted by fluorescent lamps used in housing

  - elimination of the glare caused by the source of light and all surrounding surfaces

  - establishment of the optimum distribution of brightness within a room

  - elimination of the stroboscobic effect

- reduction in flickering to such a level that visual comfort and work efficiency are not impaired.

- Under the most unfavourable conditions of discrimination, the optimum level of illumination for vision lies in the range of 20 000–30 000 lux, but this depends on whether any special visual effort is needed. For example, the following levels of intensity are optimum with fluorescent illumination: 1000–1200 lux for work requiring no special visual effort and 1300–1800 lux for work requiring fine vision (see also Table 2.16).

Table 2.16 Recommended illuminance ratios and reflections [129]

Surface	Illuminance relative to task	Space or surface	Average reflectance of surfaces within spaces
Floor	1.0	Floor cavity	0.2–0.3
Walls	0.5–0.8	Walls	0.3–0.8
Ceiling	0.3–0.9	Ceiling cavity	min. 0.6

- The code of the Illumination Engineering Society [133] recommends lighting standards for homes as follows:

	Lighting intensity (lux)
Living rooms	
General	50
Reading (casual)	150
Sewing and darning	300
Studies	
Desk and prolonged reading	300
Bedrooms	
General	50
Bed-head	150
Kitchens (working areas)	300
Bathrooms	100
Halls and landings	150
Stairs (at tread)	100
Workshops (benches)	300
Garages	50

- Visual comfort is also improved by the rational use of colour on walls, floors and ceilings inside dwellings. White, pale yellow, pale blue and pale green reflect 70–80% of the incident light and thus make rooms lighter. Yellow, green or pale blue reduce visual fatigue and help vision.

- In most work interiors where the illuminance is less than 300 lux, light bulbs of intermediate or warm colour are preferred for general lighting. Fluorescent lights of intermediate colour and appearance are usually satisfactory for use in combined electric lighting/daylight systems. Further details of colour coordination of building colours are given in a handbook by Gloag. *et al.* [134]

- To avoid glare care must be taken when designing housing to ensure that windows, electric lights and other sources are not too bright compared with the general brightness of an interior.

2.9 HOME SAFETY REQUIREMENTS

Home safety has long been recognized by the WHO and other authorities as a major healthy housing requirement. Interest in home safety has arisen partly because of changes in mortality patterns which show that fatal accidents to young persons and the elderly are now a major cause of death in many countries and are often higher than infectious or parasitic diseases. Overall, little detailed information is available on the epidemiology of home accidents in developing countries, but in several western countries about one third of all accidental deaths are believed to be caused by domestic accidents. However, the overall significance of accidents cannot just be measured in terms of mortality rates. The social and human costs also need to be considered: many useful lives are ruined by accidents, and injuries result in considerable loss of industrial production and consume scarce medical resources. Young people, the elderly, handicapped and chronically sick persons are at highest risk of fatal home accidents, but other differences also are related to gender and socioeconomic factors.

(a) Health effects
Examination of accident returns shows a fairly standard morbidity pattern by age and gender. Children (particularly boys) have a relatively high injury rate but a fairly low risk of death. Home accidents gradually rise to a peak in the toddler and lessen slightly in the 15–24-year age groups, steady in middle age and finally rise sharply in the elderly. Interestingly enough, the elderly suffer fewer accidents than children but more of the accidents end in death or serious injury. Females have a higher number of fatal home accidents than males, probably because they spend more time in the home, are often distracted by young children and may be subject to the often destabilizing effects of pre-menstrual tension.

A review of home accidents in **childhood** shows that the pattern of accidents also changes with the hazards of the environment and the stage of child development. Young babies are totally unable to protect themselves and rely entirely on adult guardians for their safety. Preschool children (who have the largest number of home accidents of any age group) are largely incapable of recognizing danger, are physically immature and yet at the same time are actively exploring their environment: they are thus at greater risk of minor accidents. For babies, the greatest hazards are to be found in the bedroom, kitchen, bathroom or any room where he or she is unattended. Suffocation and falls are the most common types of accident. However, for children aged 1–5 years the places where accidents most frequently occur are the living room, kitchen, nursery and bedroom: falls, scalds, poisoning and burns predominate. For somewhat older children, the pattern of accidents is more varied with danger in the immediate vicinity of the home being more commonplace.

Home accidents can have very serious consequences for the **elderly**, such as invalidity, extended periods of medical care and even death. In addition, pathological factors, such as acute and chronic illnesses, compound the effects of accidents. The tendency of the elderly to tire easily, to be forgetful, absent-minded and fearful of modern surroundings and equipment increases environmental hazards. [6] The side effects of medication for geriatric ailments of mental illness also interfere with normal reasoning abilities, thus increasing accident risks. Depression, lack of self-confidence or boredom may also disincline the elderly to take safety precautions.

Socioeconomic classification of accident victims has not been sufficiently refined to enable any accurate opinions to be formed. However, many surveys have shown a relationship between poverty and a high number of domestic accidents. Socially neglected families live in poorer housing that is often overcrowded, unduly cluttered with equipment and household belongings (because of limited storage space), or has inadequate cooking facilities, all of which are likely to play some part in home accidents. For instance, an information paper by the Building Research Establishment in England noted that a number of housing and social indicators are statistically correlated with incidence of fire in dwellings. Research showed a higher incidence of fires in areas of non-owner-occupied housing and thus poorer areas. [135] Clearly, in poor housing, accidents are related to the higher number of hazards present and also perhaps to less understanding of hazard risks.

Low income may also contribute to home accidents by reducing the amount of money available to remedy an unsafe physical environment or to buy safe but more expensive equipment and goods. Children of one-parent families also seem to have a higher number of accidents. Single parents generally have less income, tend to live in poorer, less safe housing, and may be forced occasionally to leave children unsupervised.

Another important epidemiological factor in the aetiology of home accidents concerns the **state of health** of the occupants. Studies of fatal accidents carried out by the Consumer Safety Unit of the Department of Trade in the United Kingdom [136] suggest that many accidents in the home occur because of the physical and mental condition of the casualty and the characteristics of the social setting. Relevant factors include alcohol, drugs, mental and physically disabling illness, tiredness, stress and inadequate supervision of children. Very low intelligence also is correlated with increased accident liability, but other handicaps in the form of decreased sight, hearing, sense of smell, skeletal deformity and spasticity also make people more vulnerable. For example, arthritis and osteoporosis (particularly of the neck of the femur) make a fall that might not seriously injure a healthy limb more likely to result in a fracture. Also, the relative immobility of the arthritic lower limb makes tripping and falling more probable.

Immigrants and ethnic minorities also may be at special risk of home accidents because of poor understanding of electrical and mechanical appliances together with a generally poorer educational background or difficulties in adjusting to a different environment.

(b) General control measures

The inter-relationship between environmental, socioeconomic and health factors in the aetiology of home accidents means that prescriptive preventive measures are exceedingly difficult to define in many cases. Undoubtedly, a combination of safe design of the home coupled with consumer product safety and education will either remove potential safety hazards or reduce the consequences of the hazard. Professor Backett concluded in his study of domestic accidents that 'the modification of human behaviour by teaching good risk-taking is so much more difficult than rendering the domestic environment at least moderately safe that there is no doubt which is the more economical short-term solution. [136]

Domestic accidents can be tackled as a health problem at two levels: centrally, in terms of laws and social policy and of the organization of health services, and locally, at the level of the family in terms of safety design.

- Each country should implement a comprehensive home safety policy aimed at reducing home accidents. To accomplish this, individual countries must monitor domestic accidents by collecting and publishing mortality/morbidity data. This would include detailed information on causal agents, place of accidents, and age and gender of victim. Policy-makers would then be able to identify vulnerable groups, dangerous products and unsafe housing environments, as well as provide invaluable information for other epidemiological studies and formulation of safety standards.

- A national home safety policy has a number of essential objectives, including legal, technical and educational strategies. Ideally, regional policies should also be adopted which take into account local trends and differences in home accident patterns.

- Checklists of safety or hazard features in the home should be drawn up on a national and/or regional basis to enable surgeons or other trained personnel to evaluate conditions. These lists need to be regularly updated by health departments to take account of changes in epidemiology. With improved knowledge of accidents in each area, it might be possible to quantify each item in the checklist linked to an intervention or performance standard. Alternatively, checklists can be used for educational purposes in households that do not meet requisite safety standards or to enable householders to assess safety conditions for themselves.

- Safety education has an important role in any home safety policy and is most effective if targeted at those with a responsibility for looking after others (e.g. carers, parents and teachers). However, safety education is likely to be largely ineffective in changing the behaviour of very young children, the elderly and chronically sick persons who often have impaired sensory or developmental ability to recognize or respond to danger signals. The elderly, even those with all their faculties, usually have long-ingrained habits and practices, some of which may be dangerous. In these cases, safety education may be only partially effective.

- Safety education policies should not place the entire responsibility for home safety onto parents or the individual. Planners, designers and architects have a responsibility for ensuring that housing or consumer products are designed to a high standard of safety design.

- Safety campaigns should reflect the epidemiology of accidents in a particular area and be targeted at a particular group wherever possible. Examples of campaigns might include the following:
  - safe use of electrical installations and applicances where electricity is available for the first time
  - campaigns on the dangers of CO poisoning might be suitable in areas with a number of possible faulty gas appliances or leaky flues, poor indoor air quality or elevated numbers of gas poisoning cases.

- campaigns on water safety in areas where there are canals, waterways or water reservoirs.

- Examples of safety education measures include the following: national media campaigns through newspapers, radio, posters and leaflet distribution; simple, clear warning labels on appliances and potentially dangerous consumer goods; safety education lectures in schools and community groups; safety training of doctors, engineers, architects, child minders and carers, nurses, sanitarians and others concerned with designing or visiting the home; establishment of voluntary and/or governmental safety organizations to advise on all aspects of home safety.

- Safety campaigns should also be tailored to the needs of ethnic minorities and those with learning difficulties. Literature should be translated into native languages where necessary. Alternatively, other methods of communication should be employed.

- It is important that new housing occupants be given written and verbal information on operating unfamiliar appliances and safety precautions at commencement of occupancy.

- All the above measures have applications for health education on other aspects of healthy housing mentioned in these guidelines.

2.9.1 Protection of the neighbourhood against hazards of vehicular traffic

(a) Health effects

Road accidents in residential areas cause a considerable number of deaths and injuries each year, particularly of young children. However, the ease with which residents can reach their homes, places of employment and community amenities within or outside the residential area are also important environmental, planning and housing considerations. Easy access to housing developments is also needed for emergency services such as fire appliances and ambulances, refuse collection vehicles, delivery vehicles, police and health services, undertakers and visitors.

Inevitably, the separation of pedestrian access from vehicular facilities for road safety means compromising on estate design and layout. For example, increasing access distance from home to vehicle pick-up may encourage unwanted access by non-residents, which could affect security arrangements and incidence of human assault.

(b) Control measures

Access arrangements depend largely upon the age distribution and the needs of the residents in a particular housing development. For example, the aged and infirm may dislike long distances to vehicle pick-up points or amenities and would find changes in levels difficult to negotiate. Conversely, children may use nearby access roads as playgrounds thus increasing the possibility of road traffic accidents and causing stress to parents worrying about their children's safety. In all cases good transport arrangements and roads are needed to enable residents to get conveniently to nearby towns, cities, schools, hospitals and wider community facilities. The object, therefore, is to accept this but to carry out a detailed audit of how the safety of roads serving, or adjacent to, housing can be accomplished.

- Pedestrian and vehicular traffic should be adequately separated in housing developments and residential areas. This can often be accomplished at the design stage by providing open space, wide pavements, fencing or barriers between roads and housing developments.

- Adequate turning space is needed for vehicles reversing and turning thus minimizing accidents to children, the elderly and other pedestrians.

- Strict vehicle speed restrictions should be imposed in roads in residential areas, including physical devices to settlement access roads. In some cases, 'sleeping policemen' (humps in the road) can be very effective in reducing traffic speed on roads passing through housing developments.

- Table 2.17 shows some typical indices for accessibility of facilities within public housing developments in the United Kingdom.

2.9.2 Avoidance of unsafe conditions in the housing environment, in outbuildings and surroundings of the home

(a) Health effects
Although the home itself is the usual source of domestic accidents, a number of accidents occur in its immediate vicinity. This particularly affects children in the older age groups who are active in exploring and playing in this environment. Gardens, sheds and outbuildings are also common sources of accidents arising from hobby and leisure activities.

(b) Control measures
- Railway lines, electrical plant, building sites, derelict buildings and other potentially dangerous sites in residential areas should be properly secured from children and vagrants.

Table 2.17 Recommended indices for accessibility of facilities within public housing developments in the United Kingdom*

Facilities	Distance (m)	Remarks
Clothes drying	18	On same level for small dwellings.
	31	From family dwellings with not more than one storey of stairs.
Refuse disposal	31	Maximum walk from kitchen door of family dwellings (including lift journey and not more than two storeys of stairs).
Overnight parking place	76	Maximum distance from family dwelling.
	31	Maximum distance from small dwellings.
	18	Desirable distance.
Vehicle pick-up points	18	Desirable distance — all dwellings.
	46	Maximum distance from family dwellings.
	31	Maximum distance from small dwellings.
Play space	30	Maximum distance from young children's doorstep.
Kickabout area	400	Maximum distance from family dwellings.
Sitting-out area	100	Maximum distance from dwellings of the elderly.

*From MOHLG. *Layout studies: interim report.* London: Ministry of Housing and Local Government, Research and Development Group, 1968 (unpublished draft layout bulletin MOHLG).

- Overhead electricity cables should be protected or be sufficiently high to ensure that they are not accessible by children.

- All wells, ditches, drains, cesspools, septic tanks, pits, ponds and pools etc., should be properly fenced off, securely covered or otherwise protected. Life-saving equipment should be available to watercourses, lakes, canals, swimming pools, etc.

- Any large trees that are dying or have heavy overhanging branches likely to fall should be trimmed or felled.

- Garages, sheds and outbuildings are traditionally used for storing tools, equipment, oil and heating fuel, which may pose a safety risk to persons using them and to young children who often explore or play in them unsupervised. Under normal circumstances, these buildings should be securely locked to prevent children from entering, but in any case all dangerous tools, objects, gardening and other chemicals, and heating fuel should be kept out of children's reach.

- Gasoline, paraffin and other inflammable substances should be stored in suitable containers.

- All power tools and appliances should be properly grounded and guarded. Electrical wiring, plugs etc., should be properly encased and comply with electrical safety standards. Earth leakage circuit breakers should be used for outdoor electrical equipment.

- Adequate lighting and ventilation should be provided in outbuildings, particularly those with heating appliances or volatiles commonly emitted from cleaners, propellants, paints, chemicals and hobby materials.

- Outbuilding construction should not pose a threat to safety or cause a fire hazard. For example, floors should be even and not present a trip hazard and integral workshops or garages should be properly fire-proofed.

- Walkways and paths need to be adequately lit at night and constructed of an even surface that is not slippery when wet or icy. Surface water should be adequately drained.

- Single external steps or unexpected ramps should be avoided at all costs. Where this is not possible, steps should be clearly marked with a change of colour and provided with a suitable handrail. All steps should be designed for easy use.

- Fences should be made difficult for young children to climb and gates should be self-closing and difficult to open. Very low rails or fences can cause tripping and falls and should always be clearly visible.

- High windows should have a 'buffer' zone immediately beneath to cushion any fall. Railings and fence palings should be avoided in this area.

2.9.3 Protection against the risks and effects of falls

(a) Epidemiology

The most important cause of accidental death in the home is falls; these cause up to two thirds of all male accidental deaths in the home and up to four fifths among women. Most fatal cases are in the elderly age group, and they increase with the number of flights or stairs to be negotiated. Accident statistics show that in the United Kingdom, 7–10% of falls are fatal for elderly persons and that about one third of falls in the 65–74-year age group occur on stairs and steps. [45] The fragility of the elderly renders them much more liable than younger persons to incur fractures in a fall, and a fracture in an elderly person is more likely to involve complications and even death. Overall, people aged 65 years and over are at much greater risk than any other age group of having a fatal accident at home, with the problem becoming particularly acute for those aged 75 and over.

Apart from falls on stairs, there are two main groups of falls: young children climbing on furniture etc., and elderly people falling while moving about the house. Falls from heights such as steps or ladders account for most of the deaths in middle-aged males, particularly when engaged on house repairs etc.

(b) Control measures

- High buildings should have suitable safety rings firmly set into walls and chimneys for outside work and maintenance with ladders.

- Balcony areas should be unclimbable by children. Balustrades should be at least 3 m high and bulky enough to support persons prone to vertigo. Horizontal dividing bars to balconies should be avoided, especially above ground level as they are often used as ladders by young children. Vertical balustrades should not be spaced more than 9 cm apart.

- Thresholds to main access doors should be so designed that they form the nosing of steps.

- Other falls are caused by carrying clothes baskets or rubbish to the clothes line or dustbin areas, respectively. In these circumstances vision is often obstructed by the goods being carried. It is therefore important to avoid any unnecessary changes of level or obstructions en route.

- Uneven and slippery floors make every household activity potentially dangerous and should be avoided.

- All rooms should have non-slip floor finishes, particularly in kitchens and bathrooms where floors are frequently wet. In these cases non-slip tiles or other suitable finishes or coverings should be used (e.g. rubber-backed non-slip carpets or certain sealers and polishes made from natural or synthetic resins that when properly used are less slippery than those made from wax).

- Failure to provide adequate damp-proofing, sub-floor ventilation, or a proper screed can lead to serious deterioration in floor finishes (e.g.

loss of adhesion in tiled finishes leading to trip hazards). Floors and floor coverings should always be kept in good repair.

- Circulation areas should not have any single steps or unexpected changes of level. Where this is not possible, they should be differentiated by a change of colour.

- A mat well should be provided in front of entrance doors to minimize tripping and accidents caused by slippery foot wear.

- Housing for elderly, infirm, chronically sick or disabled persons should preferably be on one level, and ramps should be used instead of steps wherever possible.

- In housing for the elderly or infirm, a grab rail should be placed adjacent to the WC pan. In these cases, toilet accommodation should be located on the ground floor.

- Baths should be fitted with suitable handrails to assist the elderly, children and infirm persons getting in and out. In these cases the sides of the bath should be low enough to facilitate easy access. Specially designed baths are available for disabled persons.

- To avoid falls and accidents at night, light switches should be located between the bedroom and WC so that the way ahead can be lit from either direction. Illuminated switches should be provided where necessary.

- Natural and artificial lighting to all rooms should be quantitatively and qualitatively sufficient to enable all domestic chores and operations to be accomplished without causing trip hazards. This is particularly important in kitchens and workplaces where potentially hazardous operations are carried out.

- Swings to cupboard doors and main kitchen doors should be so planned as to avoid collisions. This is particularly important if hot plates or liquids are being carried. A serving hatch between kitchen and dining areas minimizes this risk.

- High-level storage cupboards are a source of falls and other accidents, particularly by the elderly who often use steps, chairs etc., for accessing them. These should be avoided. Where possible, high-level storage cupboards should also be avoided in children's bedrooms.

Staircases are a common cause of accidents in the house, and careful thought needs to be given to their design, layout and lighting.

- Stairways should not be constructed at an angle steeper than 37°, nor should they have a tread height greater than 15 cm or a depth

Badly designed staircases are a common cause of falls.

of less than 25 cm. All should have adequate, firm handrails preferably on both sides for elderly persons. Vertical balustrades or horizontal rails should not be more than 9 cm apart.

- Single steps and winders should preferably be avoided but if required, they are best positioned at the bottom rather than at the top of a flight. Straight flight staircases are generally safer, but staircase widths, especially at landings, should be sufficient to allow furniture to be safely manoeuvred. Tapered steps should provide adequate going.

- Top and bottom steps should not encroach onto circulation areas, and doors also should not open onto stairways.

- Circular stairs with a wider to narrower width of tread along each step should not be used as elderly people often cannot judge the width at the inner end causing falls.

- Open risers are preferably avoided particularly if there are young children in the household. Similarly, open stairwells should not be climbable by children. Child-proof gates should be provided at the top and bottom of stairs where necessary.

- Staircases should be well lit. Artificial lighting should shine towards stairs to obviate shadow. Light fittings and windows should be within normal reach. Two-way light switches should be provided at the top and bottom of stairs.

- The position of windows, doorways, roof access traps and light fittings adjacent to staircases should be carefully considered to avoid the risk of falls. Ceilings over staircases should be at a level easily accessible for decorating and cleaning.

- Stair carpets should be securely attached to the treads and risers (particularly important at the top and bottom of the staircase). Loose coverings to stairs should be avoided.

Windows are a common source of danger particularly to children and people who have to clean windows from the inside. Safety locks should be fitted to all windows in rooms above ground floor which are accessible to young children. Devices should be installed to restrict window openings.

- Staircase windows should be within normal reach for cleaning and opening.

- Windows above ground floor level must be at least 80 cm from the floor. Alternatively, inward opening French windows with a balcony outside will suffice.

- All windows above third-storey height must be capable of being reglazed or cleaned from the inside (unless there are balconies).

- If horizontal and vertical pivot windows are reversible through 180° so as to be cleaned from inside, locking bolts should be provided when fully reversed. Sliding windows should be designed so that they can be removed from their frames.

- Above the third storey, windows should have a minimum internal sill height of 110 cm (as opposed to 80 cm normally). Alternatively, additional protection must be provided.

- Window controls should normally not be more than 2 m above the floor (assuming no fixed obstructions such as baths or sinks).

- Fasteners to casement and pivot windows above ground level should

Windows to upper storeys should be provided with child-proof locks.

limit the initial opening to 10 cm and provide continuous control of window movement.

2.9.4 Provision of adequate facilities to enable means of escape in case of fire and control and removal of conditions likely to cause or promote fire

Fires are mainly caused by children playing with matches, rubbish burning, smoking, arson, defective electrical appliances, defective heating/gas appliances and clothes catching fire. Overall, the causes of fire directly attributable to human failings may constitute more than one third of all causes of fires in buildings. [137]

Fires are a leading cause of death, particularly in multi-occupied housing.

(a) Health effects

Fires are a common cause of death every year, particularly in housing inadequately protected and without adequate means of escape. In the event of fire, smoke and fumes often cause people to become confused and behave irrationally. Where crowds of people are gathered, these effects may be heightened, with panic ensuing. In a burning building, smoke, fumes and heat may quickly overcome occupants who are unable to reach a place of safety quickly enough or find their escape route cut off. Most people who die in fires are killed in the early stages of the outbreak, and this may happen before an alarm has been raised. Victims usually die as a result of posioning from the fumes, sometimes before the fire itself reaches their part of the building or before they are aware that the fire has broken out.

The most common cause of fire deaths is asphyxiation from CO poisoning arising from partial combustion of combustible materials

185

and also from the effects of high concentrations of carbon dioxide which effectively increases the rate and depth of breathing, thus causing deep inhalation of any toxic gases that may also be present. [137] Asphyxiation may also occur because of the reduced oxygen content of the air or by poisoning from the burning of other chemical elements, such as sulphur or chlorine, which are toxic. Heat in the form of actual flame or radiation will cause burns and when experienced at high intensity is immediately fatal. In lesser intensities, it can cause serious injury that may lead to death from shock. [137]

(b) Control measures
(i) General provisions
These can include:

- Roadways, gateways and space around buildings should be adequate to allow access by fire services and should not be obstructed by parked cars, accumulated rubbish etc.

- Fire hydrants or other water sources should be located within reasonable distance of housing.

- Each building should be capable of containing a fire within one area and of protecting against fire from outside (compartmentation).

- Spread of fire can be controlled by separating walls, or by spacing the building away from the boundary, by the fire resistance, fenestration and non-combustible content of external walls, and by ensuring that the roof covering has adequate resistance to external penetration and surface spread of flame.

- Walls, floors, ceilings and linings should be designed to provide separation and limit fire spread. In general, doors should have the same fire resistance as the walls except that openings in external walls are not subject to the compartmentation standards, providing that distance is sufficient between walls and boundaries (i.e. provision of a protected area).

- Fires can spread through roofs and suspended ceiling spaces unless compartment walls are extended and additional fire-stopping provided where necessary. This will provide a fire-break between adjoining dwellings.

- Basements may pose additional hazards. Care must be taken to ensure that the ground floor has adequate fire resistance from the basement and that any openings in it are protected.

- Doors and staircases to storeys above the ground floor should provide a minimum half-hour fire resistance.

186

- All parts of the dwelling should have adequate means of escape to the outside. Where necessary, alternative exits should be provided.

- Windows to upper storey rooms should wherever possible be openable to allow exit in an emergency.

- Meters and gas shut-down controls should be readily accessible and adequately protected against fire.

- Suitable non-combustible materials which minimize flame-spread and release of toxic gases should be used in the building construction.

- Highly inflammable materials should not be used in high-risk areas of the house. Only furnishings pretreated against fire should be used in these areas (particularly important if any of the occupants smoke cigarettes).

- Smoke detectors are useful for early fire warning, especially at night when victims often become asphyxiated by smoke while asleep. (Research in the USA has shown that these devices reduce the death rate from fires 1.5 times.) These should be located at suitable positions in the house and arrangements made for regular servicing.

- Adequate storage arrangements should be provided for inflammable substances, such as heating fuels or chemicals. These should preferably not be stored indoors. Petrol should always be stored in an approved safety can outside the dwelling. Oil heaters are the cause of many domestic fires. Only heaters where the flames are automatically extinguished on tipping over should be used.

- Each dwelling should have at least one easy-to-operate and properly maintained fire extinguisher or fire blanket. This is probably best situated in the kitchen where most fires start.

(ii) Multiple and high-rise buildings
- It is important that a safe and secure secondary means of escape is provided with at least two escape routes leading in opposite directions. Where possible, there should be emergency access to an adjoining building across a flat roof.

- Portable oil or gas heaters and inflammable materials should not obstruct access to exits.

- Internal staircases should be enclosed in a fire-protected structure to provide adequate time for escape. Doors onto staircases should be self-closing and swing in the direction of escape.

- Similarly, all entrance and cupboard doors off halls and landings should be self-closing and adequately protected against fire. Inflammable materials should not be stored under stairs.

- In some cases, enclosed corridors should be lit with emergency exit lighting.

- Lifts and staircases, pipe openings, conduits and ducts can act as chimneys for fire unless they are properly enclosed or fire-stopped.

- Electric switch and lift motor rooms are potential sources of fire and need to be properly fire-proofed.

- Smoke/fire alarms should be installed at suitable locations.

- In tall buildings, firemen's lifts, ventilated lobbies, smoke outlets from basements and automatic roof vents or other smoke disposal methods need to be provided. Also, each storey should have dry and wet rising mains, and communication by telephone should be available for firemen between ground and high levels.

2.9.5 Protection against burns and scalds

In western countries, burning is a significant cause of accidental death among children. Between 60 and 90% of all deaths due to burns and scalds are caused by home accidents. Women are up to five times as likely to die from burns and scalds as men.

A major investigation of over 5000 burnt patients who had hospital treatment in the UK for burns showed that about 66% of burns investigated occurred in or about the home. Among these, nearly two thirds of the children were under 15 years of age, with about 30% under 5 years of age. All records indicated the special vulnerability of the elderly, for whom relatively small areas of burnt skin can be rapidly fatal. Burns from scalds are caused mainly by touching or knocking over utensils filled with hot or boiling liquids.

Appropriate **control measures** include the following:

- The flames of a cooking stove or heating appliance should not be less than 1 m from the ground to reduce the risk of burns to small children. Ovens should preferably have double doors and an inside light. Gas stoves should not be placed immediately next to a window or door and should have at least one worktop adjacent to it (preferably one on either side). Cupboards mounted immediately over a cooker or boiler are a source of burns from contact with hot surfaces or firing of clothing.

Kettles are a common source of burns and scalds to children.

- Hot-water heaters, geysers and boilers should be thermostatically controlled so that domestic water is not delivered above 54° C.

- Powered washing machines and driers should be designed to switch off automatically when the doors are opened. Child-proof safety switches also should be fitted where appropriate.

2.9.6 Protection against asphyxiation or gas poisoning from faulty heating and cooking appliances and services

All fires and fuel-burning appliances (including portable appliances) need a fresh air supply for correct combustion. This air normally enters the room and into the appliance through vents and air-bricks as well as by gaps under the door or around window frames. If the air entering a room is insufficient, the fire or heater could soon use up most of the oxygen present. This situation causes a dangerous deterioration in indoor air quality, particularly the build-up of CO; it also affects the efficiency of the combustion process. In addition, combustion products from open fires, mains gas, oil-fired or solid-fuel appliances must be expelled safely from the room by a flue or chimney (except certain portable flueless appliances). In developed countries, piped supplies of natural or town gas to appliances is the usual fuel for cooking and heating. However, in developing countries, liquefied petroleum gas (LPG) available as commercial butane or propane is usually used for cooking and heating. In essence, every domestic LPG installation consists of the gas containers, the gas-consuming appliance and the pipes and connections between them. The portable LPG heater is a self-contained cabinet with its own fuel supply, usually from 15 kg butane cylinders. Under normal circumstances, the byproducts of LPG combustion are nitrogen dioxide, carbon dioxide and water vapour. However, as with utility gas, if the oxygen supply is inadequate, poisonous CO gas can be given off. LPG may also present a fire hazard unless proper safety precautions are taken.

(a) Health effects
Several hundred cases of asphyxiation from CO have been directly associated with faulty heating and cooking appliances. Asphyxiation by CO is second or third in importance as an external cause of fatal accidents in developing countries. Generally speaking, gassing accidents are lower in homes supplied with bottled liquid petroleum gas (which does not contain CO) compared with utility gas. Gas installations are also the cause of many household fires and occasional explosions when piped gas supplies leach into the ground or into unventilated rooms.

(b) Control measures
(i) General measures

- All rooms containing fires and fuel-burning appliances should have a sufficient number of vents or air-bricks. In no circumstances should these be blocked up.

- Gas- or oil-fired boilers need to be serviced and flues swept at regular intervals.

- Flues serving appliances which burn coal, smokeless fuel or wood need to be swept out at least once a year, but more often if the fire is in constant use. Mechanical sweeping should be used to remove materials (other than soot) that may cause a blockage (e.g. loose bricks or bird-nesting material).

- Wood-burning stoves burning wet or newly felled wood can cause creosote to form in the wood burner and chimney, necessitating more regular cleaning.

- Smoke boxes and throat plates to solid-fuel heaters and cookers need to be cleaned at least once a month.

- Grilles to balanced-flue appliances must always be kept unobstructed to enable air and waste gases to circulate.

- Paraffin heaters and wicks need to be checked regularly to prevent a build-up of dust that could restrict air flow. Warning labels should be affixed to appliances cautioning users not to refill with paraffin while the heater is alight, to keep heaters away from doors and draughts, and to ensure that a good supply of fresh air enters the room.

- All heating and cooking appliances should be installed and maintained by competent, trained installers.

- Defective appliances should be replaced regularly. Leaking flues or chimneys should be repaired without delay.

- Gas fires and heaters should always be designed with automatic gas cut-off devices when the pilot light is extinguished.

- Special attention needs to be given to connecting pipes between stoves, burners and gas cylinders as these are often made of crude rubber, which soon deteriorates.

- Rubber diaphragms to pressure-reduction valves leak easily and need to be replaced at regular intervals.

- Brass gas taps and valves corrode over time and frequently stick half-way open. This means that not all burners may light when the gas is turned on, thus releasing unburnt gas into the room. Similarly, when the fire is turned 'off', the tap may continue to supply small quantities of gas to the fire. Old gas taps should preferably be replaced with automatic spring-loaded gas taps which close with a bayonet action. Gas taps should be of a type that cannot be turned on accidentally.

- Old gas piping often fractures or leaks at fittings, sometimes causing CO poisoning, and should be replaced regularly.

- Flues to gas or solid-fuel cooking/heating appliances need to be inspected by the local authority or equipment supplier to ensure they are in a safe, gas-tight condition. In some countries, compulsory inspection of gas appliances is undertaken on request or when houses or flats change hands, but some method is also needed for ensuring compulsory replacement of dangerous appliances. In some cases financial support may be needed to meet part of the costs incurred.

- In new housing construction, consideration should be given to installing gas burners of advanced design that, because of the high temperature created at the heating surface, provide flameless combustion thus ensuring that no CO is formed.

- All rooms containing a gas appliance should preferably have some form of permanent ventilation by an air-brick in a wall or sub-floor ventilator. Gas appliances above a 7 kW rating should have air vents of $4.5\,cm^2$ for each kW of input rating above 4 kW. Additional ventilation is needed where gas equipment is installed in a compartment, such as a cupboard.

- Where appliances are flued to the outside air, ventilation for combustion is still needed and can be provided by a vent opening measuring at least the same as the cross-sectional area of the flue collar.

- Unflued appliances require at least $6\,cm^2$ of free ventilation area for each 0.3 kW input divided equally between high and low level, or $97\,cm^2$ (whichever is greater). Ventilation requirements are in addition to those required by occupants and oxygen-consuming appliances and apply to each separate compartment of partitioned rooms.

- Ventilating rooms by window openings, infiltration or mechanical fans will reduce build-up of CO and other gases.

- The correct size flue should always be fitted to flued appliances and should have a draught diverter terminating vertically above the eaves of the roof in a clear, exposed position.

(ii) LPG appliances
Particular safety measures for LPG appliances include:

- To avoid damage cylinders should never be dropped off vehicles.

- Butane and propane gases are heavier than air and leakage will collect at the lowest level. Cylinders should, therefore, never be stored or used below ground level, or adjacent to cellars, basements or drains.

- Cylinders are best stored outside in an accessible, secure, well-ventilated area, suitably protected from the elements and any possible impact damage. Cylinders should be stored at a suitable distance from the buildings or boundary walls.

- In cold climates, cylinders should be raised off the ground and housed in an insulated and ventilated wooden chest.

- It is important that cylinders are not changed or checked for leaks in the presence of naked lights or lighted cigarettes.

- Connectors, washers and valves need to be inspected regularly for damage and should always be installed in accordance with manufacturer's instructions.

- A gas regulator must always be fitted at the source of supply to reduce and stabilize the gas pressure.

- Copper tubing from cylinder to fixed appliances should always be used. LPG attacks natural rubber, and only approved hoses should be used for portable installations.

- To prevent CO poisoning, atmosphere-sensing devices should be used that close off the gas supply before dangerous levels of CO are reached.

- Because of the risk of explosions or fire, LPG appliances are not recommended for use in high-rise flats.

2.9.7 Protection against electric shocks from defective appliances and services

(a) Health effects

Defective electrical appliances, wiring and fittings commonly cause electric shock and electrocution, which is often fatal in children and the elderly.

(b) Control measures

- Modern electrical installations are not normally dangerous, providing that they are installed in accordance with approved safety standards. Old installations, however, are a potential hazard in causing fires or electric shock and should be regularly inspected, serviced and replaced before they get into a dangerous condition.

- A sufficient number of socket outlets conveniently situated will obviate overloading and trailing leads.

- Electric points should be fitted with the correctly separated fuse and shock stops provided to all disused electric outlets. Socket outlets must not be situated near sinks or in bathrooms.

- All electric points and appliances should be adequately earthed and there should be no electric contacts between electricity source, the individual and water supply.

- Miniature circuit breakers should be used to automatically switch off the electric current as soon as any short-circuiting occurs. This prevents the build-up of heat in equipment and thus reduces the possibility of fires and electrocution resulting from electric circuit faults.

- All meters, main switches and fuse boxes should be easily accessible and protected against fire.

- Particular emphasis needs to be given to all electrical equipment and installations in kitchens.

- Old-type coiled electric radiant panel fires are a source of fires and burns, especially in housing for the elderly or children. In these cases, high-level electric heaters should be used in preference.

- Only cord-operated switches to electrical appliances should be used in bathrooms/washrooms. Electric light fittings should preferably be of a type to discourage connection to appliances. Only shaving sockets should be provided in bathrooms.

- Light switches should be reasonably accessible (e.g. light switches should be placed adjacent to beds and between bedroom and bathrooms). Cord switches should be located in WC compartments and bathrooms at child's height.

- Coiled leads and plastic bases to electric kettles should be used wherever possible to reduce scalds caused to children pulling boiling water down onto themselves.

- Poorly serviced electric blankets sometimes give rise to fires or electric shocks and should be replaced as necessary.

2.9.8 Protection against bodily harm from lacerations and similar injuries

(a) Health effects

Lacerations by sharp tools and objects constitute the most common non-fatal type of injury in the home. For instance, the 1980 Home Accident Surveillance report of the UK Department of Trade showed that cuts/lacerations accounted for 60.8% of injuries as shown by initial visits to accident departments of hospitals. [138] Lacerations by indiscriminate use of tools, kitchen equipment and sharp objects account for considerable pain, discomfort and in some cases serious permanent injuries. There are many obvious sources of lacerations in the home, many of which relate to accidents involving broken glass from windows, glazed doors and other glass infill panels.

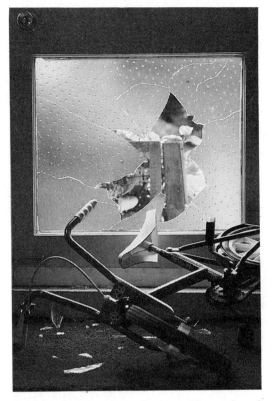

Broken glazing is the main cause of cuts and lacerations in buildings.

(b) Control measures

- Only safety glass which is laminated, toughened or heat-treated should be installed below 1 m from the floor. The glass should be sufficiently strong or thick to withstand impact damage of a fall and to minimize resultant injuries. Safety glazing should comply with international standards.

- Glass doors and panels should not be situated at the bottom of stairs or steps.

- Safety glass should always be used in glazed door panels.

- Large sheets of glass should be marked so that they are clearly visible.

- Glass which is too thin may break under pressure or blow out with the wind. Glass weight should always be specified in accordance with safety standards, depending on the size and situation of the window.

- Off-centre pivot doors should always be detailed so as to avoid trapping of fingers.

- All high-speed cutting devices should be properly guarded, and can openers should not leave raw metal edges. Knives and other cutting implements should be kept out of reach of children.

2.9.9 Protection against poisoning from dangerous drugs, medicines and household chemicals

A study by the UK Department of Trade into child poisoning from household products (excluding drugs) showed that turpentine, bleach, paraffin, disinfectant, perfume and nail polish remover accounted for

Poisons and medicines should be kept in a lockable cupboard out of a child's reach.

40% of all child poisoning. Overall, almost 100 household substances were implicated, about half of which were in bottles or jars and mostly in liquid form. Nearly half of the incidents in the bathroom or toilet involved bleach or toilet cleaners, with the kitchen and outside sheds or garden being the two most common locations of poisoning incidents. About half of the cases involved products that were not in their normal place of storage at time of accident. [21] Canadian research found the following breakdown in poisoning cases in the home: aspirin, 16%; barbiturates, 3%; other medicines, 26%; household materials, 23%; and other substances, 22%.

MacQueen [139] and others found the greatest risk of poisoning to young children was from drugs and medicines. Child-resistant containers reduce child poisoning accidents by about 80% [6]. By contrast, lockable cupboards and safety education measures have had limited effect on accident reduction.

Some household chemicals and adhesives may be used by adolescents for glue-sniffing. Solvent abuse is now a major problem in some countries, and it is therefore especially important that these chemicals be kept in a lockable cupboard.

(a) Control measures

- Suitable and sufficient storage facilities should be provided in all houses for storing dangerous, inflammable and/or poisonous household chemicals and pharmaceutical products. In general terms, this means lockable cupboards or cabinets for chemicals and medicines in rooms where the products would normally be used or stored. Child-proof catches to cupboards provide some protection against very young children opening them.

- Inflammable substances such as turpentine, oil and petrol should only be stored in rooms or cupboards that are adequately protected against fire.

- Householders should be encouraged to use child-resistant containers for bleaches, medicines and drugs.

2.9.10 Protection against poisoning from plants and fungi

Poisonous plants, berries, fruits and fungi are a serious source of potential poisoning in residential areas. Where this is a problem, suitable eradication measures should be instigated. These include selective use of herbicides, removal and a regular system for inspecting infected areas, supported by an education programme targeted at children and parents.

2.9.11 Protection against poisoning from heavy metal and other contaminants from soil

Soil composition is an important consideration when choosing suitable sites on which to build housing. Some soils are contaminated with heavy metals either through natural corrosion of metal-rich ores or by past industrial operations or dumping. Contaminants include arsenic, lead, copper, zinc and a whole range of trace elements and chemicals (including pesticides), which may be poisonous if they contaminate water supplies or are ingested by children through hand-to-mouth activities. Other contaminants include methane, which is commonly given off following the putrefaction of organic and vegetable matter. Apart from fire risk, methane can also give rise to nuisance complaints. In particular, problems have arisen when houses have been built on, or adjacent to, garbage disposal sites. It is therefore recommended that housing is not built on such sites and that soil composition is routinely tested for heavy metals and other contaminants before choosing a site for development. Checks should be made on the history of sites to ascertain whether any previous industrial or other potentially toxic operations have taken place. In some cases it may be possible to remove toxic topsoil and replace with clean soil. Alternatively the site could be concreted over or otherwise sealed to reduce risk of poisoning through ingestion or contamination of food crops such as vegetables during the growing season.

2.10 SPECIAL HOUSING REQUIREMENTS

Many groups have special housing needs in relation to their health. These should be considered to be additional to the general healthy housing requirements described elsewhere in these guidelines. The institutional arrangements for meeting these needs will vary considerably from country to country, depending upon special housing provision, health care facilities and community self-help infrastructures. Similarly, the question of whether to adapt the existing housing environment to meet the special needs of the individual or to move the individual to another suitable environment must depend upon a number of factors including the availability of special housing and the willingness of occupants to move. However, a proportion of the housing stock should be adapted to meet special needs. In many cases, relatively minor changes in design at the planning stage will accommodate a wide number of special housing needs (e.g. widening doorways to enable wheelchair or pram access). In this context the overriding objective must be to match housing provision with health needs and to adopt a flexible approach to provision of design features which will accommodate both general and special needs in the future.

2.10.1 Provision of housing suitably adapted to meet the needs of children, women with children and single parents

(a) Children
(i) Health requirements

During the first years of life, the body, brain functions and character are rapidly developing and are much more subject to environmental influences than at any later age. At this time of life, the social environment of the mother and family are of paramount importance, especially the dwelling environment since it influences the health and behaviour of all members of the family, which directly or indirectly influences the physical, psychological and social development of the child. [8] It is therefore important that hygienic housing conditions be provided which can satisfy the special health needs of babies and children.

Children are especially vulnerable to enteric diseases, respiratory and chest infections, digestive disorders and also certain non-communicable diseases such as lead poisoning, accidents and some allergic conditions. Children living in poor housing are more likely to be retarded in their development and more susceptible to these diseases than children living in better housing.

Research studies have also indicated the following associations: overcrowded housing conditions and incidence of respiratory diseases; lack of sanitation and incidence of enteric disease; increased childhood accidents and overcrowded and otherwise poor housing environments; elevated blood-lead levels in children and lead-polluted housing; and impaired personality and educational development in children and apartment living. [140] Many non-housing factors contribute to the aetiology of these diseases, not least the social and economic environment of the family, degree of parental supervision, social class of parents, state of nutrition and sometimes cultural factors. However, there are also medical reasons why the housing environment can have a direct bearing on child health. Differences in disease and illness patterns between children and adults can be attributed largely to differences in biological, psychological and social health needs, and exposure to causative agents. For example, young children often have less immunity to many infectious diseases than adults (e.g. infantile diarrhoea), are less able to cope with a given dose, and are more prone to contracting infections because of characteristic unhygienic habits (e.g. faecal–oral contacts) and have increased exposure to disease agents such as occurs when children play in water or soil polluted by harmful bacteria, parasites or chemicals.

To take another example, young children are more susceptible to lead poisoning than adults: their lower body weight means they cannot tolerate the same dose as adults; effects of low lead intoxication (reduced concentration, intelligence and educational attainment) are higher in children than in adults; they absorb more lead into their bodies (particularly bones) as part of their physical development and they are more exposed to lead than adults because of their tendency to lick or chew old lead paintwork or eat dirt or dust containing lead. [72]

Children are generally considered to be more vulnerable than adults to carcinogens such as asbestos [17] because they differ in body metabolism and tolerance to given stimuli, they have a longer life span than adults, giving cancers with long latency periods more time to develop (mesothelioma has a latency period of 20–30 years), they are closer to the ground than adults and are thus more likely to disturb and breathe in asbestos fibres in floor dust or disturb asbestos materials during play or exploration.

Children also have impaired thermoregulatory ability compared with adults. Thus in cold climates children need warmer rooms than non-elderly adults in order to avoid hypothermia, and in hot climates children are more prone to hyperthermia unless precautions are taken to maintain a suitable thermal environment. [121]

(ii)   Basic housing requirements

The residential environment plays an important part in healthy child development: unpolluted air; access to open spaces, parks and play facilities; and provision of health care centres, shops, schools, nurseries and other communal facilities where mothers and children can interact outside the home.

High child densities in human settlements are a source of dissatisfaction to parents, children and other residents, particularly in high-rise housing. Relatively small rooms limit play space, mothers are afraid to let younger children play on the balconies (many of which are walled only to waist height), and neighbours complain of noise if children play in corridors or lift halls. Also, the ground is too far away for convenient supervision and lift controls are often too high for even junior-age school children to operate. As a result, many children and mothers become isolated in their own homes. For instance, a UK Government-commissioned survey in 1970 showed that attempts made by mothers to keep young children quiet in flats were likely to impair personality development. A Glasgow study concluded that young children living in flats failed to acquire a sense of security, and had their curiosity and later ability to explore and experiment stifled. [22] Sensible housing allocation policies and adoption of appropriate child density norms are two specific measures which can minimize this particular problem (e.g. by allocating families with young children to the lower floors of tower blocks or reducing child densities to a specific level). The outside play environment also needs to provide stimulation and challenges to mental development, but without being unnecessarily unsafe.

Children also have special housing needs inside dwellings: for example, additional space is needed for play, mental stimulation and development. In addition, avoidance of overcrowding will reduce transmission of communicable diseases and child abuse. A sanitary means of excreta disposal and waste water disposal will reduce the incidence of enteric and parasitic diseases, and personal washing facilities will reduce faecal–oral disease transmission. Furthermore, good indoor air quality and climate will reduce childhood respiratory diseases and home safety requirements will reduce child accidents arising from a child's natural tendency to play, explore and experiment in potentially dangerous situations. Child poisoning caused by the use of toxic materials (such as leaded paintwork) in the home can be prevented by choosing non-toxic building materials. Young children also need an appropriate, quiet and peaceful place to sleep — even during the day — and if possible suitable uniform temperatures in all rooms of the house where they spend most time.

Finally, children's health/housing needs change as adulthood approaches. Adolescents often want more privacy and independence from the rest of the family and have different social, recreational and space requirements. Also, neighbourhood noise is likely to interfere with adolescent sleep and study, thus affecting educational performance. These examples illustrate the need to consider differential health needs of children in relation to housing and the environment, particularly when assessing housing needs, developing housing standards or allocating family housing.

(b) Mothers with children
(i) Health requirements
There is generally thought to be little difference in healthy housing needs of women compared with men, but the housing needs of women with children differ considerably from those of childless women. In fact, the customary bond between mother and child means that the housing needs of mothers are inextricably linked to the housing needs of their children. For example, the susceptibility of women to neurosis and depression may be aggravated by a poor housing environment, and this is likely to have a direct adverse effect on children in terms of gross neglect, emotional starvation and possibly child abuse.

(ii) Basic housing requirements
A mother with a young family needs somewhere to sit and relax while she watches her family at play. For a family with small children, a garden attached to a dwelling or a park or communal area, will be the solution. In multi-storey housing, playground wardens or community members who can supervise young children at play will relieve mothers of the worry of unsupervised children playing out of sight. It also gives the

mother a break from the constant demands young children make on her within the home. Community day nursery schemes and crèches assist working women with children to provide additional financial support to the family.

(c) Single parents

The housing problems of single parents (both women and men) include lack of time and opportunity for child supervision while working, which can result in increased child accidents and laxity in child hygiene practices. Non-working single parents usually have extremely limited financial means and inevitably live in poorer housing and are less able to improve their situation by moving to better housing. Community and institutional support are particularly important to these groups. Special priority needs to be given to assisting single-parent families living in poverty, financial hardship and in unsatisfactory housing.

2.10.2 Provision of housing suitably adapted to meet the requirements of the elderly

(a) Health requirements

A number of normal developments in the ageing process make the elderly more susceptible to specific housing-related agents or conditions compared with other groups. However, considerable variation in health/housing needs can be expected among elderly persons: some may be completely healthy and independent, and some afflicted by a variety of ailments and thus highly dependent upon others. Overall, the elderly have more critical physical, physiological and psychological health requirements compared with younger members of the community.

The main **physical effect** of old age is reduced mobility. For instance, mobility may be impaired by processes affecting the neurological, sensory or musculoskeletal system. Indirect effects may occur through degenerative diseases of the cardiovascular and cardiopulmonary systems. Also, chronic diseases of the gastrointestinal, cardiovascular, renal, cardiopulmonary, neurological or musculoskeletal system may diminish the tolerance of an elderly person to exposure to various agents. For example, asphyxiants such as CO may be more potent in the presence of pre-existing chronic hypoxemia or coronary artery disease, and pre-existing chronic obstructive/restrictive airway diseases may be exacerbated by exposures to a variety of airborne chemical and biological agents.

Medications taken to control the symptoms of chronic illnesses may enhance or potentiate the action of a hazardous exposure. For example, antihypertensive drugs with bronchial side effects may initiate or exacerbate asthmatic symptoms and psychotropic drugs with anticholinergic or antiadrenergic actions may interfere with accommodation to heat or cold. Also, elderly people have reduced host defence through degeneration or dysfunction related to ageing. [9]

Finally, the elderly are more susceptible to accidents in the home, particularly falls. These falls often result from a loss of balance because the sense of balance deteriorates with age.

In terms of **physiological needs**, the elderly tend to need higher indoor temperatures than young healthy adults to compensate for poor circulation and less efficient thermoregulatory control mechanisms. Generally speaking, they need a room temperature about 2–3° C warmer than that needed by younger adults, but which roughly corresponds to the heating requirements of small children. Also, elderly persons require a more uniform distribution of heating from floor to ceiling to prevent chilling of legs and feet. In contrast, the elderly, particularly those with cardiac disease, cannot endure high temperatures or moderately high temperatures accompanied by high humidity. Impaired eyesight, smell and hearing, susceptibility to fatigue and diminished movement are other examples of potentially disabling conditions in the elderly.

The elderly have special **psychosocial needs** and require privacy not only during periods of acute or chronic illness, but also to permit sedentary recreation and meditation. Elderly people often become forgetful or absent minded. This might be symptomatic of the ageing process or might be related to something more serious, such as Alzeimers disease. Senile dementia can present very serious housing problems relating to safety, personal hygiene and general health. It is therefore important that the elderly are not isolated from the rest of the community – particularly young persons – as this often leads to loneliness, depression and poor social well-being. Also, apart from the medical problems, the effects of ageing, losses of friends, loved ones, and independence, together with reduced income and possible job satisfaction on retirement, may adversely affect behaviour, attitudes, self-esteem, self-interest, appetite and sleep. A poor residential and social environment may exacerbate these feelings and result in unhappiness or worry.

(b) Basic housing requirements

Dwelling units for the elderly should preferably be integrated with those occupied by younger persons to create a balanced and mixed residential microdistrict (see also section 2.1.2). Every effort should be made to encourage elderly people to occupy housing where they can retain their independence, be close to relatives and friends, and feel to be an integral part of the community to help combat loneliness. Residential units need to be located near public transport, shops, health centres, churches and other community facilities. Pedestrian crossings are needed over busy roads. Alternatively, the elderly can live in 'sheltered' or 'collective' housing. In these cases, special accommodation for the elderly is provided in service apartments, with warden supervision to assist residents with errands, mail distribution, cleaning, laundry, infirmary functions, and communal restaurant and social facilities. Such accommodation is often part of a mixed-community development scheme.

Inside the home, housing needs to be designed so that elderly people do not feel 'cut off' from the wider community by positioning windows where they can see people (e.g. children playing) in the distance. The environment also must enable efficient heat regulation, and humidity control mechanisms are needed to prevent stress on physiological responses (i.e. a deep body temperature of not less than 35° C and not more than 39° C with controlled humidity is needed to prevent hypothermia and hyperthermia, respectively).

Since elderly persons frequently have difficulty climbing stairs, they should preferably be allocated single-level ground floor accommodation. Where this is not practicable, dwellings occupied by the elderly above the ground floor should be served by a lift. In any circumstances, steps and ramps must be equipped with handrails. The design should reduce necessary bending, reaching or other physical strain during homemaking activities (e.g. by providing easy access to storage space and easy-to-operate windows and doors). Home accidents also can be reduced by good housing design: avoiding steep, badly lighted stairs and providing adequate handrails to minimize falls and avoiding high shelves and cupboards, slippery or defective floors and coverings and badly designed cooking apparatus (see section 2.9).

The first Expert WHO Committee on Housing also recommended that lighting in dwelling units for the elderly be 'quantitatively and qualitatively adequate', since the elderly need more and better light than a younger person to do the same task. It also pointed out that other persons with impaired ability to see and smell may not be aware of a fire, and may be unable to move rapidly to escape from it. [12] In these cases, fire hazards can be reduced by the proper choice of building materials, furnishings, careful planning of circulation and location of facilities. To prevent fires and CO poisoning from heating and cooking appliances, adequate vents, guards and other safety controls must be installed (see section 2.9.6).

Finally, the importance of noise insulation is common to all groups in the community, but since many elderly persons have hearing difficulties this may lead to complaints from younger neighbours about loud conversation, radios etc., in poorly insulated dwellings. Conversely, noise from children or other sources can distress elderly persons, especially if they are unwell or trying to rest (see section 2.4.6).

2.10.3 Provision of housing suitably adapted to meet the requirements of disabled people

The United Nations estimate that 450 million people worldwide have some form of physical or mental impairment, i.e. any loss or abnormality of psychological, physiological or anatomical structure or function. [141] However, impairment by itself does not necessarily lead to 'handicap', which has been defined as 'loss or limitation of opportunities to take part in the normal life of the community on an equal level with others'. Whether this happens or not will depend on the nature of the disease, attitude towards the impairment, social demands, and last but not least the work and **housing environment**.

The current policy of the WHO and the United Nations in general is that disabled persons should not be segregated but be integrated as much as possible within the general population. Thus, the built environment should be so designed that it does not handicap those persons disabled by physical or mental impairment. The nature of preventive or remedial action will depend largely upon the nature of the disablement, and design criteria should be consulted before making decisions about standards and policy. However, the United Nations [141] has laid down some general considerations in relation to healthful housing needs of disabled persons which are summarized below.

(a) Persons with movement difficulties

Mobility difficulties may be caused by a number of factors, including congenital conditions, accidents, disease and ageing. Some diseases, such as polio and leprosy, which are common in developing countries will also inhibit movement if not properly treated.

The main problem faced by disabled persons with movement difficulties is gaining access to public buildings, educational establishments, and the home and workplace. Thus, disabled persons often become prisoners of the unadapted built environment, which socially and economically isolates them from the rest of the community. This can affect mental health and well-being. Environmental measures, such as provision of ramps, adequately sized door openings and special adaptation of bedrooms, sanitary appliances, fittings and cupboards are examples of suitable remedies. Allocation of persons with limited mobility to ground floor, single-storey accommodation may also be of assistance, but it should be remembered that there is a greater security risk on ground floors and an upper floor dwelling may give a more pleasant view. Additional heating may be needed in cold climates to compensate for impaired blood circulation. Disabled persons with restricted movement in arms and hands may need special fittings to enable them to use windows, appliances, doors etc.

Electrically operated ramps provide easy access for disabled people.

(b) Persons with vision difficulties

Blindness or acute visual disability may be caused by disease, accidents or congenital factors. Visual acuity is usually related to age. Diseases such as measles, trachoma and cataracts may cause blindness if not properly treated in time. Lack of vitamin A in a child's diet also may cause blindness.

Persons with seeing difficulties have problems with orientation and mobility: reading difficulties may increase orientation difficulties. However, orientation can for some people be aided through the use of colour, illumination and in certain cases the texture of building materials. Building design and layout which is simple and straightforward will assist orientation.

(c) Persons with hearing and/or speech difficulties

Deafness may be caused by diseases such as otitis and mastoiditis that if not treated properly will lead to hearing difficulties. These persons are seriously impaired without showing any outward signs of their disability. Since persons with hearing difficulties have problems in comprehending sounds or words in noisy environments, rooms should be acoustically well designed and insulated. People with impaired hearing may rely on lip reading for communication,

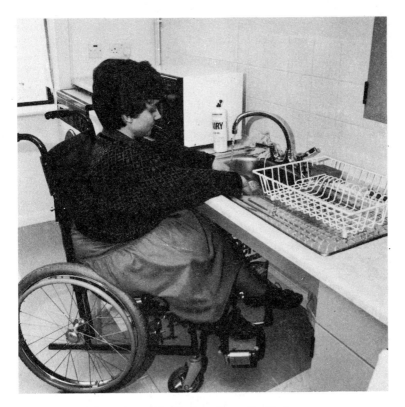

Adaptations of a kitchen for a disabled person.

a technique that is helped by good general natural and artificial lighting.

(d) Persons who have fits

Fits are generally caused by epilepsy, a symptom of electrical disorder in the brain, and may be associated with a number of different conditions (e.g. head injury, stroke, brain tumour, lack of oxygen during birth). Persons who have fits are more common in developing regions and most of them are children. People who have fits have a tendency to fall and injure themselves: to obviate severe injury, sharp edges and corners should be avoided where possible. For instance, in many traditional houses, open fireplaces constitute a risk for epileptic persons who may fall into the fire and receive severe burns; such fireplaces should be guarded.

207

(e) Persons with learning difficulties

Learning difficulties may result from genetic, medical or nutritional factors. The built environment must be organized in a simple layout that facilitates orientation, which is especially important for persons who have learning difficulties.

(f) Persons with mental illness

Traditionally, mentally handicapped and mentally ill persons have been institutionalized in large hospitals with little or no contact with the community at large. Although these hospitals provided intensive nursing care, the hospital environment was often dehumanizing and unsuitable for rehabilitation. The present approach, which is supported by the WHO, is for mentally ill persons to be housed in the community wherever possible but with back-up support from community health-care services. Such a policy must involve not only the community itself but also considerable joint planning and collaboration between the hospitals, health and housing authorities. This means developing a comprehensive local service aimed at enhancing the autonomy and independence of the individual with a network of professional services of properly trained staff employed where the patient or resident lives. This would enable mentally ill persons to develop the greatest independence and autonomy of which they are capable.

The physical housing requirements for mentally ill persons are similar to those for the long-term chronically sick. As far as possible, the mentally ill should live in ordinary housing within the community rather than be divorced from it. For instance, experience in the UK has shown that hostel accommodation is little better than hospitals for housing the mentally ill. Small housing units with wardens or live-in health-worker provision have been found to be the most suitable. However, the type of accommodation required will depend upon the nature of the mental illness and degree of adaptation to the housing environment. Small, closely knit communities are usually better at accommodating mentally ill persons than remote urban centres, which are often totally unsuitable.

(g) Persons with allergies

Persons with allergies may be sensitive to dust, house mites, mould, pollen, animal hair, formalin, turpentine etc., in the home and environment. Others are sensitive to contact with substances such as nickel, chromium and rubber. [142] Removal of the cause will usually prevent sensitivity to these allergens (see section 2.7.1h).

Special housing requirements

2.10.4 Provision of housing suitable for the chronically sick and others with special health needs

The chronically sick are another group who spend much time in the home and residential environment. In this instance, the concern is not just preventing poor housing from **causing** illness, but providing suitable housing as a therapeutic aid to health recovery. These people are generally under long-term medical treatment and medications taken to control the symptoms of chronic illness may exacerbate the action of hazardous housing exposure.

Good indoor thermal climate, good indoor air quality, noise insulation, privacy and pleasant outlook are especially important factors in aiding recovery. Access to health centres and medical facilities are also needed, but family and community support is especially important in providing care and other assistance. Chronically sick persons may also have special housing requirements peculiar to their medical condition. Generally, they will need to be housed on ground floor accommodation without stairs and will benefit from a separate room or segregated room area. The aim is a humanizing community care service which can integrate and reintegrate people into society, to desegregate and to offer valued settings in which all individuals can develop and sustain social relationships and lifestyles. This can only be achieved in decent, well-designed housing (see also section 2.3.3).

2.10.5 Provision of housing suitable for the homeless, rootless and long-term unemployed persons

Young people are often forced to leave their home areas and search the cities for shelter and, where possible, work: many fail to find either. As a result, they often become itinerant while the rootless find life even more difficult because of the lack of any community ties whatsoever. Many homeless people have severe mental health problems which makes any further integration even more difficult. They are also likely to have physical health problems relating to lack of shelter, lack of access to sanitation and washing facilities, poor nutrition and possible injuries to hands and feet. They mostly have very limited access to health care facilities. Homelessness and long-term unemployment are now major problems in most developing countries and formed the theme for the 1986 United Nations International Year of Homes for the Shelterless.

The growing numbers of long-term unemployed persons in developing countries are likely to bring about significant changes in social institutions and health patterns. Unemployed persons with shelter are likely to spend a lot more time at home, perhaps initially creating new

For some homeless persons shelter may just be a cardboard box.

tensions within the family. Discontent and lack of self-esteem, coupled with low income, are common characteristics among the involuntarily long-term unemployed and can lead to depression, worry and anxiety in family members. Social well-being is also often affected by unemployment because of reduced spending power for social occasions and diminished contact with other social groups outside the home (e.g. work colleagues). Thus, for the unemployed, the home and family become the focus of social and recreational activity. Also, since diminished income levels are usually correlated with poor housing, the unemployed and their families are more likely to present housing-related illnesses. Income maintenance payments, provision of publicly subsidized hygienic housing and availability of recreational social facilities for the unemployed would help minimize the health and social effects of long-term unemployment.

3

Operational and organizational
requirements

Most countries have now committed themselves to the WHO's strategy of Health for All by the Year 2000. If these goals are to be achieved, increased emphasis must be placed on housing hygiene programmes which embrace all facets of health, including the physiological, psychological and mental health needs of occupants. Thus, a comprehensive healthy housing strategy should be adopted by all governments, municipalities and local agencies to provide a policy guide and programme for meeting national and local targets over a given time span. This strategy should embody and inter-relate with other pursuant economic, social, cultural, health care and educational policies which impinge on housing hygiene. Policies should aim to maintain a housing environment that minimizes the transmission of infectious agents and the occurrence of accidental injury, provides protection and security from external, natural and man-made hazards, creates and maintains a favourable indoor micro-climate, and provides an adequate amount of living and sleeping space and a safe and healthful residential environment for the occupants. The WHO is committed to improving housing and related environmental health but acknowledges the need for countries to set priorities to deal with the worst problems first. According to its programme of work for 1986–1987, now encompassed into its current programme:

> The magnitude of the investment required to resolve the problems of housing shortages, however, far surpasses the capacities of national economies. It is thus more rational to focus on national needs that are amenable to solution through housing and sanitation improvements, taking into account community involvement, especially through self-help programmes; intersectoral linkage, particularly the health and education sectors; improvement of the surroundings of housing units; and the introduction of new financing mechanisms.

This chapter examines some of the operational and organizational requirements for introducing a healthy housing strategy.

3.1 REGULAR INSPECTION AND APPRAISAL OF THE HOUSING STOCK TO ASCERTAIN HYGIENIC QUALITY

The housing stock is the major capital resource asset to the state, regardless of ownership or tenure patterns. Information on the condition of the housing stock assists policy-makers in making decisions concerning possible intervention measures, such as provision of financial assistance, assessment for rehousing, rehabilitation and slum clearance. It could also be usefully linked to epidemiological surveys.

All housing appraisal and assessment schemes rely on a detailed initial survey of properties to assess conditions, extent of overcrowding, provision of amenities, state of repair, environmental deficiencies etc. In addition, useful back-up information can be obtained from statistics usually included in census returns. From these surveys, it should be possible to get some indication of which properties are fit or unfit for human habitation, and which have the greatest priority for action.

The type of inspection procedure varies widely between countries: some use a standard checklist for surveyors to record occupancy, rent levels, provision of amenities and state of repair etc. Each factor can be given a coded weighting that can be computed to provide the requisite information on conditions, costs and prospects for action. Such information is extremely useful for providing some uniformity and prioritization of housing hygiene programmes and does not require a high degree of professional expertise by the inspecting officer.

The drawback to comprehensive assessment schemes is that they take a long time to complete, by which time the information may be out of date, and they are thus inappropriate for situations requiring immediate action or for responding to complaints. In the latter cases, the inspection expertise of a trained environmental health officer or surveyor is used to determine and implement remedial action. Where an area has been identified as being substandard or in a priority category, periodic house-to-house inspections should be made of all dwellings. These inspections are concerned primarily with basic sanitation, occupancy and physical conditions, usually resulting in enforcement of a housing hygiene code. If no code exists and there is no other basis for intervention, these inspections can still provide an invaluable opportunity for educating occupants and owners in appropriate preventative or remedial action. On other occasions, inspections are carried out following complaints, usually by a tenant where the owner or landlord is unwilling to carry out essential repair work or services. Thus, inspecting officers need to be trained not only in housing hygiene and surveying practice but also in handling complex social and legal problems as they arise.

The main value of periodic inspections is enabling tenants and others living in poor housing to get their problems investigated and hopefully remedied. They are also helpful for drawing up detailed lists of work, which can be used to prevent premature obsolescence, particularly if repairs are incorporated into a planned maintenance programme.

3.2 ADOPTION OF APPROPRIATE POLICIES FOR DEALING WITH SLUMS AND INSANITARY HOUSING

Removal of slum or otherwise insanitary housing effectively eliminates associated conditions that are detrimental to the health, comfort and well-being of the occupants. Hygienic housing improves personal health, resulting in savings in primary health care costs; it also raises self-esteem, personal satisfaction, comfort and opportunities for social relations. These benefits are enjoyed by the individual and the community alike. Remedial measures should also help remove deep-seated feelings of deprivation, despair and social injustice commonly experienced by slum dwellers. Such action is important for maintaining social and political stability but could also be defended on purely humanitarian grounds. In addition, there may be economic advantages: obsolescent housing represents a cost-deficit on housing capital and revenue accounts. Removal of such housing is an economically rational strategy for relieving the national budget of the expensive burden of excessive capital repair and amortization costs. Finally, the community enjoys many advantages arising out of clearance and rehabilitation schemes. Opportunities are often created for improving the environment, reducing high residential densities, and providing new employment and community facilities.

The choices of action for dealing with insanitary housing include: repair/maintenance of existing defects and conditions; improvement of housing amenities and facilities by conservation measures; upgrading of environmental amenities and services, and clearance of slum housing and selective or comprehensive redevelopment action. However, in all cases, cost-benefit considerations usually determine policy proposals (i.e. whether the costs of repair/rehabilitation are reasonable by reference to capital and/or rental values, and whether these costs are lower than slum clearance and redevelopment schemes).

However, more attention is now being given to non-economic factors, such as the social, ecological and environmental effects of rehabilitation, compared with redevelopment. Cultural and historical considerations are also important factors in determining the action taken. This is particularly relevant in older city areas where conservation of historical buildings is especially important to tourism and maintenance of

Simple improvements to older housing can prevent slum clearance.

community values. In these cases, conservation of buildings and the micro-environment usually outweighs cost-benefit assumptions about the future of the area.

The implementation of repair/improvement schemes largely depends upon available finance, whether the housing is in public or private owner-ship, and the ability/willingness of health-housing administrations to enforce minimum standards through informal or legal action. Basic healthy housing requirements are often prescribed in codes or legislation, but implementing non-essential repair/improvement works that arguably improve only the occupants' comfort is more difficult to justify. In the latter case, it is sometimes difficult to distinguish between 'health' and 'comfort'.

No hard-and-fast rules exist for dealing with individual insanitary housing – each case must be considered on its merits after wide discus-sion and consultation with all health-housing disciplines and the communities directly affected by the proposals. However, residential areas with high incidence and concentration of child illnesses, postnatal diseases, enteritis, respiratory diseases or home accidents and other more obvious and quantifiable housing/health illnesses, will almost certainly be known to health and housing practitioners, doctors etc., in the area. The provision of health care services and resources in these areas will initially require detailed assessment of the level and magnitude of each problem, its identifiable causes and possible alternative remedies. On this basis, housing renewal and improvement programmes, area programmes, action programmes and subprogrammes could be implemented during the planning period. At a more detailed level, proposals relating to such matters as organization changes, staffing, manpower resource levels and expenditure levels could be re-assessed. Finally, it should be possible to disaggregate long- and medium-term plans down to the level of a more practical annual programme which could serve as a detailed guide to current activity in each service field. For this to succeed, a high degree of service coordination is needed at the level of policy formulation and service delivery

3.2.1 Comprehensive slum clearance and redevelopment schemes

These schemes usually involve clearance of several hundred insanitary houses deemed unfit for human habitation together with other housing (not necessarily unfit), shops, commercial buildings etc., as part of a comprehensive urban renewal programme. The areas selected are usually situated in the older, inner city areas and comprise houses that were initally built to a low standard of housing hygiene or badly arranged in relation to other housing or buildings.

Essentially, slum houses are unfit for human habitation by reference to healthful housing criteria and are usually situated in a crowded district of a town or city inhabited by very poor people in streets, alleys or courts, forming a thickly populated neighbourhood or district of a squalid and wretched character. In other cases, slums consist simply of blocks of badly planned houses in varying stages of disrepair and lacking essential conveniences and sanitation. Finally, there are individual slum houses atypical of the area as a whole that need to be treated differently from the rest of the area.

Large-scale slum clearance and redevelopment schemes were commonplace after World War II, but in recent years emphasis has shifted from large-scale clearance and redevelopment towards a more selective approach mainly because of the social and community disruption associated with comprehensive development schemes. In any event, many countries have by now completed wide-scale development schemes and

215

now find it is generally better only carry selective clearance as part of an urban renewal programme. This includes improvement/rehabilitation options, infill development or mixed policies of gradual renewal. For these reasons, redevelopment schemes of a manageable size commensurate with economies of scale, existing environmental conditions and staff/labour resources are often preferable to large-scale schemes.

(a) Advantages

- Comprehensive redevelopment provides an opportunity to establish healthy housing and environmental conditions commensurate with employment, supporting services and housing reallocation priorities.

- New housing stock can be planned in accordance with age distribution, family size and special housing needs.

- The displaced population can be redistributed into socially manageable areas and infrastructures (e.g. by providing a better balance between the employed and unemployed, the young and the elderly, and professional and unskilled groups in the redeveloped area).

- Residential densities can be reduced, and more open space, recreational amenities and community services (e.g. new health centres, shops and schools in the microregion) can be provided.

- Renewal schemes may facilitate traffic flow through improved traffic management or road-widening schemes.

- The progressive and cumulative reduction in the capital valuation of the housing stock and the associated accumulative increases in annual capital repair and amortization costs associated with economically obsolescent housing are terminated.

- The high initial capital expenditure costs are offset by considerable reductions in capital and revenue outlays in future years. These capital savings can be fruitfully invested into wealth and employment-generating industries, resulting in higher levels of national and personal income.

- Comprehensive urban renewal schemes may indirectly improve monetary benefits by increasing market values or reducing accidents and associated time loss from work.

- Existing commercial premises in the area can now be developed, extended or adapted to facilitate new businesses, thus providing jobs for local unemployed workers.

216

(b) Disadvantages

- Permanent rehousing into a new environment creates adjustment costs for outgoing residents.

- Community infrastructures, social relationships, employment options, health, education and transportation systems are seriously disrupted or destroyed.

- There is no guarantee that new housing will provide a better quality of life than housing demolished or that people will want to live in it.

- New housing, schools, health services and possibly employment opportunites are needed immediately for persons displaced from slum areas.

- Redevelopment schemes create an alien and unfamiliar perspective within existing areas. This maladjustment can initally create tension between long-established communities and new ones which are often treated with mistrust and suspicion until they are accepted into the wider community.

- Mass building schemes seriously disrupt existing amenities and quiet enjoyment while work is going on. Transport systems may not be able to cope with additional lorries and road traffic.

- Redevelopment schemes require very high levels of capital expenditure to pay for site clearance and new building works.

- Existing utilities, such as water supplies, sewerage systems, roads, shops and factories, may be unsuitable or unadaptable to new development schemes.

- A high level of trained staff is needed to carry out the managerial, professional and administrative functions of the redevelopment process.

- Well-trained building labour and suitable building materials are needed to build new housing and services.

Slum clearance schemes pose practical problems associated with the administration and programming of site clearance, relocation of residents, reallocating dwellings and/or redevelopment of sites. In particular, a high degree of management and trained personnel are needed to administer the schemes. Compensation payments may also be necessary to assist with removal/resettlement costs, as well as to pay social and community costs.

The main problem associated with slum clearance schemes is having a sufficient stock of vacant dwellings to rehouse displaced occupants. This problem is exacerbated when initial residential densities are high, usually resulting in a shortfall in dwellings if the new scheme is built

Typical badly planned new development scheme.

at a lower density. In these circumstances, policy-makers are confronted with an extremely difficult situation: redevelop at a lower density, which would be acceptable on social and environmental grounds but which would slow the rate of slum clearance, or build at higher densities with all the attendant social, environmental and health problems.

3.2.2 Small-scale redevelopment schemes

Redevelopment schemes usually involve building new houses, roads and services etc., on a site previously cleared of slum housing and ancillary buildings.

These small-scale schemes are less costly to implement, do not result in social alienation of residents and need fewer management resources. These schemes are therefore generally preferred to grandiose comprehensive renewal programmes. However, all redevelopment schemes require considerable public interest and funding if they are to succeed.

3.2.3 Infill redevelopment schemes

Infill redevelopment schemes are mostly used to clear small pockets of

slum housing to provide additional space for environmental amenities, open space or new housing construction. Such schemes are
far less disruptive on services and communities than comprehensive
schemes, particularly if clearance is staggered as part of a long-term
development programme. Infill development is particularly beneficial
if linked to area rehabilitation schemes that provide local housing
accommodation for displaced residents. They often form part of a mixed
redevelopment/rehabilitation programme of gradual urban renewal.

Infill development schemes enjoy similar benefits to comprehensive
redevelopment programmes. However, they also share many of the
disadvantages of comprehensive development schemes; many of the
residents may not want to move, thus necessitating some form of
compulsion; residents may not be able to afford to buy or rent new or
newly improved accommodation; and accommodation may not be
available in the area where they have family, community or employment
ties.

3.2.4 Area improvement schemes

Improvement areas mainly comprise dwellings which are insanitary

Area improvement schemes have several advantages over comprehensive
redevelopment options.

in many respects, lack basic amenities and usually in need of considerable repair work. Despite this, the housing is structurally sound, well planned in relation to other properties and the micro-environment, and has not yet reached a condition of economic and physical obsolescence and therefore still has improvement potential.

The objective of housing improvement schemes is to rehabilitate and repair housing before it reaches a state where slum clearance would be the most appropriate option. This would enable dwellings to be modernized by installing amenities such as piped water supplies, washing facilities, inside toilets, bathrooms, space heating, and extensions to make more living space available to reduce indoor space densities.

In other cases rehabilitation is applied to conserve housing of historic, cultural or architectural interest, thus preserving the character of the area. At a basic level, this involves preserving the outside appearance and structure of the housing (enveloping) or additionally taking action to remedy insanitary conditions inside the dwelling including the provision of additional amenities. Action may also be taken to improve the environment of the area such as tree planting, pedestrian streets or making additional open space and off-street parking facilities available.

(a) Advantages

- Rehabilitation of older areas of existing housing is often cheaper than wholesale redevelopment schemes and halts the decline in capital values and costs of repairs.

- The social problems connected with clearance and redevelopment schemes, such as disruption of communities, resettlement difficulties and adjusting to a new way of life, are eliminated.

- Environmental improvements are usually easier to achieve. For instance, new alien structures associated with comprehensive redevelopment schemes are avoided by maximizing existing environmental features and ecological considerations.

- The need for new community services and infrastructures is usually obviated.

- Improved housing encourages mobile, younger and economically stronger families to remain in the area.

- A surplus pool of empty housing is not needed for relocating people from areas scheduled for redevelopment.

- Organizational and manpower problems connected with planning and implementing redevelopment schemes are less demanding.

(b) Disadvantages

- Residents are temporarily disturbed while their housing is improved. Some residents, particularly the elderly, may not be prepared to tolerate the noise and disturbance generated by extensive rehabilitation works. In addition, lifetime habits and low expectations of the elderly mean that they may see little tangible benefit from improvement work.

- There is usually limited opportunity to reduce residential housing densities or provide additional open space, community services or off-street car parking without selective demolition of existing housing or other buildings.

- The majority of people living in insanitary and run-down housing are on fixed or low incomes, meaning that they are unable to finance the costs of rehabilitation work. The elderly are less able to carry out major renovation work themselves.

- Considerable difficulties have arisen in countries where financial assistance has been available for improvement work. In particular, many applicants have difficulties understanding the legal, administrative and financial complexities of improvement grant or subsidy schemes. Many schemes are subject to interminable delays while applications are awaiting processing. This has deterred many would-be applicants from seeking out financial assistance and carrying out rehabilitation work.

- Renovation policy is solely remedial. There is usually no preventive element to ensure that housing does not deteriorate into disrepair or that renovated dwellings are kept in good order.

- Public money spent on renovation schemes reduces money available for new building works or maintenance of the existing housing stock, which could result in a deteriorating housing stock in the future.

(c) Administration of improvement schemes

In the public sector, housing improvement schemes can be programmed and phased over a given period dependent on finance and staff resources. In the private sector, programming of improvement schemes is not so easy to achieve and usually proceeds on a more piecemeal basis.

Most schemes give priority to installing basic amenities such as water supply, sanitation, sanitary appliances and hot water, with the proviso that the houses should be in good repair and fit for habitation for a specific number of years. Such improvements bring the highest and quickest returns in terms of improved housing hygiene. Area improvement schemes rely on an accurate assessment of housing conditions following house-to-house surveys. Work costs need to be closely monitored and public consultation at all stages is essential in gaining cooperation of owners and tenants both at the planning and operational stages.

Other improvement schemes, such as 'enveloping', tackle only the problems of exterior environmental and urban decay. 'Enveloping' of properties has recently been tried in England by renewing roofs, windows and doors, removing porous brickwork and external renderings, guttering, and implementing measures to prevent rainwater penetration and external disrepair of older properties. The costs of enveloping are met entirely by the local authority and the state. This leads to improved environmental and social conditions as well as individual conditions. However, the schemes have been criticized for not dealing with interior conditions, which may be extremely poor.

3.3 REHOUSING THE HOMELESS AND PERSONS FROM SLUMS AND INSANITARY HOUSING

Obviously, occupants must be moved from the slum housing prior to demolition and redevelopment. However, whether the responsibility to provide alternative accommodation rests on the family, the housing owners, landlord or the state is purely a value judgement. Much will depend upon social, economic and political considerations. However, the availability of suitable alternative accommodation is often at a premium. Provision therefore may need to be made for temporary accommodation to be made available until permanent housing can be found. Another constraint is the availability of accommodation that rehoused persons can afford to rent or buy and the convenience of accommodation in relation to employment or family ties.

Criteria for rehousing are usually determined by a points scheme for assessing housing needs and the relative priority for rehousing. Where a shortage of sanitary housing exists, new house building programmes should be initiated to meet the deficit. Consideration should be given to providing prefabricated housing units, mobile homes and caravans as an interim step to long-term building programmes. Unless such action is taken, slum clearance and redevelopment schemes are likely to be non-starters. In addition, some countries give priority consideration to rehousing on medical grounds (as certified by a community physician or medical practitioner), regardless of whether the housing is in a slum clearance area or not.

Muir Grey [143] gives six situations where priority for rehousing on medical grounds might be considered:

- housing conditions definitely causing physical disease

- housing conditions possibly causing physical disease

- housing conditions possibly causing mental disease

- physical diseases or infirmity making previously satisfactory housing unsuitable

- effects of disease making housing conditions difficult

- housing conditions affecting social well-being in terms other than disease or infirmity.

In theory, this enables individual and special health needs to be assessed independently of normal assessment criteria. However, in practice, there are considerable difficulties in making decisions based on these criteria, since the housing environment is only one (albeit important) aspect which may be responsible for poor health. Because most housing allocation schemes are too inflexible and insensitive for assessing rehousing on health grounds, medical practitioners can play an important part in a healthy housing strategy by ensuring that housing authorities give priority to people with medical needs.

3.4 INTERSECTORAL COOPERATION FOR CORPORATE PLANNING AND MANAGEMENT OF HEALTHY HOUSING POLICIES

The health authority, such as the Ministry of Health, has a wide range of responsibilities in relation to housing. Its prime duties should include monitoring the prevalence, morbidity and aetiological factors of housing-related diseases, to promote good health wherever possible and to ensure that primary health care services are adequate for meeting health needs. It also has an important advocacy role with other ministries/departments, particularly in ensuring that the health basis for housing is incorporated into national policies and programmes.

However, to be effective the health authority must command the support of the other agencies involved and be able to coordinate intersectoral cooperation. Clearly, countries differ in how they distribute responsibilities (e.g. social services may or may not be part of the health authority and housing is usually part of a Housing Ministry with its own executive powers). Housing hygiene tends to spill into many other disciplines that may be dealt with by a plethora of ministries and departments. The scope for an uncoordinated approach towards planning and implementation of services is therefore enormous (e.g. in scheduling building development with sanitary provisions).

Lack of clarity regarding the role of the respective agencies involved often leads to internal strife, power struggles and interdepartmental rivalry and mutual suspicion. As a result, information or plans are not exchanged or shared, and the approach towards project planning is uncoordinated and inefficient. The WHO has been attempting to get its Member States to adopt intersectoral cooperation and coordination of health policies for several years, often without much success. [144]

However, the need to involve the active participation of the community means that there must also be full cooperation and understanding between the statutory agencies, ministries and voluntary organizations, community groups and prominent community leaders. A corporate approach that uses consultation and participation at the pre-planning stage is probably one of the most important operational and organizational tools available for improving service delivery and cost-effectiveness in achieving healthy housing goals.

3.5 BASIC HOUSING STANDARDS, LEGISLATION AND CODES TO FULFIL FUNDAMENTAL HUMAN HEALTH NEEDS

Housing standards can express the quantitative and qualitative aspects of housing hygiene in different ways, but implicit to all standards is an assumption that housing variables can be measured by empirical assessment and comparison on a codified or numerical scale. However, although quantitative housing entities, such as number of rooms, housing density or provision of amenities, are relatively easy to measure, qualitative aspects, such as the effects of housing on mental and social well-being, are more difficult to assess. As a result, quality is often ignored altogether in housing standards or at least treated with scant regard.

In addition, the functional basis of housing standards is determined largely by diverse and often incompatible values:

- societal values: what society believes ought to be provided or will accept

- political values: what priority politicians and government place on housing provision

- economic values: what society is able or prepared to pay for housing

- uniformity: what is needed to standardize housing conditions

- equality: the role of standards in redistributing wealth.

All of these inputs depend on the value placed on them; and where values are constantly changing, a situation could easily arise where the functional basis for the standard may disappear and, therefore, the standard becomes unnecessary, obsolete or unacceptable to the housing consumer.

To overcome this, housing standards need to be periodically re-examined to determine whether they fulfil any meaningful purpose especially in relation to basic housing hygiene needs. This is particularly important when designing new housing, which is a capital-intensive asset in providing suitable accommodation for many years — usually 100 years or more.

Housing codes and standards must also reflect the prevailing economic, social and cultural background of the country and region if they are to be relevant: housing codes and standards based on other countries' models are rarely fully transferable and need to be field-tested before acceptance. Even within a given country, local housing hygiene standards may need to be devised to allow for differences of climate, geography etc. Consideration also must be given to epidemiological and economic factors when drawing up housing standards. Cultural and social factors are also important although health education can be used to encourage people to adapt their lifestyle and practices to their housing standards.

In some countries, minimum housing standards do not exist, are incomplete or exist but without policies or enforcement procedures for implementing them. In other cases, 'performance standards' are adopted that, while stating objectives, do not always furnish criteria for measuring and enforcing field observation and inspections. Therefore, the basic objectives have to be reduced to specific criteria that can be measured and observed. In many cases, this basis for comparison will be a rule, code or official guide suitable for the country and region in which they are applied as mimimum requirements for new housing and new residential areas. Where standards and codes are prescribed, enforcement machinery and personnel available to implement them must be adequate. This is particularly important in the public housing sectors where the state has a moral, if not legal duty to protect the health and safety of its housing tenants. But, wherever they are applied, housing standards and codes can provide basic rights in relation to housing provision and health requirements. Ideally, all minimum housing standards should satisfy absolute health housing needs regardless of ownership or tenure.

This should be regarded as a first priority for policy-makers both in developed and developing countries.

3.6 INCORPORATION OF ENVIRONMENTAL HEALTH AND HEALTHY HOUSING REQUIREMENTS INTO PLANNING POLICIES

The interplay of social, political and economic factors means that an interprofessional approach to planning and environmental health in terms of development and implementation of policies is of the utmost importance to establishing and maintaining a healthy environment, particularly in urban areas where environmental health problems are most acute. The acceptance in many developed countries of a rational approach to social and economic development and establishment of long-range economic, social and physical planning at national, regional and local levels has been extremely effective for dealing with short-term problems in metropolitan areas. The American Public Health Association has enumerated four basic levels of public health concerned with the residential environment:

- ensuring the elements of simple survival

- preventing disease and poisoning

- maintaining an environment suited to more efficient performance

- preserving comfort and enjoyment of living.

The increasing attention given to these areas through concerted and integrated action in the economic, social and physical planning fields has given some prospect of achieving these goals. However, many developing countries have no national policy for urban or regional development and no physical planning agencies at either the governmental or municipal level. Thus, the problems of water supply, sewage and waste disposal, the unhygienic condition of housing and the residential environment, the poor selection of sites and layouts for housing and industry, and the pollution of the environment by noxious chemical and microbiological agents are major considerations in these areas.

Other problems closely related to environmental health include land-use zoning, urban renewal, school and recreational facilities and vehicular traffic schemes. Seen in this context, the hygienic condition of the 'shelter' is but a microcosm of environmental hygiene as a whole, and the planning of the urban environment, therefore, requires close collaboration and cooperation between environmental health workers, architects, planners and government institutions within a broad spectrum of disciplines if metropolitan housing problems are to be resolved.

The possible lines of action for more effective environmental health planning programmes fall into three main categories: citizens and community groups; institutions of higher learning, research centres and professional organizations; and governmental and intergovernmental agencies including international groups. [2]

The WHO scientific group on the development of environmental health criteria for urban planning identified two major environmental health/housing goals in relation to urban planning. One goal is correction: the elimination or modification of present hazards of the environment that affect the health and social well-being of urban residents. Here standards are concerned with correcting past errors due to no planning, poor planning, planning that used inadequate criteria or planning that ignored criteria altogether. The other goal is prevention: the efficient management of environmental resources of an urban area in such a manner as to promote or enhance health and well-being and avoidance of hazards. [3]

A United Nations report on metropolitan planning and development in 1963 [145] identified seven areas that governments should consider:

- National health policy should give special attention to the problems created by metropolitan growth and its overcrowding, poor housing and poor sanitary conditions, deficient nutrition and high physical and mental strain on a large percentage of the population.

- Health administrators and technicians should participate in physical and general planning for urban and metropolitan areas from the earliest stages of such planning.

- The health administration should be adequately represented in the department or ministry in charge of planning and development policies for the metropolitan area, in order to include health and sanitation specialists in planning and development boards.

- Health services should be adequately financed as part of the capital investment policy of the metropolitan area and the country as a whole.

- Health services should be coordinated with those of other departments in the urban and peripheral areas.

- Further research is needed on the health and social aspects of urbanization, with particular regard to the problems of migrants.

- A balanced health policy should be developed for urban and rural areas.

These measures go well beyond the realm of housing but provide a

227

framework in which housing hygiene issues can be accommodated as part of a strategic, overall environmental health/planning policy. Such goals are a feature of the WHO health for all 2000 strategy.

3.6.1 Physical planning

The aim of metropolitan planning is firstly to create a physical environment congenial to the individual, the family and the community, and secondly, to establish a physical environment which will effectively promote economic development. In the context of metropolitan development, a plan has been expressed as a **model** of an intended future situation with respect to specific economic and social activities, their location in the region affected, land areas required, and the structures, installations and landscape environment for these activities.

A plan is also a **programme of action** and predetermined coordination of legislative, fiscal and administrative measures, formulated to achieve a certain situation represented by the model. [2]

The basic elements of a plan may consequently be taken to be activity planning, environmental planning, location planning, land-use planning and administration. However, of fundamental importance in connection with metropolitan planning is the close integration of economic and social planning with physical planning. [146]

Physical planning consequently involves developing and changing the physical environment so as to permit the proposed economic and social development to take place without causing individual hardship or social dislocation.

Physical planning usually proceeds in stages, and its progress is reflected in a number of separate plans. First, a general outline is usually formulated, extrapolating general development trends over a relatively long period of time, say 15–25 years. Such a plan must be based on the best available economic and demographic projections for the region and must be drafted against the background of proposed or anticipated national development. It is normally expressed in terms of a land-use plan for the different economic, social and cultural functions and activities to be located in the region, and for the different forms of cultivation and exploitation of regional resources based on land characteristics, mineral resources, water, soil and other related surveys. The different functions and activities must in turn be interconnected by means of a network of transportation, water, sewerage, drainage and utility lines, linked, where appropriate, to neighbouring or national networks.

At a later stage, a more detailed master plan is drafted for a shorter period, say 5–10 years. At this stage, land-use plans may include such communal facilities as parks, open areas, playgrounds, schools, libraries, cultural centres, hospitals, clinics and health centres. In this phase, feasibility studies should be made for power, transport, water, sewerage and drainage projects and for the different programmes to be carried out in the economic and social development sectors. Capital investment programmes based on such studies should include the probable sources of required capital. However, these general plans and investment programmes must be continuously reviewed in the light of changing conditions and current achievements.

In the final stage, detailed territorial and sector plans are prepared to supplement the more general plans and investment programmes formulated in the first two stages. These include neighbourhood or urban development plans ready for execution and plans for environmental health, transport or other facilities required to support the different economic, social and cultural functions in a given area. These detailed plans are usually developed in an order of priority dependent on the resources available and representing the current short-term development programme or capital investment budget covering a period of 1–5 years. In the light of the concrete achievements of this short-term programme, both the master plan and the long-term outline plan must be periodically reviewed, evaluated and suitably revised. [2]

Important factors concerning the physical planning of the housing environment include the following.

(a) Planning control

- regulating new industrial, commercial or housing development in accordance with local plans and criteria

- preserving buildings of particular architectural or historic interest

- regulating pollution and effluents from industrial sources.

(b) Community facilities

- providing shopping facilities, schools, other educational establishments, hospitals, health centres, recreational, play and sports facilities, and transport and communication systems including roads, railways, and other public transportation sytems

- providing social service establishments, day nurseries, day centres etc., for the elderly, mentally and physically handicapped persons, children and others to enable members of the community to meet and mix

- providing cultural and religious facilities

- providing civil protection facilities of police, fire, and rescue services (including civil defence).

(c) Environmental facilities

- providing water supplies and sewage disposal systems
- providing electricity and gas services
- providing services for collection and disposal of solid wastes.

(d) Employment facilities

- providing and encouraging employment opportunities within reasonable travelling distance of housing
- providing service industries, such as building construction and maintenance services and professional services, to meet community needs.

(e) Housing

- planning and designing new housing in accordance with housing hygiene principles
- redeveloping slum or otherwise unhygienic housing
- improving and rehabilitating areas of older housing.

3.7 PLANNING OF RURAL IMPROVEMENT AND SPATIAL DEVELOPMENT SCHEMES

All over the world residential housing environments are undergoing fundamental changes as a result of the rapid increase in the urban population. This is having many effects, for example, on housing provision, environmental health facilities, open space and transportation provisions. Conversely, rural areas are also undergoing a fundamental transformation from agricultural and rural life to a highly urbanized way of living. The implications of these changes in causing urban sprawl, overcrowding and shanty towns are described elsewhere in these guidelines. However, since urban problems often mirror poor economic and employment conditions in rural areas, an assessment should be made of the effects of changes in farming and agricultural practices in rural employment and income from the land. These problems have been largely responsible for deteriorating housing conditions in rural areas and causing rural–urban drift, which has led to a shortfall of housing in urban areas and the creation of slum shanty towns and congestion of existing urban conglomerations.

Constraints on primary preventative measures include the following: inertia and self-reinforcing force of poverty, which denies the social and material means for improvement; uncontrolled population growth, which exceeds the pace of economic development and the equitable distribution of the benefits of development; restrictions on land tenure, which affect prospects for economic self-sufficiency as well as for adequate habitation; massive and uncontrolled urbanization, which overwhelms governmental and social capacities to provide for minimal health needs; limited powers of intervention by governments and communities; inadequate attention to social development as it interacts with economic development or stagnation; and unstable political and military conditions that impose circumstantial and economic limits on the possibilites of adequate habitation.

Clearly, urbanization is a trend that is probably unstoppable as long as urban centres continue to provide employment and/or shelter, which although poor are usually better than that provided in rural settlements. However, in theory the trend can be partly reversed by intervention measures to improve rural conditions, particularly employment opportunities (e.g. by relocating industry, providing income support measures for farm workers and/or subsidizing farm produce).

Spatial development schemes may provide a mechanism whereby intermediate centres can be established between existing rural and urban centres. New town and satellite development schemes enable population and industry to be redistributed from under-resourced rural areas and from overcrowded, congested, polluted and/or slum urban areas, thus creating new balanced communities of manageable size with easy access to employment, health, social and community facilities.

New town development schemes provide an ideal opportunity to optimize housing hygiene, planning and environmental health requirements, without having to fit in with existing conditions and restrictions. However, new towns are extremely costly to provide and although industry may be prepared to pay some of the initial development costs, a considerable capital deficit is still likely. It is therefore essential that public finance be made available to help pay development costs of municipal facilities, schools, hospitals, utilities, roads, etc.

In the early stages of resettlement, community ties will likely be very weakly established, which could result in feelings of alienation, loneliness, depression and mental illness among parts of the population. Social problems are also likely to arise due to an imbalance in the age distribution of new town communities (i.e. a preponderance of young working people in the early stages of new town development and an excessive number of elderly people 30–40 years later). These changes are likely to pose disproportionate and variable demands upon social and health facilities at every stage of new town development.

Also, transferring jobs and people from one part of the country to another causes problems, and considerable persuasion is needed to achieve it. There is also no guarantee that vacated overcrowded housing and industry from the originating area will not be filled by others moving in, unless steps are taken to acquire the land or premises or prevent them from being reoccupied.

However, despite all the difficulties, new and expanding town schemes can be an extremely effective means of relocating jobs and housing from overcrowded areas, especially if financial subsidies, interest-free loans, compensation payments and other incentives can be given to defray removal and development costs.

In some cases, there are considerable advantages of developing existing towns or urban centres by expanding industry and housing that can be used to relocate populations from overcrowded areas with high unemployment levels. Usage of the existing nucleus of community life offers considerable social advantage over new town development schemes, and existing road, rail and water and sewerage facilities reduce development costs and time.

3.8 SPECIAL PROVISION FOR SHANTY-TOWN UPGRADING AND PREVENTION

Rural and urban environments are both deteriorating under the impact of rapid growth. Physical congestion and blight are affecting vast areas, apparently defying efforts towards improvement and presenting seemingly insoluble problems of planning, organization and financing. The social and physical symptoms of this growth are reflected in bad housing and poor community services, absence of sanitation, choked-up city traffic, filth, squalor, disease, and various forms of group and personal maladjustment. Large numbers of migrants fail to become integrated into the urban community and its institutions, forming 'squatter' settlements, which have multiplied in cities of all sizes in many parts of the world and which, in a number of metropolitan cities, already contain as much as half of the total population of these cities.

3.8.1 Health effects

The immediate impact of uncontrolled urbanization on housing hygiene includes increases in communicable disease within overcrowded areas (especially enteric, parasitic and respiratory diseases), deterioration in mental health conditions resulting fom urban deprivation and poor environmental conditions, and an increase in air and water pollution in mixed residential/industrial areas. In these urban fringe and shanty-town areas, morbidity and mortality rates are high, especially where poor sanitation is combined with high population densities. In particular, infant mortality is high in these areas. For example, in Portugal during the 1971 to 1974 cholera outbreaks, the most critical problems appeared in urban fringes near the capital cities of Lisbon and Oporto. [147] Facilities for personal washing, food preparation, etc., are also usually absent which can have major implications for hygiene, self-esteem and nutrition. Accidents are also likely both within and outside the shanties.

3.8.2 Control measures

People living in these areas are normally in low-income and other-wise disadvantaged groups; many are migrants, travellers or expatriates and are often unable, by themselves, to improve significantly their housing situation. Control measures must therefore take into account the economic reality of the situation and the particular features of the slums. Shanty housing undoubtedly poses the major challenge to housing hygiene and public health. The improvement and upgrading of shanty-town housing is therefore likely to reduce major health threats.

A WHO workshop held in Split in 1983 [28] concluded that:

> To resolve the problems associated with shanty towns and squatter settlements, new approaches must be developed by governments and other agencies to deter their further growth and development, to rehabilitate existing substandard housing that is economically worthy of such an effort and to demolish housing units that are grossly substandard. Such programmes will involve the construction of large numbers of healthful dwellings to rehouse those persons who are displaced.

The workshop made the following specific recommendations:

- A more vigorous attack should be initiated by all governments to prevent the spread of squatter settlements or shanty towns. They should investigate all of the causative forces that bring about these living conditions and identify practical means of preventing this type of housing.

- Cooperative programmes should be undertaken to develop practical plans of action consistent with the principles of urban planning, to limit future growth of existing squatter settlements or shanty towns, and to eliminate those already in existence where the housing is deemed hazardous to the health and well-being of the occupants.

- A vigorous campaign of health education in basic sanitation should be launched through various media to teach urban dwellers (particularly newcomers to urban areas and residents of squatter settlements and shanty towns) that they have a responsibility to maintain their home and its environs in as clean and sanitary a condition as practicable to reduce the hazards associated with the transmission of infectious agents and accidental injury.

- An interim hygiene programme for urban dwellings should include the following characteristics:

  - security of tenure of a dwelling on a plot of land, provided through leasehold or freehold titles

  - dwellings should be situated on plots of land measuring at least 60 m^2 per dwelling unit

  - the size of building should provide at least 4 m^2 of floor space per occupant with an ultimate goal of 8 m^2 of floor space per occupant

  - occupants of dwellings should be provided with security against intruders and protection from the elements

  - sanitary methods of excreta disposal should be provided for the private use of each household (e.g. a sanitary, fly-proof pit privy, a flush water closet with a sanitary disposal system or a similar device)

  - appropriate facilities should be provided for the sanitary storage, collection and disposal of all rubbish and household refuse

  - adequate protection should be provided against insect and rodent vectors and reservoirs of disease

  - dwellings should be located so that they are served by community medical, social, educational, welfare and cultural facilities.

The primary health care approach is suitable for improving conditions in this kind of human habitat because its main objective is to make 'essential care universally accessible to individual families in the community in an acceptable and affordable way and with their full participation'. [148]

In addition, **sites-and-services schemes** can sometimes be adopted for squatter prevention or upgrading schemes. These schemes have been successfully implemented on an experimental basis in some developing countries where shanty-town housing is a problem. However, there have been many other occasions where such schemes are not suitable, e.g. sites would normally exclude shanties erected on the sides of hills or other inaccessible positions. Roads, water supplies, sewerage systems and electricity are provided with financial assistance from the United Nations Centre for Human Settlements or other funding agencies. Assistance and advice are also given to improve environmental health conditions. Providing that additional development and population can be controlled, improving long-term hygiene conditions of individual shanties should be possible. Although sites-and-services schemes do not attempt to eradicate all the problems associated with shanty-town housing, they undoubtedly help reduce mortality and morbidity caused by enteric and respiratory diseases that are often endemic in these areas. There is no evidence to suggest that adoption of sites-and-services schemes institutionalizes shanty-town housing. On the contrary, such schemes provide policy-makers with two long-term options: to upgrade the site into a permanent settlement or to 'buy' time to provide alternative housing accommodation with eventual redevelopment of the shanty-town site. However, evidence from a WHO workshop held in Ankara in 1985 [149] suggests that traditional planning controls have been unable to prevent squatter settlements in urban fringes. The most successful schemes have been those where cost-effective sites-and-services partnership arrangements and community participation have been maximized.

3.9 PROVISION OF INSTITUTIONAL, ORGANIZATIONAL AND OPERATIONAL ARRANGEMENTS FOR IMPLEMENTING HEALTHY HOUSING POLICIES

Organizational and operational arrangements for implementing housing hygiene policies vary considerably between countries, depending on the degree of central or local control over administration of housing programmes. Similarly, intervention and enforcement measures reflect varying attitudes towards the role of the state *vis-à-vis* the individual in 'solving' the housing problem.

However, health and housing administrations can contribute technical skills and human understanding to housing and residential environment programmes at all levels of government regardless of stage of country or area development. [150]

Physical planning and sanitary administration infrastructures, such as water supply, solid waste and sewage disposal, are examples needing institutionalized administration. Individual action would be insufficiently coordinated or resourced to make the necessary decisions or actions in these cases. Health administrations are most experienced at pursuing preventative medicine; by applying this principle to housing, they can encourage programmes which prevent the construction of new slums. This approach, coupled with intersectoral coordination of other related disciplines and encouragement of health education and community participation programmes, would maximize the resources of all who contribute to the planning, building, rehabilitation and enforcement of housing hygiene codes and environmental health policies.

3.10 PROVISION OF ADEQUATE FINANCIAL RESOURCES FOR REMEDYING INSANITARY HOUSING CONDITIONS

Housing finance is a major policy consideration of any housing hygiene strategy, particularly in developing countries where money is in short supply. Housing finance cannot be considered in isolation from other investment needs and is inextricably linked with other economic factors such as amount of private investment, economic growth, state expenditure on other social services, land prices, costs of building materials, labour and rent levels in relation to income and levels of unemployment.

In developing countries, policy-makers have to decide how best to share scarce public resources for a number of competing and arguably equally important needs (e.g. education and health services). As far as revenue is concerned there is likely to be considerable savings in medical and health-care costs where housing hygiene has been improved. Indeed, the savings may pay for the improvements in housing conditions in some cases, e.g. provision or upgrading of sanitation and water supply. As far as capital investment is concerned, this may be channelled into growth-producing industries rather than into consumer projects such as housing. Decisions also have to be made on qualitative aspects of new housing construction such as capital unit costs, which have an important bearing on the future life of buildings, levels of future repair expenditure and housing hygiene.

Too often, capital costs are reduced so that more dwellings can be constructed out of the same budget. This usually has the effect of increasing revenue costs (e.g. maintenance charges or running costs). In other cases, repairs are neglected in order to pay costs of more new construction. The progressive decay of old urban neighbourhoods cannot usually be halted without financial stimuli (subsidies, loans, etc.) from the capital market. However, since many residents in these areas have restricted income or live in poverty, public intervention is likely to be necessary at both central and local levels to assist with the costs of improvement works. The financial burden of this assistance can be partly offset by providing employment and work for building workers, component manufacturers and ancillary industries. Also, by providing financial assistance, the government can plan or otherwise influence the course of the urban renewal process to common benefit.

Many countries give some form of financial assistance towards improving the housing stock. Canada, for instance, gives financial assistance to house owners whose income is below a certain limit, to landlords of dwellings who agree to rent control and to non-corporations and cooperatives. In Finland, help is given to owner-occupiers in the form of low-interest loans. In the Netherlands, financial help is given by the State to local authorities to meet the costs of assessing and selecting improvement areas, financing the preparation of improvement plans and sharing the costs with the local authorities of improvement works. In the United Kingdom, improvement grants can be given by local authorities for repairing and improving houses that can normally comply with a set of standards upon completion and have an expected 30-year life. These grants, which are based on eligible expense limits, can be given individually or pursued on an area basis in improvement zones or housing action areas. Because most people living in areas of poor housing have insufficient means to finance repairs and improvements themselves, capital must be provided from private and/or public funds from outside the area.

In some countries, positive fiscal incentives are given to encourage private investment in new housing. In most socialist countries, new housing is usually built and paid for by public funds. Rent control policies are sometimes applied to prevent landlords from profiting from scarce housing resources, which has had the effect of discouraging landlords from investing in new housing for letting or performing essential repairs. Where rent controls have not been applied, houses often remain empty because nobody is prepared or able to pay the rents required. Rent control policies should therefore provide reasonable security of tenure but prevent exploitation by private landlords charging excessive rents. However, they should not punitively discourage owners from making housing available for letting, i.e. they should provide for reasonable returns on capital outlay and cost of repairs and maintenance.

Better financial incentives should be provided to encourage new sanitary house building for owner occupation and private renting (e.g. by interest-free loans, improvement grants, housing subsidies or tax incentives). Housing cooperatives and self-build groups should be actively encouraged through fiscal arrangements, making land for building available at reasonable prices, providing subsidized building materials, and giving technical advice and assistance on housing construction.

These examples illustrate the complexity of formulating a rational housing finance policy and the control role which the state plays in encouraging or discouraging investment. Ideally, financing of housing should be organized to stimulate the building of new dwellings and to relieve the housing shortage and so eradicate slum conditions. Sufficient capital or easy-term loans should be made available for private and public construction. In general terms, housing investments should be a major policy commitment but planned in line with economic growth and resources and other priorities.

3.11 ADOPTION OF SUITABLE PLANNED AND ROUTINE REPAIR AND MAINTENANCE POLICIES FOR PREVENTION OF INSANITARY HOUSING

Housing in a state of disrepair but which can be remedied at reasonable cost should be repaired before it deteriorates further. Effective enforcement machinery and resources need to be made available to local public health administrators to get repairs done (i.e. appointment of environmental health officers, sanitarians or housing inspectors). This enforcement role can be supported by financial incentives to owners to repair or maintain their housing. Experience indicates that legislation and enforcement machinery on its own is rarely effective in maintaining a good standard of repair of the housing stock: there must be the financial wherewithal to pay for it.

The owner or landlord of the property is normally responsible for repairs, but sometimes a tenancy agreement stipulates that the tenant is responsible. In many countries, landlords of private housing are legally required to carry out repairs within a reasonable period of time. If the repairs are not performed, the local authority may prosecute the owner, who can be fined on conviction. Alternatively, the authority may do the repairs itself in default and recover the costs from the owners. Similar powers are often given to local authorities under public health legislation to deal with premises that could be harmful to the health of the occupants or likely to cause a nuisance. Tenants of public housing may also have a legal right to repairs although UK experience would say that the enforcement machinery is less effective than for private tenancies.

In both the public and private sectors, repair obligations should be carefully set out in tenancy agreements between landlord and tenant. However, although tenants may be responsible for minor repairs, private landlords or the local authority as public landlords are often liable for major or structural repairs, to keep the structure and exterior of the dwelling in good repair and additionally to keep in repair and proper

238

working order the installations in the dwelling for the supply of water, gas and electricity, sanitary conveniences and fitments.

Reactive action in relation to repairs is rarely satisfactory since it usually indicates that a building component has failed, which can then adversely affect other building components thus increasing the cost of repairs. Planned maintenance programmes should therefore be initiated wherever possible so that components are replaced before the end of their useful life rather than afterwards. Such programmes greatly extend the life of housing (providing that the infrastructure is sound) and in the long term are very cost-effective. Examples of programmed maintenance items include renewal of roofing, windows and doors, external painting, repointing of brickwork and replacement of fixtures such as heating appliances.

3.12 INVOLVEMENT AND PARTICIPATION OF THE COMMUNITY AND WOMEN IN HEALTHY HOUSING POLICIES

Community involvement and participation in housing hygiene policies can be conducted at several levels. At its simplest level it is a consultation exercise to enable professional staff and housing agencies to get feedback on policy options and community views (e.g. in deciding upon slum clearance, redevelopment and rehabilitation options). At a more sophisticated level, communities may be directly involved in organizing, planning, financing and managing housing development, perhaps using a labour pool or cooperative model to build housing for their own occupation. In developing countries the organization of direct participation through community self-help schemes has been shown to be the only realistic way for the community to obtain housing suited to its financial means. Such participation is not just a practical economic necessity but is bound up in wider ideological judgements concerning the housing role of formal institutions *vis-à-vis* the community. John Turner's experience in Peru clearly led him to believe that self-help schemes were preferable to state models as summed up as follows:

When dwellers control the major decisions and are free to make their own contribution to the design, construction or management of their housing, both the process and the environment produced stimulate individual and social well-being. When people have no control over nor responsibility for key decisions in the housing process, on the other hand, dwelling environments may instead become a barrier to personal fulfilment and a burden on the economy. [151]

Self-help maximizes freedom of choice, motivation and community participation but by no means excludes state and formal housing agencies from providing supervision, advice, education or training, and ensuring that the standard of workmanship meets housing hygiene requirements. Effective partnership arrangements between the state and the community is often an efficient way of maximizing scarce housing resources. Indeed, in many cases, effective community participation is the only way that essential facilities, such as safe and adequate water supply, sanitation and low-cost housing, can be provided. In particular, the participation of women in housing hygiene policies is to be encouraged at every level. Women usually have the main responsibility for household activities and child rearing. Women also often spend long hours labouring in the fields or, in town, undertaking other work to assist family finances. However, their status depends greatly upon national, ethnic and social class traditions. The WHO is actively encouraging a more positive role for women's organizations in the developing world to act as pressure groups for the community and encourage participation in health care activities such as nutrition, family planning, immunization and rural water supply and sanitation schemes. [150] The education of women in housing hygiene is especially important in encouraging hygienic practices in children, helping them to adapt to current housing conditions and instigating physical improvements to the housing environment. Women can provide immense pragmatic experience concerning housing design and should be actively consulted when embarking on new development or improvement schemes.

3.13 EDUCATIONAL MEASURES TO SUPPORT HEALTHY HOUSING PROGRAMMES

Most families in developing countries are themselves responsible for providing housing: in the main, housing is self-built and self-designed. However, planners, architects, builders, and health/sanitary workers may all be involved in some way with the type of housing provided or approved. Educational measures are instrumental in bringing about improvements in housing hygiene, especially those that do not rely upon high capital outlay. Housing hygiene principles can be applied to a number of different targets for health education and/or training initiatives.

Householders are the largest group to be educated because families often build their own dwellings and, by definition, are the users of housing. The prime educational objective should be to increase understanding of what provisions are needed in the home to foster the health of the family (within its financial limitations) and the personal and domestic practices of hygiene, maintenance, hazard reduction and accident prevention. These initiatives also need to be included in school health education programmes. While education provides the cognitive basis for householders to improve housing conditions, it may not be sufficient to induce the action itself. Support from within and outside the local community may be needed to convert knowledge into positive attitudes and effective action.

Architects, builders and material manufacturers and suppliers require education in design and construction techniques that promote healthy housing. Health information should be integrated into the professional and technical education curricula, and current practitioners should be reached through continuing education, and through professional and trade associations.

Health workers, ranging from community-based physicians, sanitary engineers and sanitarians, to primary health care auxiliaries, should be educated to understand the health principles of housing and to integrate educational and other remedial measures into their health service work. Workers in other sectors, including those in agriculture, rural development and social work, may also be able to help household efforts towards economic and housing hygiene improvement.

Policy leaders, development planners, managers, and local officials should be educated on the health implications of human shelters, and various approaches they can use to affect health outcomes.

These educational efforts can be extensive, and challenging, for they require the collection of a 'body of knowledge' that is relevant to national conditions and goals, development of educational materials and messages which are suitable and meaningful to these various targets, identification and mobilization of channels to carry the educational message, and the induction of teachers and trainers in health and housing. Apart from formal educational settings, emphasis should be given to the use of the mass media, both for direct educational purposes and for creating a climate of awareness favourable to health objectives.

In dealing with the needs and problems of human habitats, community involvement at all levels should support the process of self-help and communal cooperative action.

The strongest supports are those that come from the community or neighbourhood itself. Such indigenous supports range from collective ideals and attitudes, through community-based service programmes, to physical activities of neighbour-help and communal resource development. Often, the development of these supports must be cultivated through deliberate efforts to raise consciousness, mobilize opinion and encourage local cooperative capabilities to formulate ideas and proposals, to devise ways to implement them and to share costs in money or contributed goods and labour. In this way healthy housing targets can develop organically in a climate of common objectives and purpose. New goals can be set in accordance with the WHO health for all strategy. Given the support, resources and effort, healthy housing can move from being a theoretical proposition to the practical reality which it clearly deserves to be.

References

1. American Public Health Association. *Basic principles of healthful housing*. APHA, 1939.
2. WHO Technical Report Series, No. 297. *Environmental health aspects of metropolitan planning and development*. Report of an Expert Committee, 1965.
3. WHO Technical Report Series, No. 353. *Appraisal of the hygienic quality of housing and its environment*. Report of an Expert Committee, 1967.
4. WHO Housing and Health, as agenda for action, 1987.
5. WHO Regional Office for Europe EURO Reports and Studies, No. 21. *Health aspects related to indoor air quality*. Copenhagen, 1979.
6. WHO Regional Office for Europe. *The prevention of accidents in the home*. Report on a symposium, Copenhagen, 1968.
7. WHO Regional Office for Europe. *Noise control in buildings*. Document ICP/CEP 702. Copenhagen, 1977.
8. Martin, A.E. & Oeter, P. *Environmental health aspects of human settlements*. Document ICP/BSM 002. Copenhagen, WHO Regional Office for Europe, 1978.
9. WHO Regional Office for Europe. *The effects of indoor housing climate on the health of the elderly*. Report of a working group. Document ICP/BSM 002(S). Copenhagen, 1982.
10. Yew. Urban low-income housing in south-east Asia. In Richards,P.J. & Thompson, A.M., *Basic needs and the urban poor*. London, Croom Helm, 1984.
11. Cericez, F. Report to WHO workshop on *Housing hygiene in Mediterranean countries*. 1983 (see ref. 28).
12. WHO Technical Report Series, No. 225, *Public health aspects of housing*. First report of the Expert Committee, 1961.
13. WHO Technical Report Series, No. 544. *Use of epidemiology in housing programmes and in planning human settlements*. Report of an Expert Committee, 1974.
14. Wilner, D.M. *et al. The housing environment and family life: a longitudinal study of the effects of housing on morbidity and mental health*. Baltimore, MD: John Hopkins University Press, 1962.
15. WHO. Preamble to WHO constitution. In *WHO basic documents*.

References

12th edn, Geneva: World Health Organization, 1961.

16. Parsons, T. *The social system.* Gencoe, Ill: Free Press, 1950.
17. Martin, A.E. *Housing, the housing environment and health. An annotated bibliography.* WHO Offset Publications, No. 27. Geneva: World Health Organization, 1976.
18. Sacher, G.A. Energy, metabolism and thermoregulation in old age. *ASHRAE Transactions* 1979, **85**:775–783.
19. Fanning, D.M. Families in flats. *British Medical Journal* 1967, **4**:382–386.
20. Littlewood, J. *et al. Families in flats.* London: HMSO, 1981.
21. Stewart, W. *Children in flats: a family study.* London: National Society for the Prevention of Cruelty to Children, 1970.
22. Jephcott, H.P. *Homes in high flats.* London: Oliver and Boyd, 1971.
23. MoHLG. *The density of residential areas.* London, HMSO, 1952.
24. *Building standards (Scotland) regulations.* London, HMSO, 1971.
25. *A design guide for residential areas.* Essex: Essex County Council, 1973.
26. Bassett, W.H. & Davies, F.G. *Clay's handbook of environmental health.* London: H.K. Lewis, 1981.
27. *Greater London development plan.* London: Greater London Council, 1976.
28. WHO Regional Office for Europe, 1983. Document ICP/BSM 002(5). *Housing hygiene in Mediterranean countries.* Report on a WHO meeting, Copenhagen, 1983.
29. *UN compendium 1975–1977.* New York: United Nations, 1980.
30. A.N. Sysin Institute, WHO Regional Office for Europe, Document ICP/BSM 002. *Health aspects of indoor climate.* Copenhagen, 1982.
31. Stein, L. A study of respiratory tuberculosis in relation to housing conditions in Edinburgh. *British Journal of Preventive and Social Medicine* 1950, **4**:143–169.
32. Benjamin, B. Tuberculosis and social conditions in the metropolitan boroughs of London. *British Journal of Tuberculosis and Diseases of the Chest* 1953, **47**:4–17.
33. Anderson, E. Skeletal maturation of Danish school children in relation to height, sexual development and social conditions. *Acta Paediatrica Scandinavia* (Supplement) 1968, **185**:1–31.
34. Strotzka, H. Housing quality and mental health. *Wohnungsmedizin* 1973, **3–4**:25–27.
35. Essen, J. *et al.* Childhood housing experiences and school attainment. *Child Care, Health and Development* 1977, **41**:41–58.
36. Wilner, D.M. *et al.* How does the quality of housing affect health and family adjustment? *American Journal of Public Health* 1956, **46**:736–744.
37. Wilkinson, A.W. & Jackson, R.H. eds. *Children, the environment and accidents.* London: Pitman Medical, 1977.

References

38. Brandon, S. Violence in the family. *Royal Society of Health Journal* 1977, **5**:201–205.
39. United Nations Economic Commission for Europe. *Utilization of space in dwellings.* Geneva, 1959.
40. *Uniform housing code.* Pasadena, CA: International Association of Building Officials, 1958.
41. Lebegge, M. *Fundamentals of a healthful residential environment: space and occupancy requirements.* Geneva: WHO, 1961.
42. APHA-CDC. *Housing maintenance and occupancy ordinance.* Washington DC: US Dept. of Health, Education and Welfare, Public Health Service, 1976.
43. Department of the Environment. *Homes for today and tomorrow.* London: HMSO, 1961.
44. Sosnovy, T. *Housing conditions and urban development in the USSR.* Washington DC: US Government Printing Office, 1966.
45. ROSPA. *Home safety in retirement.* Subscriber Biefing No. 3. London: The Royal Society for the Prevention of Accidents, 1983.
46. DoE. *The value of standards for the external residential environment.* London: Department of Environment, 1976.
47. UN. *Redesign, repair and strengthening of buildings in seismic regions.* Document ECE/HBP/43. Geneva: Economic and Social Council, 1982.
48. Anderson, *et al.* Effect of air humidity and sulfur dioxide on formaldehyde emission from construction materials. *Holzforch Holzverwerfung* 1976, **28**:120–128.
49. Martin, A.E. Mortality and morbidity statistics and air pollution. *Proceedings of the Royal Society of Medicine* 1964, **57**:969–975.
50. Ashley, D.J.B. Environmental factors in the etiology of lung cancer and bronchitis. *British Journal of Preventive and Social Medicine* 1969, **23**:258–262.
51. Lawther, P.J. *et al.* Air pollution and pulmonary airway resistance: a pilot study. *Environmental Research* 1973, **6**:424–435.
52. WHO Regional Office for Europe, Document EURO 1143. *Health effects of air pollution.* Report on a symposium, Prague, 6–10 November 1967. Copenhagen, 1967.
53. WHO, Environmental Health Criteria No. 8 *Sulfur oxides and suspended particulate matter.* Geneva: WHO, 1979.
54. NRPB. *Human exposure to radon decay products inside dwellings in the United Kingdom.* Oxon: National Radiological Protection Board, 1984.
55. NRPB. The incidence and origin of radon and its decay products in buildings. Oxon: National Radiological Protection Board, 1984.
56. O'Riordan, M.C. *et al. Human exposure to radon decay products inside dwellings in the United Kingdom. A memorandum of evidence to the Royal Commission on Environmental Pollution.* London, Her Majesty's Stationery Office,

References

1983 (National Radiation Protection Board Report, No. R152).
57. Rudnick, I. Propagation of sound in the open air. In Harris, C.M. ed. *Handbook of noise control.* New York: McGraw-Hill, 1957.
58. WHO, Environmental Health Criteria, No. 12. *Noise.* Geneva, 1980.
59. Committee on Appraisal of Societal Consequences of Transportation Noise Abatement. *Noise abatement policy: alternatives for transportation.* Washington DC: National Research Council, 1977.
60. Watt, J. *et al.* Diarrhoeal disease control studies. 1. Effects of fly control in a high morbidity area. *Public Health Reports* 1948, **63**:1319–1334.
61. McCabe, L.J. *et al.* Diarrhoeal disease control by improved human excreta disposal. *Public Health Reports* 1957, **72**:921.
62. WHO. *Specifications for pesticides used in public health,* 5th edn. Geneva: WHO, 1979.
63. Coleman, A. *Utopia on trial, vision and reality in planned housing.* London: Hilary Shipman, 1985.
64. Health and Safety Executive, Her Majesty's Inspectorate. *Probable asbestos dust concentrations in construction processes.* Technical Data Note 42. London: HMSO, 1976.
65. Commission of the European Communities, Directorate-General for Social Affairs, Health and Safety Directorate. *Public health risks of exposure to asbestos.* Report on a working group of experts. Oxford: Pergamon, 1977.
66. WHO Regional Office for Europe, EURO Reports and Studies, No. 81. *Biological effects of man-made mineral fibres.* Copenhagen, 1983.
67. WHO Regional Office for Europe, EURO Reports and Studies, No. 78. *Indoor air pollutants: exposure and health effects.* Copenhagen, 1983.
68. National Research Council, Committee on Indoor Pollutants. *Indoor pollutants.* New York: National Academic Press, 1981.
69. WHO, Environmental Health Criteria, No. 3. *Lead.* Geneva, 1977.
70. Sachs, H.K. Effect of a screening programme on changing patterns of lead poisoning. *Environmental Health Perspectives* 1974, **7**:41–47.
71. DHSS. *Lead and health. Report of a DHSS Working Party on Lead in the Environment.* London: HMSO, 1980.
72. Waddington, J.I. The international drinking-water supply and sanitation decade in Europe. *Royal Society of Health Journal* 1983, **103**:108.
73. WHO Regional Office for Europe. Document W3/62/3. *Rapid assessment of the situation of drinking water and sanitation in Europe.* Copenhagen, 1981.
74. WHO Regional Office for Europe. EURO Reports and Studies No. 44. *Surveillance and control of acute diarrhoeal diseases.* Copenhagen: WHO, 1981.
75. Schliessman, D.J. *et al.* Relation of environmental factors to the

occurrence of enteric disease in areas of eastern Kentucky. *American Journal of Public Health* 1958, **45**:354–362.

76. Schliessman, D.J. Diarrhoeal disease and the environment. *WHO Bulletin* 1959, **21**:381–386.

77. Watt, J. Diarrhoeal diseases in Fresno County, California. *American Journal of Public Health* 1953, **43**:728–741.

78. Goodman, A.H. Contamination of water within buildings. *Royal Society of Health Journal* 1984, **104**:109.

79. WHO. *Guidelines for drinking water quality. Volume 1. Recommendations*. Geneva: WHO, 1984.

80. WHO Technical Report Series, No. 544. *Uses of epidemiology in housing programmes and in planning human settlements*. Report of an Expert Committee on Housing and Health, 1974.

81. Sykes, J.F.J. *Public health and housing*. London: P.S. King & Sons, 1901.

82. Britten, R.H. New light on the relation of housing to health. *American Journal of Public Health* 1942, **25**:21–26.

83. Graves, L.M. *et al.* Housing problems in a southern city. *American Journal of Public Health* 1935, **25**: 21–26.

84. Beck, M.D. *et al.* Diarrhoeal disease control studies. The relationship of certain environmental factors to the prevalence of *Shigella* infection. *American Journal of Tropical Medicine and Hygiene* 1957, **4**: 718–723.

85. Kalbermatten, J.M. *et al. Appropriate technology for water supply and sanitation: a planner's guide*. Washington DC: International Bank for Reconstruction and Development/World Bank, 1980.

86. Okum, D.A. & Ponghis, G. *Community waste water collection and disposal*. Geneva: WHO, 1975.

87. Wagner, E.G. & Lanoix, J.N. *Water supply for rural areas and small communities*. WHO Monograph Series, No. 42. Geneva: WHO, 1959.

88. WHO Technical Report Series, No. 484. *Solid wastes disposal and control*. Report of an Expert Committee, 1971.

89. Sterling, T.D. & Kobayashi, D.M. Exposure to pollutants in enclosed living space. *Environmental Research* 1977, **13**:1–35.

90. *Ventilation air conditioning*. London: CIBS, 1972.

91. WIIO. Environmental Health Criteria, No. 13. *Carbon monoxide*. Geneva: WHO, 1979.

92. Ferris, B.G. Health effects of exposure to low levels of regulated pollutants — a critical review. *Journal of the Pollution Control Association* 1978, **28**: 482–497.

93. NAS. *Nitrogen oxides*. Washington DC: National Academy of Sciences, 1977.

94. Melia, R.J.W. *et al.* The relationship between respiratory illness in primary school children and the use of gas for cooking. I. Results from a national survey. *International Journal of Epidemiology* 1979, **8**:333–338.

References

95. Spiezer, F.E. *et al*. Respiratory disease rates and pulmonary function in children associated with NO_2 exposure. *American Review of Respiratory Disease* 1980, **121**:3–10.

96. WHO. Environmental Health Criteria, No. 4. *Oxides of nitrogen*. Geneva: WHO, 1977.

97. Bakov, A.N. *et al*. Sanitary and chemical elevation of polyvinyl acetate seamless floors with addition of carbamide resin. *Gigiena i Sanitariya* 1965, **30**:30–35.

98. Yodaiken, R.E. The uncertain consequences of formaldehyde toxicity. *JAMA*, 1981, **73**:1677–1678.

99. Harris, J.C. Toxicology of urea formaldehyde and polyurethane foam insulation. *JAMA* 1981, **73**:234–246.

100. Chanet, R. *et al*. Genetic effects of formaldehyde in yeast. II. *Mutation Research* 1976, **35**:29–38.

101. Feldman, M.Y. Reaction of nucleic acids and nucleoproteins with formaldehyde. *Progress in Nucleic Acid Research and Molecular Biology* 1975, **13**:1–49.

102. National Research Council. *Formaldehyde and other aldehydes*. New York: National Academic Press, 1981.

103. Olsen, J. *et al*. Formaldehyde-induced symptoms in day care centres. *American Industrial Hygiene Association Journal* 1982, **43**:5–12.

104. DHEW. Publication No. (PHS) 79-50066. *Smoking and health — a report of the Surgeon General*. Washington DC: Dept. of Health, Education and Welfare, 1979.

105. Hoegg, V.R. Cigarette smoke in closed spaces. *Environmental Health Perspectives* 1972, **2**:127–129.

106. Royal College of Physicians of London. *Air pollution and health*. London: Pitman Medical and Scientific Publishing Co., 1970.

107. Tager, I.B. *et al*. Effect of parental cigarette smoking in the pulmonary function of children. *American Journal of Epidemiology* 1979, **110**:15–26.

108. Hirayama, T. Nonsmoking wives of heavy smokers have a higher risk of lung cancer: a study from Japan. *British Medical Journal* 1981, **282**:183–185.

109. Weber-Tschopp, A. *et al*. Objektive und subjektive physiologische Wirkungen des Passivrauchens. [Objective and subjective physiological effects in passive smoking]. *International Archives of Occupational Health* 1976, **37**:277–288.

110. Fischer, T. *et al*. Lufverunreinigung durch Tabakrauch in Gaststätten. [Pollution from tobacco smoking in restaurants]. *International Archives of Occupational Health* 1978, **41**:267–280.

111. Grimmer, G. *et al*. Zum Problem des Passivrauchens: Konzentrationsmessungen von polycyklischen aromatischen Kohlenwasserstoffe in

References

Inner aumen nach dem maschinillen Abrauchen von Zigaretten. [About the problem of passive smoking: Concentrations of polycyclic aromatic hydrocarbons from cigarettes measured inside rooms after air ventilation]. *International Archives of Occupational Health* 1977, **40**:83–92.

112. Dockery, D.W. & Spengler, J.D. Personal exposure to respirable particles and sulfates. *Journal of the Air Pollution Control Association* 1981, **31**:153–159.

113. Cocklin, G. *The weather-conditioned house.* New York: Reinhold, 1958.

114. Goodlow, R.V. & Leonard, F.A. Viability and infectivity of microorganisms in experimental airborne infection. *Bacteriological Reviews* 1961, 25:182–187.

115. *Gas safety regulations.* London, HMSO, 1970.

116. Drapeau, A.I. & Junkcovies, S. *Manual of the microbiology of the environment.* Geneva: WHO, 1977.

117. Uglow, C.E. *Air quality and ventilation in dwellings.* Garston, UK: Building Research Establishment, 1985.

118. Backenkova, F.D. *et al.* Some aspects of hygienic evaluation of working conditions in buildings without natural lighting and windows. *Gigiena Truda i Professional'nye Zabolevaniya* 1970, **11**:40–43.

119. Yaglou, C.P. *et al.* Ventilation requirements. *ASHRAE Transactions* 1936, **42**:133.

120. McIntyre, D.A. *Indoor climate.* London: Applied Science Publishers, 1980.

121. Goromosov, M.S. *The physiological basis of health standards for dwellings.* Public Health Papers, No. 33. Geneva: WHO, 1968.

122. Fanger, P.O. *Thermal comfort, analysis and applications in environmental engineering.* Copenhagen: Danish Technical Press, 1972.

123. Tyrell, D.A. *Common colds and related diseases.* London: Edward Arnold, 1965.

124. Collins, K.J. Hypothermia and thermal responsiveness in the elderly. In Fanger, P.O. *et al.*, Eds. *Indoor climate.* Copenhagen: Danish Building Research Institute, 1979.

125. Malyseva, A.E. *Health problems or radiative heat exchange between man and his environment.* Moscow: Medgiz, 1963

126. *Homes for the future.* London: Institute of Housing/RIBA, 1983.

127. Olesen, B.W. Thermal comfort requirements for floors occupied by people with bare feet. *ASHRAE Transactions* 1974, **83**:11–16.

128. Ismailova, D.I. Setting of hygienic standards for a radiant factor of microclimate for panel radiant heating and cooling of residential and public buildings. Thesis, Moscow University, 1970.

129. *Thermal, visual and acoustic requirements in buildings.* Building Research Establishment Digest, No. 226. Garston, UK: Building

Research Establishment, 1979.

130. Chibuk, J.H. *Energy and urban form*. Document HBP/SEM 17/R.48. Ottawa: ECE Committee on Housing, Building and Planning, 1977.

130a. *Heat losses from dwellings*. Building Research Establishment Digest, No. 190. Garston, UK: Building Research Establishment, 1976.

131. Dancig, N.M. *et al*. The resistance of animal organisms to infection under the influence of ultraviolet radiation. In *Ultraviolet radiation*. Moscow: Medgiz, 1958.

132. Cernilovskaja, F.M. *Health significance of fluorescent lighting in industry*. Leningrad: Medicina, 1964.

133. *IES: Code for interior lighting*. London, CIBS Lighting Division, 1984.

134. Gloag, H.L. *et al. Colour coordination handbook*. London: HMSO, 1978.

135. Chandler, S.E. *Residential fires in London related to housing conditions and social factors*. Garston, UK: Building Research Establishment, 1980.

136. Backett, E.M. *Domestic accidents*. Public Health Papers, No. 26. Geneva: WHO, 1965.

137. Marchant, E.W. *et al. Fire and buildings*. Lancaster, UK: MTP Publishers, 1972.

138. Consumer Safety Unit. *Child poisoning from household products*. London: Department of Trade, 1980.

139. MacQueen, I.B.G. *A study of home accidents in Aberdeen*. Edinburgh: Churchill Livingstone, 1960.

140. Essen, J. *et al*. Childhood housing experiences and school attainment. *Child Care, Health and Development* 1968, **4**:421–48.

141. *Designing with care. A guide to adaptation of the built environment for disabled persons*. New York: United Nations, 1981.

142. WHO Regional Office for Europe. Health Aspects of Chemical Safety, Interim Document No. 12. *Allergic responses and hypersensitivities induced by chemicals*. Copenhagen, 1983.

143. Muir Grey, J.A. Housing, health and illness. *British Medical Journal* 1978, **2**: 100–107.

144. WHO Public Health Papers, No. 74. *Intersectoral coordination and health in environmental management*. Geneva, 1981.

145. *Metropolitan planning and development*. Document ST/TAO/Set C/64. New York: United Nations, 1963.

146. WHO Technical Report Series, No. 511. *Development of environmental criteria for urban planning*. Report of a WHO Scientific Group, 1972.

147. Labato de Faria. *Housing hygiene and environmental health problems in urban fringes*. WHO Workshop, 1985.

References

148.   WHO/UN. *Primary care — a joint report by the Director-General of the World Health Organization and the Executive Director of the United Nations Children's Fund.* Geneva: WHO, 1978.
149.   WHO Regional Office for Europe. Document TUR/RUD 002. *Housing hygiene and environmental health problems in urban fringes.* Report on a workshop. Copenhagen, 1985.
150.   *Women, health and development. A report of the Director-General.* WHO Offset Publication, No. 90. Geneva: WHO, 1985.
151.   Turner, J.F.C. *Housing by people.* London: Marion Boyars Publishers Ltd, 1976.

Appendix
Criteria for healthy housing

AUDITING HEALTHY HOUSING

The primary purpose of carrying out housing inspections is to collect information relating to health and safety conditions in the property, e.g. state of repair, freedom from dampness and hazards, layout and size in relation to occupancy; to ascertain provision of amenities and to assess compliance with any housing and public health legislation, e.g. fitness for human occupation. Such inspections often follow a complaint by a resident to the local municipality or health administration, although they may be carried out as part of a systematic survey.

The outcome of such inspections is usually to determine whether any legal action (i.e. service of a legal notice requiring works to be carried out) or other intervention (such as an award of a housing grant) is necessary. In the main, the choice is between rectification of any faults together with improvement (i.e. provision of additional amenities) or closure and/or demolition in the case of the worst properties. In larger surveys, i.e. house-to-house or area surveys, such information is helpful in allowing policy-makers to make wider decisions concerning possible intervention measures, such as declaration of improvement areas, provision of financial assistance, assessment for rehousing, rehabilitation, slum clearance and special housing needs. It is also helpful in gaining some overview about the condition of the housing stock both locally and nationally. In the latter cases it is usual to collect additional information relating to socio-economic characteristics, demographic profiles and occupancy (e.g. residential density, number of persons per room, income, age and sex profiles, ethnicity and employment etc.). All of this is likely to be put into an economic planning and/or social perspective. If local information is available on mortality and morbidity rates it should also be possible to use a survey approach which takes into account epidemiology. However, morbidity is difficult to measure and data are often only available for specific population groups such as school children or working people. These data are therefore subject to considerable error and there are methodological difficulties ascribing illnesses to housing conditions anyway. However, relevant indicators which might be initially indicative of poor housing conditions include enteric infections, respiratory disease, physiological stress and accidental injury. If such health data are available then they could be used as an aid to making informed choices for action. Collaboration with local doctors, health clinics and the public health division of the local health authority (which might well have information about health patterns in the area) would be essential to this approach. However, in some cases the community itself might be monitoring incidence of illness, accidents, etc., which can be utilized.

Once a survey approach has been decided upon, it is usual to carry out a pilot survey of a defined housing sample. This may be randomized or stratified by housing type, area or socio-economic characteristics. The choice of the area to be surveyed may be influenced by health and socio-economic data relating to the chosen area. For example, child density indices, numbers of elderly people, degree of unemployment, incidence of upper respiratory disease, enteric disease or home accidents may all be factors which would affect selection of a housing sample. The size of the sampling frame will depend upon the degree of statistical accuracy required, available resources and size of area being surveyed. However, it is not unusual to inspect 10% of the housing stock during a pilot survey. This would then enable some priorities to be established for follow-up inspections.

However, before any survey work commences it is necessary to decide what information is to be collected and just as important, *why* it is needed, i.e. what outputs would the information be put to. If the health and safety audit is being conducted to determine future action or requisite assistance (e.g. financial help or rehousing), then some attempt may be made to ascribe a score to various housing factors to establish the scale and priorities of particular housing conditions. Different scores can be given to individual items which reflect the health priorities for tackling them, e.g. the absence of water supplies to a house would normally have a higher priority points rating than a house provided with *inadequate* water supplies; overcrowding coupled with absence of means to escape in case of fire in shared housing would be given a higher priority points rating than a single occupied house (because the fire risk is lower). All these decisions are dependent upon having some agreed rationale about the expected health outcome and its application through points ratings and priorities. However, enforcement machinery, codes, legislation, finances and other resources need to be available if any meaningful outcome is to be gained from the exercise. To achieve this, an audit of the policy, organizational, legal, financial, economic, educational and institutional framework for

253

implementing housing hygiene objectives could prove beneficial (see Chapter 3).

At a technical level, a survey form or checklist is useful as an 'aide memoir', and avoids the frustration which every inspecting officer feels when finding that she or he has missed a vital piece of information during the inspection so necessitating a re-visit.

Ideally, survey forms and checklists should be designed to meet very specific objectives in accordance with the type of housing, local situations and likely outcomes of measures taken, e.g. legal action or health education. The following checklist is an example of the sorts of questions a housing surveyor might ask (either consciously or subconsciously) when trying to make some assessment of health and safety of housing. However, the checklist could and should be modified to meet specific needs and practical usage. For example, a different sort of checklist might be used for new housing as opposed to that for existing housing. Nevertheless it hopefully provides a starting point to an inspection and appraisal approach compatible with the parameters for the healthy housing previously outlined in this guide.

A1 HOUSING LAYOUT REQUIREMENTS (2.1)*

A1.1 Provision of housing of suitable height to enable normal family use and social activities to be performed (2.1.1)

- What percentage of housing stock is high-rise?
- What planning policies exist to restrict building height?
- What is the storey height?
- Are families with young children (<5 years) or the elderly housed above the sixth floor?
- Is accommodation used for housing rural immigrants? If so, what provision has been made for education and needs assessment?
- What provision is there for rehousing vulnerable groups?
- Are lifts provided in high-rise housing?
- Is lift provision satisfactory (sufficiency, maintenance, cleanliness)?
- What community facilities are provided to high-rise housing (education, recreation, health and social services)?
- Are any communal facilities provided on intervening floors above ground level?
- Are play facilities for children provided?

---

*The references relate to chapter sections within the guidelines.

- Is noise insulation provided to flats?
- Are there adequate facilities for drying clothes?
- Is space provided for parking cars, bicycles etc?
- Are there facilities available for hobbies?
- Are arrangements for refuse disposal adequate?
- What provisions are made for fire-protection?
- Are security measures adequate?

A1.2 Provision of housing and suitable dwelling size mix to enable community and social interaction (2.1.2)

- What dwelling size mix is provided within the housing development?
- Is dwelling size mix suitable for socio-economic characteristics?
- Is suitable provision made for housing the elderly and families with young children?

A1.3 Provision of housing with sufficient space between housing blocks so as not to intrude on view, privacy or impede insolation and air circulation (2.1.3)

- What is the minimum distance between housing blocks and adjoining buildings?
- Do planning standards stipulate minimum space between buildings? If so, are these standards satisfactory?
- Is spacing between buildings adequate (privacy, air circulation, overshadowing)?

A1.4 Provision for good orientation of buildings compatible with climatic conditions (2.1.4)

- In which direction does the housing block face?
- Is the orientation satisfactory (overheating, underheating, privacy)?

A2 SPACE AND DENSITY REQUIREMENTS (2.2)

A2.1 Provision of housing built to suitable residential housing densities compatible with good environmental conditions and social and recreational needs (2.2.1)

- Do any residential density standards apply in new housing development or improvement schemes?
- What is the maximum residential density (habitable rooms/hectare)?

- Do density standards make allowance for families with children?
- Do housing densities take account of environmental, social and recreational needs?

A2.2 Provision of housing of suitable size and sufficient usable floor area to satisfy human requirements for health, safety, family life, privacy, rest and domestic, recreational and social activities (2.2.2)

- How much habitable floor space per person is provided?
- Is the floor area ergonomically designed for carrying out household tasks?
- Is the floor area overcrowded or does it pose safety hazards?
- Is provision made for separation of sleeping apartments for the sexes?
- What space standards are applicable (e.g. WHO (EURO) <12 m² habitable space per person)?
- What provision is made for storage space?

A2.3 Provision of sufficient open space for active and passive recreation and aesthetically pleasing environment (2.2.3)

- How much open space is provided (per person) within housing development or serving it?
- What uses is open space put to (recreation, food crops, allotments, parks)?
- Does open space act as a barrier between housing and industrial developments or major roads?
- Do land policy and planning laws make provision for open space?

A3 SOCIAL REQUIREMENTS (2.3)

A3.1 Provision of facilities for normal family life, hobbies, recreation, play and social activities (2.3.1)

- Does the shelter provide opportunities for children's play, homework, domestic activities, entertaining friends and privacy for other family members?

A3.2 Provision of facilities for normal community and wider social life (2.3.2)

- Is settlement planned with recognizable spatial limits so that people can identify with their locality?

- Do neighbourhoods, districts and sub-communities have easy communal contact routes within and between them?
- Are schools, shops and recreational facilities provided?
- Is through traffic segregated from community infrastructures?
- Is provision made for safe and easily identified access to units in the residential neighbourhood?
- Are provisions made to keep the community together in a familiar environment?

A3.3 Provision of facilities for rest and recuperation from sickness or ill-health (2.3.3)

- Are community care facilities provided for people recovering from sickness or illness?
- Are medical care facilities adequate?
- Are medical aids available to enable disabled people to adjust better to their environment?
- Does the home provide peaceful, pleasant surroundings and privacy when recovering from sickness or ill-health?

A3.4 Provision of reasonable conditions of privacy (2.3.4)

- What privacy requirements are desired by the family?
- What is the space between housing and adjoining buildings?
- Is privacy compromised by buildings overlooking housing?
- Is privacy afforded during bathing or toilet operations?
- Are opportunities available to household members for privacy in performing personal pursuits and activities?
- Is it necessary for parents to share the same sleeping accommodation as their children?

A3.5 Provision of opportunity for achieving aesthetic satisfaction in the home and its surroundings (2.3.5)

- Do physical planning and design measures provide for a pleasant view from main windows?
- Does housing overlook industrial developments?
- Are backyards enclosed or is there any overshadowing from adjoining buildings?
- Are there any ugly screens, hutments or outbuildings impeding view?
- Is there provision for a distant view of the countryside or greenery and vegetation in the short view?

A3.6 Provision of opportunities to enable work activities to be carried out at home (2.3.6)

- Is the home suitable for carrying out work activities?
- Are there any hazards in the home associated with work activities (fire, asphyxiation, injuries, poisoning)?
- Are there any special health and safety precautions which would need to be implemented?

A4 SHELTER REQUIREMENTS (2.4)

- Is local information available on climate, topography, and geographical features in relation to housing developments?
- Has any evaluation been made of consequences of external elements and natural hazards (seismic and wind forces, meteorological and hydrological data, disease-transmitting life)?

A4.1 Provision of suitable shelter to ensure that housing is windproof and weathertight and otherwise protected from external elements and natural hazards (2.4.1)

- Is the shelter free from damp (rising, penetrating, condensation)?
- Is the shelter designed and constructed in such a way to keep out dampness (integrity of roof coverings, walls, floors, damp courses, sills and gutters)?
- Are measures taken to prevent local flooding (surface water drainage, flood barriers, stilts)?
- Are lightning conductors provided to tall buildings?
- Is the shelter sufficiently windtight to prevent excessive draught or infiltration?
- Are buildings located correctly in relation to topography and prevailing winds?
- Are the main structural elements strong enough to resist typical wind speeds?
- Are lowpitch roofs (15°–30°) used? If so, can roof coverings be dislodged?
- Is roof sufficiently strong to withstand snow-loads?
- In cold climates, is the site sufficiently protected against frost damage?
- Are foundations and service pipes sufficiently deep underground to be protected from frost damage?

A4.2 Provision for admission of direct sunlight and protection against excessive insolation (2.4.2)

- Are buildings orientated so that doors and windows do not face mid-day sun but take advantage of prevailing summer winds?
- Are green belts, trees, climbing plants and water reservoirs (or flat roofs) used to reduce temperatures of walls and roofs?
- Is light-coloured paint used on walls to reflect solar radiation?
- Is building constructed of materials which do not absorb heat quickly?
- Are living rooms designed that are long in relation to width and with adequate ceiling height (3.5 m optimum)?
- Do flat roofs have a ventilated space between roof deck and ceiling?
- Are devices for producing shade used to control sunlight penetration? (e.g. window blinds)
- Are verandas installed?
- Is there a cool area in the garden to rest and relax?
- Is openable window area adequate and does it provide cross-ventilation to all rooms?
- Is metalized lavisan film used on windows?
- Does open area of windows extend close to ceilings?
- Is there provision for natural night ventilation?
- Is a circulating or extractor fan installed?
- Is air conditioning provided? If so, is it adequate?

A4.3 Protection against seismic activity (2.4.3)

- Has risk assessment been carried out of risks and magnitude of earthquakes within each region?
- Have design measures been implemented to provide optimum protection against seismic movement?
- Are prefabricated or industrialized housing systems grouped together increasing seismic hazards?

A4.4 Protection against air pollutants (2.4.4)

- Have pollution control measures and legislation been implemented to ensure the efficient burning of hydrocarbons?
- Have smokeless zones or measures to prohibit coal burning been enacted?
- Can WHO standards for SO_2 and smoke be achieved (>100 $\mu g/m^2$)?
- What measures have been taken to reduce exposure of housing to lead emissions from industry or road traffic?

- Are allotments and vegetable gardens adjacent to busy roads, lead smelters or other sources of lead emissions?
- Are streets, playgrounds and other areas frequented by children swept regularly to remove dust and lead-bearing road dirt?

A4.5 Protection against radioactive emissions (2.4.5)

- Is housing sited in areas where radon ground levels are high?
- What radiological monitoring has been undertaken?
- Is sub-floor and room ventilation adequate to reduce radon levels?
- Have building materials containing deposits of radioactive materials been used?
- Where radon is diffusing into buildings through the ground, has a vapour barrier been installed between the ground and the living space above?
- Have floors and walls been sealed so as to prevent radon emission?

A4.6 Protection against excessive noise and vibration from within and outside the dwelling (2.4.6)

- Are residential areas separated from industry and transport by noise buffer belts?
- Are nearby industrial buildings and machinery insulated against noise?
- Are highways so planned that through-traffic bypasses residential areas?
- Is housing separated from main streets by wide green belts of thickly planted trees?
- Is vehicular traffic prohibited or reduced in residential streets particularly at night?
- What provision is made for regulating train and aircraft noise in the vicinity?
- Are grass areas used instead of parking and other hard surfaces outside housing developments?
- Are play areas for children planned away from dwelling?
- Are rooms with shared walls and floors used for similar purposes?
- Is there a noise buffer between living rooms and stairs, hall, and kitchen?
- Do bedrooms adjoin balconies or are they sited underneath them?
- Is the water closet located over living rooms and bedrooms?
- Are partitions between WC compartment and living rooms or bedrooms insulated (<35 dB)?
- Are WC cisterns fixed on partitions? If so, are they fitted with silencer pipes?

- Are drain pipes carried in ducts next to living rooms and bedrooms?
- Are refuse chutes placed next to living rooms and bedrooms? If so, do hoppers, chutes and containers have sound-deadening linings?
- Are surfaces of staircases in housing blocks made with sound-absorbing materials?
- Are lift motors mounted on resilient supports?
- Are access doors from machine rooms to internal staircases well fitting and of solid construction?
- Are devices fitted to entrance and garage doors to limit banging?
- Is adequate sound insulation provided to walls, floors and ceilings (solid walls, cavity fillings, wall linings, suspended ceilings, floating floors)?
- What noise protection is provided by window construction (thick glass, double glazing)?
- Are main entrance doors to common balconies designed to a high standard of noise insulation?
- Are ventilation ducts adequately insulated?
- Are ventilation fans designed to run at lowest possible speeds?
- Is there any noisy machinery badly sited so as to cause noise nuisance?
- Do tenancy agreements restrict times or conditions of use for amplified music systems?
- Do ambient noise levels meet WHO standards (>45 dB(A) L_{eq} background and > 35 dB(A) L_{eq} bedrooms)?
- Do airborne sound insulation, impact sound levels and reverberation times meet WHO recommendations?

A4.7 Provision of suitable shelter against disease vectors, pests and vermin (2.4.7)

A4.7.1 Insects
- Is there any evidence of infestation by pests and vermin (state names)?
- Is general sanitary design, maintenance and house-keeping adequate to discourage insect and other animal disease vectors?
- Is there prompt and efficient disposal of waste and rubbish?
- Are food stocks protected against vermin infestation?
- Are doors and windows to larders screened against fly infestation?
- Are insecticides used against vermin infestation? If so, can they be used safely?
- Are there breeding sites for mosquitoes in the vicinity?
- Are drains, ditches, ponds and swampy areas drained to discourage mosquitoes?
- Are biological agents used to control mosquitoes?
- Are mosquito nets available in sleeping quarters (where necessary)?

- Are all gaps in skirtings, pipe ducts and dados closed off against cockroaches and other insects?
- Are openings around fireplaces and kitchen ranges sealed off?
- Do heating and ventilation ducts provide harbourage for cockroaches?
- Is there evidence of bedbug or flea infestation?
- Are mattresses and bedding cleaned regularly?
- Have cats and other domestic animals been treated for flea infestation?
- Is relative humidity below 45% to reduce house-mite infestation?
- Are furnishings vacuumed regularly?
- Are bedding and furnishings aired in sunshine regularly?
- Is there evidence of woodworm infestation? If so, has this been treated with suitable biocides?

A4.7.2 Rodents
- Are there any accumulations of rubbish providing harbourage and food for rats and mice?
- Are there proper hygiene measures in the kitchen?
- Are housing and other buildings designed and repaired to make them rat-proof?
- Is the building site covered with site concrete?
- Are there any rat bridges to buildings such as cables, tree branches or other objects?
- Are eaves of roofs and ventilation pipes covered with wire mesh and balloons?
- Are metal pipe guards used to prevent vertical scaling by rats and mice?
- Are air-bricks, ventilators, doors, windows and other openings treated with fine wire mesh?
- Are openings at least 1 m from ground where necessary?
- Are metal kick plates fitted on bottom of entrance doors where necessary?
- Are disused drain runs filled up with concrete?
- Are drains, inspection chambers and air inlets in good repair?
- Are food storage facilities adequately protected against entry of rats and mice?
- Has provision been made for rodent control through poisoning or trapping?
- Is there a regular baiting programme in sewers?
- Do pesticides for rodent control meet WHO specifications?

A4.7.3 Other pests
- Is housing properly protected against ingress of pigeons and other birds?
- Are water storage tanks covered to keep out birds?

- Is there a control programme for other animal pests infesting housing?

A4.8 Protection against intrusion by humans or dangerous animals (2.4.8)

A4.8.1 Humans
- Are housing developments designed so as to avoid hiding places for intruders?
- Are walkways and approach roads well lit at night?
- Are policing and security patrols adequate?
- Are security devices to doors and windows adequate?
- Are security alarms provided?
- Do ground-floor flat rooms have eye level windows for effective surveillance?
- Do front doors impede line of vision from windows?
- Are there any high obstructions obscuring the view of the street from windows?
- Do back gardens abut onto alleyways or paths?

A4.8.2 Animals
- Is housing adequately secured against intrusion by dangerous or poisonous animals?

A5 DESIGN AND CONSTRUCTIONAL REQUIREMENTS (2.5)

A5.1 Provision of facilities which are designed to optimize performance of household tasks without causing undue physical or mental fatigue (2.5.1)

- Do environmental and housing facilities optimize the performance of household tasks?
- Is the provision of household appliances adequate?
- Do furnishings and finishes aid aesthetic and psychological satisfaction?

A5.2 Provision of building components with sufficient strength, stability and durability to enable effective maintenance, repair and cleanliness (2.5.2)

- Are floors, walls, ceilings and work surfaces constructed of smooth impervious materials capable of being easily kept clean?

- Are all parts of housing accessible for cleaning?
- Are hygienic facilities provided for storing domestic goods, and personal belongings etc?
- Is building structure sufficiently strong to avoid collapse?
- Are foundations strong enough to resist subsidence or slipping?
- Has remedial action been taken to ensure that walls are not badly bulged or leaning dangerously?
- Are there any loose roof tiles or chimney pots?
- Are structural timbers badly weakened by fungal or insect attacks? If so, have they been treated?
- Are ceilings loose, badly bulged or otherwise insecure?
- Is there any broken glass in windows?
- Are foundations designed to take account of possible ground movement?
- Is any topsoil used for covering foundations?
- Are foundations laid at a suitable distance below ground level to combat effects of soil shrinkage?
- Are there any mature trees close to foundations?
- Are building foundations suitable for type of housing?
- Is housing built on made-up soil? If so, is soil toxic?
- Are there any water-soluble sulphates in the soil which may attack foundations?
- Is the water-table near to ground level? If so, is frost heave a problem?
- Are foundations sufficiently strong to take building loads?
- Does wall construction take account of design factors such as strength, stability, durability, fire resistance, protection against rain and humidity, thermal insulation and noise insulation?
- Do floors provide sufficient stability, strength, moisture resistance, durability, fire resistance, thermal properties, resistance to sound transmission and adequate sound absorption?
- Are floor finishes smooth, impervious to liquids, chemicals and grease, easy to clean and non-slip?
- Do roof coverings provide sufficient stability, strength, exclusion of rain and wind, durability, fire resistance and good thermal properties?

A5.3 Provision of non-toxic or injurious building materials, furnishings and consumer goods (2.5.3)

- Are polymers used in building materials or furnishings?
- Are there special cleaning agents, toxic varnishes or other harmful chemicals used in the house?
- Are asbestos products used in construction or consumer goods within the house?

- Does asbestos present any current or potential health risk (condition, friability, treatment, accessibility, content)?
- Can asbestos be treated or should it be removed?
- Are glass fibres or other mineral fibres used for thermal insulation or fire proofing?
- What sources of lead (if any) exist in the house or environment?
- Is there any evidence of children chewing lead paint?
- Is lead paint flaking from woodwork or not?
- Have lead water pipes or storage tanks been used? If so, what is the pH value of the water?
- Have water supplies been tested for lead content?
- Should lead water pipes or storage tanks be replaced?
- Is lead-glazed earthenware used for cooking or food storage?
- What is the lead content of soil in gardens or residential environment? Is it suitable for growing food crops?

A6 SANITATION REQUIREMENTS (2.6)

A6.1 Provision of sufficient, clean water supply reasonably accessible to the dwelling and protected against pollution from outside and within the dwelling (2.6.1)

- Are potable water supplies wholesome, with acceptable physical appearance, taste and odour and not containing anything deleterious to health of the consumer?
- Have surveys been carried out into sufficiency of drinking water, water quality and treatment?
- Is there an integrated water supply, distribution, disposal and drainage and sewerage development plan?
- Are institutional frameworks, manpower, training and management systems established?
- Are water supplies quantitatively and qualitatively adequate at source?
- Are wells, streams, springs, reservoirs contaminated with sewage or toxic chemicals?
- Do water supplies meet international standards (WHO/EC)?
- Are water supplies tested regularly to ensure compliance with standards?
- Are piped water supplies chlorinated at source?
- In urban areas are water supplies continuous, adequate, safe and supplied under sufficient pressure?
- Is adequate provision made to avoid cross-connection between potable and non-potable water supplies?

- What provision is made for water treatment in rural areas?
- Are stand-pipes or public hydrants available and sufficient for shared public use?
- Are water storage tanks always kept covered?
- Are materials used for water services a source of bacterial or chemical contamination?
- Is legislation adequate to control the design and construction requirements of water installations and services?

A6.2 Provision of sanitary means of waste and surface water disposal (2.6.2)

- Are waste-water collection/carriage systems installed at same time as new piped water supply systems?
- What methods are used for waste-water disposal? Are they adequate?
- Do piped carriage systems leak or not?
- Are provisions for waste-water disposal adequate (soakaways, streams, piped systems)?
- When soakaways are used are they below the highest natural level of the water-table?
- Is rainwater and surface water disposal adequate?
- Is access to drains and sewers adequate?
- Is waste-water plumbing system self-cleaning and vented against syphonage?
- Do venting stacks discharge foul air without causing nuisance?
- Are water traps used in plumbing fixtures?
- Are materials used in plumbing systems of sufficient strength, durability and able to resist corrosion?
- Are underground drains and sewers of sufficient size to accommodate number of properties serving them?
- Are underground drainage pipes constructed of suitable materials?
- Are house drains laid straight and enabling a self-cleansing velocity to be achieved?
- Do house drainage pipes have rigid or flexible joints and are they adequately encased and protected against damage or breakage?
- Do all parts of house drainage/sewerage system have a free passage of air through each part of the system?
- Is adequate drainage provided for rainwater run-off to courts, yards or paved areas?
- Is drainage and plumbing system regularly inspected and maintained?
- Are legal and enforcement codes or ordinances adequate to control design and construction of new drainage?
- Is there legal provision for regulating the use and maintenance of existing drainage and sewerage system?

A6.3 Provision of toilet facilities of such a nature as to minimize the danger of transmitting disease (2.6.3)

- Does every dwelling unit have its own separate inside sanitary accommodation?
- Is sanitary accommodation regularly cleaned to reduce the risk of spreading infection?
- Is there an intervening lobby between sanitary compartments and other rooms (especially kitchens)?
- Is outside toilet accommodation reasonably accessible to the dwelling unit?
- Is sanitary compartment constructed with hygienic and impervious surfaces for ease of cleaning?
- Is lighting and ventilation to sanitary compartments adequate?
- Where mechanical ventilation is used is it properly maintained to provide at least three air changes per hour?
- Do WCs provide self-cleansing of closet receptacle?
- Are toilet seats hygienic?
- Is WC properly connected up to drainage system?
- Do earth or chemical closets pose any health hazards or nuisances?

A6.4 Provision of sanitary facilities for excreta disposal (2.6.4)

- Is there provision for sanitary disposal of excreta and means of preventing cross-contamination of water supplies?
- Are insanitary methods used for excreta and waste water disposal (ditches, streams, conduits)?
- What provision is made for sanitary discharge of sewage effluent?
- Are sewage treatment plants situated with settlements able to achieve desired quality in the plant efficiently?
- Does sewage effluent meet international standards before discharge to land, watercourses or the sea?
- Are septic tank installations automatic, free from nuisance either of sight or odour and designed to require minimal attention and maintenance?
- Is the soil suitable to allow effluent from septic tanks to be disposed of evenly and harmlessly?
- Are settlement or septic tanks of suitable size and capacity for use and properly ventilated and constructed for emptying and cleansing?
- Are septic tanks situated away from trees and protected from falling leaves?
- Are cesspools of sufficient capacity ($>18 \text{ m}^3$), impervious to surface water and adequately ventilated and sited to enable emptying?

- Are pit latrines positioned near to underground water supplies?
- Do methods of excreta disposal comply with international standards (WHO/EEC)?

A6.5 Provision of sanitary arrangements for domestic washing and drying of clothes (2.6.5)

- Is each dwelling provided with a suitable sink, draining board and hot and cold water?
- What facilities are provided for clothes drying? Are these adequate (airing cupboard, sunshine, drying room)?

A6.6 Provision of sanitary arrangements for personal washing and bathing (2.6.6)

- What facilities are provided for personal washing and bathing?
- Is there a separate wash-basin, bath or shower with hot and cold water supplies provided?
- Is wash-basin situated near to a WC compartment?
- Is bath or shower situated in its own room?
- Are the walls and floor surfaces of shower compartments easily cleaned and non-slip?
- Is there a minimum 1 m head above highest position of shower? If not, is pump assistance provided?
- Is there adequate access provided for emptying and cleaning traps to fixed appliances?
- Are sanitary appliances made of hard, smooth, impermeable and hygienic materials?

A6.7 Provision of hygienic facilities for the storage, preparation and cooking of food (2.6.7)

- Are all walls, floors, ceilings, work surfaces and food preparation areas in good repair and constructed of materials not providing harbourage for dirt, grease and bacteria?
- Is a suitably sized work surface provided adjacent to the cooker for preparation of food?
- Is kitchen properly lighted and ventilated?
- Are adequate facilities provided to keep food rooms cool and at correct humidity?
- Are adequate facilities provided for the hygienic storage of fresh food products at correct temperature?

- Is provision made to prevent cross-contamination between cooked and uncooked foods?
- Are dry, clean and hygienic storage facilities provided for packed, canned and other dry foods?
- Is kitchen suitably protected against vermin and pest infestation?
- Are adequate facilities provided for cooking and heating of food?
- Do food handlers have access to adequate personal washing facilities?
- Are easy-to-clean rubbish bins with tight-fitting lids provided for waste food and rubbish?

A6.8 Provision of sanitary facilities for the storage, collection and disposal of solid and household waste (2.6.8)

- Do building codes and ordinances provide for the hygienic storage, collection and disposal of solid waste?
- Are there adequate facilities for storage and space for on-site treatment?
- Are suitable solid-waste storage containers provided for each dwelling?
- Are containers located in the open air and away from windows and ventilated and sheltered from sun?
- Can waste collector get access to containers easily and without having to pass through dwelling (maximum distance 25 m)?
- If paper/plastic sacks are used, are these suitably guarded and firmly attached to holders?
- Do all refuse containers have tight-fitting lids?
- Are refuse containers in good repair and placed on a hard impervious free-draining surface?
- Is a refuse shelter provided which is an integral part of the building? If so, can lids be removed easily and will shelter accommodate two bins?
- Where chutes are provided are they within 30 m of all dwellings?
- Are communal waste storage containers provided with a platform to give ready access to top of container?
- Are sufficient communal chutes provided?
- Are communal chutes designed to carry waste without blocking up (>450 mm diameter)?
- Are chutes continued full bore to external air? If not, is there a ventilating pipe from top hopper?
- To avoid noise nuisance are chutes situated away from habitable rooms? If not, are chutes adequately insulated?
- Are hoppers situated within a dwelling or stairway enclosure?
- Do hoppers provide one half-hour fire resistance, have self-closing doors and provide at least six air changes per hour?

- Are hoppers accessible to occupants and not cause noise nuisance?
- Are chambers for waste storage containers adequate and hygienic-ally designed and properly ventilated without causing a fire hazard?
- Is water supply provided for cleansing refuse chambers?
- Is there provision for storage of bulky waste?
- Do roads provide reasonable convenience for refuse collection vehicles (including turning space)?
- Is there provision for cleansing and maintenance of chutes, hoppers and ventilation shafts?
- Is there hygienic provision made for sanitary disposal of solid waste off-site?

A6.9 Provision of separate sanitary arrangements for housing of pets and domestic animals (2.6.9)

- Is living accommodation shared with domestic animals or is separate housing provided?
- What pet animals are kept inside the house. Are hygienic arrangements adequate for their housing and care?
- Do pet animals receive regular veterinary care?

A7 INDOOR AIR QUALITY REQUIREMENTS (2.7)

A7.1 Provision of an indoor atmosphere which is free from excessive chemicals, toxic and/or noxious odours, water vapour, pathogens and other air contaminants or pollutants (2.7.1)

A7.1.1 Gases
- Are the general measurements for controlling indoor air pollutants adequate (removing source, controlling emissions, expellation)?
- Is there any evidence of even low concentrations of CO in dwelling?
- What measures have been taken to minimize CO?
- Are there any sources of nitrogen oxides in dwelling?
- Are flueless gas appliances vented to outside air?
- Can electric cookers or heaters be used as an alternative to gas?
- Are draught settings to stoves correctly set?
- Do nitrogen dioxide concentrations exceed WHO recommendations ($>0.05-1.0\,\mathrm{mg/m^3}$)?
- What materials used in the dwelling emit formaldehyde?
- Are specially coated resin-based chipboards used? Can alternative materials be used instead?

- Is urea formaldehyde foam used for cavity wall insulation? If so, are cavities and internal brickwork properly sealed?
- Do formaldehyde emissions comply with maximum allowable concentrations proposed by WHO ($>0.12 \, \text{mg/m}^3$)?
- Is there evidence of high odour concentrations in dwelling? If so, what is likely source?
- What measures can be taken to reduce odour concentrations?
- Are cooking and personal hygiene facilities adequate?
- Are tobacco smoke concentrations excessive ($>0.15 \, \text{mg/m}^3$)?

A7.1.2 Water vapour and condensation dampness

- Is there evidence of excessive water vapour levels (condensation) inside rooms?
- Have measures been taken to reduce penetrative dampness?
- Have vapour barriers been installed?
- Has proper ventilation been provided to kitchens and other rooms used for washing/drying clothes or cooking?
- Has an extractor fan been provided in these rooms?
- Is there a cooking hood over stoves?
- Is permanent ventilation provided in rooms and voids?
- Are joisted flat roof-spaces cross-ventilated?
- Are airing cupboards ventilated to the outside and heated to enable clothes drying?
- Are portable paraffin or flueless gas heaters used? If so, are rooms well ventilated?
- Are rooms continually heated?
- Are walls, floors, ceilings and other surfaces adequately insulated to prevent water condensing onto cold surfaces?
- Have walls been insulated with dry-lining and suitable water vapour backing?
- Is there any evidence of cold bridging? If so, can any remedial action be taken?
- Are there any cold impermeable surfaces?
- Have condensation channels or strip ventilators been provided to windows?
- Are cold-water tanks and pipes insulated to prevent condensation formation?
- Would electrically operated dehumidifiers be appropriate to remove moisture from the air?
- Does relative humidity exceed 60%?
- Are U values (insulation values) adequate?

A7.1.3 Airborne pathogens

- Are hygiene measures adequate to help reduce spread of pathogens

(sunlight, ventilation, relative humidity and cleaning/disinfection)?
- Are space and personal segregation facilities adequate?

A7.1.4 Allergens

- Are there any persons in the home who are sensitive to allergens?
- What possible allergens exist in the home which might give rise to sensitivity (house mites, dust, mould, birds, animals, materials)?
- Can the causal factors giving rise to sensitivity be removed?
- Is there any evidence of mould growth or dust mite infestation? If so, can these be treated?
- Are insect, rodent and other allergen infestations being treated with suitable insecticides and rodenticides?

A7.2 Provision of sufficient ventilation to maintain comfort, air quality and hygrothermal requirements (2.7.2)

- Are all habitable rooms, halls, common stairways, kitchens, bathrooms and WC compartments provided with adequate ventilation either by openable windows or other devices?
- Are rooms provided with through ventilation?
- Is trickle ventilation into rooms sufficient (0.5–1.00 AcH)?
- Does window design allow for easily operated and controllable ventilation?
- Are open fireplaces provided? If so, are flues fitted with exhaust ventilators or cowls?
- Are ventilator pipes coupled with exhaust ventilators provided?
- Are permanent ventilators provided (air-bricks, slats)?
- Are air inlets to mechanical extractor fans properly situated to avoid draught and nuisance to neighbouring properties?
- Is air-conditioning provided? If so, is it properly designed, regularly cleaned and maintained?
- Do ventilation rates comply with WHO recommendations (18 m^3/h in temperate climates)?

A8 INDOOR CLIMATE REQUIREMENTS (2.8)

A8.1 Maintenance of a thermal environment which will not impose any significant strain on the thermoregulatory mechanisms of the body (2.8.1)

- Is ambient air temperature sufficient to provide thermal comfort for occupants (optimum 18–30° C; optimum indoor air temperature 16–32° C)?

- Is optimum temperature achieved at knee height (0.5 m from ground)?
- Is mean radiant temperature less than 3° C below an assumed optimum indoor air temperature of 20° C?
- Can minimum optimum temperature of 22° C at knee height be achieved for persons of subnormal vitality?
- Are there any excessive horizontal and vertical differences in air temperature (>1–2° C horizontal; 2–3° C vertical)?
- Can bathrooms be kept at a temperature 2–3° C higher than other rooms?
- Are surface temperatures of walls, floors, ceilings and other surfaces same as optimum air temperature?
- Is there excessive air mobility in rooms (winter 0.1–0.15 m/s; summer 0.3 m/s is acceptable)?
- Is relative humidity (RH) of rooms adequate (<60% and >30%)?
- What form of heating is used (radiant, convection)?
- Where warm-air systems are used, is there efficient circulation of heat?
- Do warm-air systems cause noise or dust nuisance?
- Where central heating systems are used, is provision made for topping up heat by radiant fires?
- Is heating provided which is affordable by occupants?
- Are heating systems easy to control?
- Is there provision for an alternative form of heating if the primary source fails?
- Is financial assistance available to help low-income groups with heating bills?
- Is thermal insulation provided? If so, is it sufficient?
- Is sufficient draught-proofing provided around window, door and other openings?
- Is cavity wall, roof and floor insulation provided?
- Are heating appliances designed to minimize heat loss through the flue?

A8.2 Provision of adequate daylight, artificial illumination and avoidance of glare (2.8.2)

- Is natural lighting provision adequate?
- Are there any adjacent tall buildings overlooking dwelling?
- Is orientation and spacing between buildings adequate?
- Is the sky visible from most places within habitable rooms?
- Are open-patterned streets with spaces between the buildings provided?
- Is natural lighting provided to WC compartments?
- Does lighting meet physiological and health requirements (optimum

intensity, similar brightness, protection against glare, avoidance of shadows, adequate contrast, biological activity of light)?

- Does artifical lighting resemble sunlight?
- Is fluorescent indoor lighting adequate on health grounds?
- Do overall illumination and glare levels meet international WHO recommended standards?
- Do colours of wall and other surfaces reflect 70–80% of incident light?

A9 HOME SAFETY REQUIREMENTS (2.9)

- Are any occupants disabled or chronically sick (state details)?
- Do any occupants receive regular medication (state details)?
- Are any occupants known alcoholics, heavy drinkers, drug addicts or senile?
- Are all members of family mobile?
- Have there been any previous accidents in the home (state sources)?
- Are small children regularly left unsupervised?
- Have children been screened for lead?
- Are telephones or other methods of communication easily available? If so, do people most at risk (or in charge) know how to use them?
- Do any of the occupants understand first aid and resuscitation?
- Is there an established fire-drill?
- Are all members of family covered by insurance for all accident risks, medical care and income compensation?
- Are medical care facilities and first-aid services available (state location)?
- Do occupants know location of medical care facilities?

A9.1 Protection of the neighbourhood against hazards of vehicular traffic (2.9.1)

- Does layout separate pedestrian and vehicle traffic adequately?
- Is parking and traffic turning space adequate?
- Are sleeping policemen used to restrict traffic speed?

A9.2 Avoidance of unsafe conditions in the housing environment, in outbuildings and surroundings of the home (2.9.2)

A9.2.1 Environment
- Is the house subject to periodic flooding, earthquakes, or landslip?
- Are there any obvious dangers near to the house (state source)?

- Is the property adequately fenced to adjacent dangers?
- Are all wells, ditches, drains and pits properly covered or otherwise guarded?
- Are overhead electricity supply lines accessible to children?
- Are there any large dead or dying trees likely to fall?
- Are there any dangerous or poisonous animals, insects in area?
- Are any ponds, canals or swimming pools fenced off or suitably guarded?
- Are water tanks properly covered?
- Are external paved surfaces, steps and ramps non-slippery when wet?
- Is drainage provided to paved areas?
- Are paths even and properly lit at night?
- Are there safety rings set into high walls and chimneys for outside working?
- Are snow barriers provided at eaves to steep pitched roofs?
- Are balcony areas unclimbable and bulky enough to give reassurance (min. 2.1 m high)?
- Are balcony balustrades spaced at correct intervals (max. 90 mm spacing)?
- Are thresholds to main access doors designed to form the nosing of steps?
- Are dimensions of external steps so designed to be easy to climb?
- Are there single external steps or unexpected ramps? If so, are they provided with a handrail and marked by a change of colour?
- Are fences and gates so designed that young children cannot climb over or open them?
- Are very low fences clearly visible?
- Is the route to the clothes line and rubbish bins direct and free from unnecessary changes of level?

A9.2.2 Outbuildings
- Are power tools and appliances adequately earthed and guarded?
- Are tools, chemicals and other objects accessible to children?
- Is petrol stored adequately?
- Is lighting satisfactory?
- Is ventilation adequate?
- Can car engine be run easily when garage doors are closed?
- Is the floor level?
- Is room adequately protected against fire?
- Are electric rotor motors provided with automatic circuit breakers?

A9.3 Protection against the risks and effects of falls (2.9.3)

A9.3.1 Staircases
- Are floor coverings non-slip?

- Is there a mat well at entrance door?
- Are the stairs too steep (>37°)?
- Are they regular, straight and of uniform height?
- Are there any shallow steps <73 mm height?
- Are tapered steps too small making them difficult to climb?
- Are there any winders or tapered treads?
- Do top and bottom steps encroach onto circulation areas?
- Are there any open risers?
- Are the balustrades <90 mm apart?
- Are there firm suitable handrails on both sides of stairs unobstructed by handrail fittings?
- Is the stair carpet pinned securely to the floor at the top and bottom of staircase?
- Do any doors open onto stairs or landings?
- Are the stairs well lit?
- Are windows and light fittings within normal reach?
- Are there two-way light switches at top and bottom of stairs?
- Does artificial lighting shine towards stairs?
- Are there any open stairwells? If so, are they unclimbable?
- Does staircase provide protection against fire?
- Are there any inflammable or dangerous chemicals stored under stairs?
- Are gates provided at top or bottom of stairs?
- Are there fixing positions for stair gates?
- Are there any radiators at base of stairs? If so, are they protected (rounded top edges without welded seams)?

A9.3.2 Halls, landings and circulation areas
- Are light switches between bedroom and WC so placed that the way ahead can be lit from either direction?
- Are there any single steps or unexpected changes of level? If so, are they differentiated by change of colour?
- Are thresholds to internal doors so detailed as to minimize tripping?
- Is lighting adequate?
- Are illuminated switches provided in circulation areas?
- Is access to roof spaces by fixed ladder?
- Does roof space have a boarded floor or cat walk?
- Is roof space properly lit?

A9.3.3 Living rooms
- Is the floor polished?
- Are non-slip floor coverings provided?
- Are edges of floor coverings securely fixed?
- Are ceiling and door heights sufficient?

A9.3.4 Kitchens

- Are there high-level storage cupboards? If so, how are they reached?
- Is lighting adequate for room and work surfaces?
- Are floor surfaces slippery?
- Are doors to kitchen so placed as to minimize through traffic?
- Are swings to doors and cupboard doors so planned as to avoid collisions?
- Is cooker immediately next to a window or door?
- Is there a minimum 300 mm width of work surface on either side of cooker?
- Are any hobs in peninsular or 'island' units?
- Are work surfaces flush with level of cooker hob?
- Do worktop fronts have square edges?
- Is the kitchen sufficiently large so that no route through kitchen impinges on the sink/fridge/cooker work triangle?
- Is there at least 1200 mm between the fronts of fitments to allow passage?

A9.3.5 Bathrooms/WC compartments

- Are floor coverings adequate and non-slip?
- Are handrails installed?
- Does shower tray have a slip-resistant finish?
- Does wash basin overhang the end of the bath?
- Does wash basin have secure bolt fittings?
- Does bath have safety grab handles and a slip-resistant moulded surface?
- Is toilet reached by going up and down stairs?
- Are locks capable of being opened from outside?
- Are pull switches low enough for a child to reach?
- Are locks on bathroom/WC doors openable from outside in an emergency?
- Is there a bell or could a call be heard in an emergency?

A9.3.6 Windows

- Are windows above third storey at least 1100 mm above floor?
- Are windows above third storey capable of being cleaned and reglazed from inside?
- Are all hand-operated window controls less than 2000 mm from floor?
- Do windows allow continual control of movement?
- Do windows have independant fastenings far beyond a child's reach (where applicable)?
- Do windows below 1350 mm from floor have an automatic device to restrict aperture of 100 mm?
- Are high-level bolts used on windows above ground floor?

- Do windows which reverse for cleaning have devices to lock them in the fully reversed position?
- Are window sills in children's rooms not easily climbable?

A9.3.7 Doors

- Do doors encroach space where a child may be playing?
- Are sliding/folding doors used where space is restricted?
- Is door furniture at sufficient height to enable children to open internal doors safely?
- Are high-level bolts used to prevent the openings of internal doors safely?
- If door closers are used are they likely to cause trapping of fingers?

A9.4 Provision of adequate facilities to enable means of escape in case of fire and control and removal of conditions likely to cause or promote fire (2.9.4)

A9.4.1 Single- or two-storey dwellings

- Are roadways, gateways and space around buildings adequate to allow access by fire brigade?
- Are fire hydrants or other water supplies reasonably near building?
- Are suitable non-combustible materials used in building construction?
- Is there a suitable fire-break between adjoining buildings?
- Is there suitable means of escape to outside (including alternative exits)?
- Are doors and stairs to upper storeys protected against fire?
- Do windows to upper storeys allow easy exit?
- Are suitable fire extinguishers (e.g. in kitchen) and hoses available?
- Are smoke alarms installed?
- Are highly inflammable materials used in furnishings etc?
- Are wiring, fuses and connections to electrical appliances satisfactory in use?
- Are there any dangerous oil heaters or outdated electric heaters in use?
- Are storage arrangements for inflammable substances satisfactory?

A9.4.2 Multiple dwellings (additional precautions)

- Is secondary means of escape provided?
- Are at least two escape routes leading in opposite directions provided to access ways?
- Is there emergency access to adjoining premises (e.g. to roof)?
- Do stairs between dwellings provide at least 30 min fire resistance in event of fire?

- Are all access ways to exits free from obstruction and inflammable materials?
- Are all entrance and cupboard doors of halls and landings self-closing and adequately protected against fire?
- Are windows and emergency exits unlocked, easily openable and large enough for access?
- Is emergency exit lighting provided?
- Are electric switch rooms properly fire-proofed?
- In tall buildings, are firemen's lifts and ventilated lobbies provided?
- Are smoke/fire alarms installed?
- Are smoke outlets provided to basements and automatic roof vents in tall buildings?
- Are any other smoke dispersal methods provided?
- Are dry and wet rising mains on each storey provided?
- Is there means of communication by telephone for firemen between ground level and higher storeys?

A9.4.3 Miscellaneous
- Is a ceiling airer situated over the cooker?
- Is there a fire blanket or extinguisher next to cooker hob?
- Are there ceiling-mounted cupboards directly over a cooker or boiler?
- If kerosene is used, is it stored safely?
- Are there any oil or gas heaters in passages?
- Are ashtrays of the bowl type and totally enclosed?
- Does the furniture pass current fire safety standards?

A9.5 Protection against burns and scalds (2.9.5)
- Is domestic water delivered at under 54° C?
- Are open flames from cooking stoves and heating appliances less than 1 m from ground?
- Can electric kettles not be pulled over easily?
- Are all cooking utensils broad at base with suitable handles?
- Is there an open fire?
- Are heaters and fires adequately guarded?
- Do showers have thermostatically controlled mixer valves?
- Is a bath easily accessible to children?
- Is surface temperature of convector radiators effectively controlled?

A9.6 Protection against asphyxiation or gas poisoning from faulty heating and cooking appliances and services (2.9.6)

A9.6.1 General
- Are gas appliances checked for leaks and regularly maintained?

- If utility gas is used, is there adequate ventilation?
- If utility gas is used, are pipes, taps and fittings functioning correctly?
- Are gas appliances vented to the outside?
- Do ovens have double doors and an inside light?
- Are open fires well ventilated?
- Are ventilation and safety devices to gas heaters operating satisfactorily?

A9.6.2 Liquified petroleum gas installations
- Are cylinders stored in a safe, accessible, well-ventilated area outside?
- Are cylinders, connectors, pipes, valves, gas regulators and cut-out devices in good condition?
- Are there any signs of leaks?
- Are LPG appliances inspected and regularly maintained?
- Are the appliances properly flued to outside air (where applicable)?
- Is adequate ventilation provided to rooms containing appliances?

A9.7 Protection against electric shocks from defective appliances and services (2.9.7)
- Are electrical appliances safe and up to standard?
- Are any electric points accessible to young children?
- Are shock stops provided on all unused electric outlets?
- Are there any electric contacts between source of current, the individual and water supply?
- Are all electric points fitted with the correct separate fuse?
- Are any socket outlets situated near to sink?
- Are sufficient sockets provided, i.e. are any overloaded?
- Are there circuit breakers on mains supply?
- Are all sources of electricity suitably earthed, insulated and safe?
- Is there an old, poorly serviced electric blanket in use?
- Are any electric heaters used? If so, are they safe?
- Can any electric point or switch be reached whilst in contact with water?
- Are any light fittings situated over the bath?

A9.8 Protection against bodily harm from lacerations and similar injuries (2.9.8)
- Is glass weight sufficient for size and position of window?
- Are all large sheets of plate glass easily visible?
- Do windows project over path and circulation areas?
- Are windows above ground floor level at least 800 mm from floor or otherwise adequately protected?

- Are all high-speed cutting devices properly guarded?
- Do can-openers not leave raw metal edges?
- Are kitchen knives and other dangerous appliances out of reach of children?
- Do powered washers and driers switch off automatically when opened?
- Are appliances regularly checked for safety and properly maintained?
- Is safety glazing used to doors, especially lower panes, patio doors and windows, within 800 mm of the floor?
- Are glass doors easily seen?
- Are off-centre pivot doors or closers detailed to avoid trapping of fingers?
- Is safety glazing provided to shower or bath screens?
- Are there mirrors or mantel shelves fixed above open fireplaces?

A9.9 Protection against poisoning from dangerous drugs, medicines and household chemicals (2.9.9)

- Is a small, lockable, high-level medicine cupboard provided?
- Are shampoos, soaps, cosmetics and cleaning materials out of reach of children?
- Are household cleaners and chemicals stored safely?

A9.10 Protection against poisoning from plants and fungi (2.9.10)

- Are there any poisonous berries or fruits in the area? If so, what steps have been taken to eradicate them?
- Can occupants identify poisonous plants?

A10 SPECIAL HOUSING REQUIREMENTS (2.10)

A10.1 Provision of housing suitably adapted to meet the needs of children, women with children and single parents (2.10.1)

- Are sufficient space and play facilities provided for children inside and outside the home?
- Are crowding indices satisfactory?
- Are sanitary facilities adequate to prevent enteric infections of children?
- Is the home safe for children?
- Has leaded paint been used? If so, is there any evidence of chewing of paintwork?

- Is there provision for children to do homework peacefully?
- Are children housed in high-rise tower blocks?
- Are facilities provided for mothers with young children to interact with others outside the home?
- Has any special housing provision been made for single-parent families?
- Are there crèches available for working mothers?

A10.2 Provision of housing suitably adapted to meet the requirements of the elderly (2.10.2)

- Are elderly persons integrated into the community?
- Can elderly people retain independence and be close to relatives and friends?
- Is housing close to community facilities, public transport, health centres etc?
- What provision is made for sheltered accommodation?
- Is efficient heating provision available?
- Is elderly accommodation situated on the ground floor? If not, is a lift available?
- Is housing safe for elderly people? In particular, are design measures to prevent falls adequate?

A10.3 Provision of housing suitably adapted to meet the requirements of disabled persons (2.10.3)

A10.3.1 Persons with movement difficulties

- Has provision been made for access to public buildings by disabled persons?
- In the home, have ramps, adequately sized door openings and adaptations to bedrooms, stairs, WC compartments and bathrooms, been carried out?
- Are sanitary appliances, fittings and cupboards suitably adapted for ease of use?
- Has additional heating been provided?
- Do disabled occupants require ground floor accommodation? If so, is such accommodation available?

A10.3.2 Persons with visual difficulties

- Is use of colour, illumination and texture of building materials suitable for persons with visual difficulties?
- Is building design and layout simple, safe and straightforward in regard to orientation?

A10.3.3 Persons with hearing and/or speech difficulties

- Are rooms acoustically well designed and insulated?

A10.3.4 Other disabilities

- Is housing suitably safe for persons subject to epileptic fits?
- Is the built environment laid out in a simple way to facilitate orientation of persons with learning difficulties?
- Is sheltered housing available for persons suffering from mental illness?
- Are measures taken to reduce allergens in housing accommodation?

A10.4 Provision of housing suitable for the chronically sick and others with special health needs (2.10.4)

- Is indoor thermal climate, indoor air quality, noise insulation, privacy and outlook adequate for chronically sick people?
- Is ground floor accommodation available without stairs?
- Do chronically sick people have access to a separate room or segregated room area within the home?
- Is family and community support available?
- Is 'special need' or sheltered housing available?

Index

Index

Index

Sunlight 53-6
  impedance 21-3
Suspended ceilings 65
Suspended particulates 57
Syphilis 117

Taenia saginata 112
Taenia solium 112
Tapeworms 112
Temperature
  control 156
  core 157
  and the elderly 203
  indoor 159-61, 203
  mean radiant 161
  operative 159
Terraced housing 20
Tetanus 68, 128
Thermal comfort
  control measures 159-66
  diurnal and seasonal variations
    158-9
  during sleep 159
  health effects 155-9
Thermal insulation 165-6
  of floors 86-7
  of roofs 88
  of walls 84
Thermoregulatory control 156
Timber walls 85
Tobacco smoke 135, 136, 137-8
Toilet facilities 107-10
Tonsillitis 29
Toxocara 129
Toxocariasis 129
Toxoplasmosis 129
Trachoma 206
Traditional housing 20-1
Traffic, vehicular 176-7
  accidents 25
Trichinella spiralis 112
Trichinosis 75, 130
Tuberculosis 8, 10, 29-30, 77, 128,
  129
Tularaemia 75
Turkey, urban population 27
Turpentine 208
Typhoid 68, 70, 99, 108, 117, 118

Ultraviolet radiation 168
Unemployment 4

long-term 209-10
United Kingdom
  Department of Environment 42
  financial assistance 237
  National Radiological Protection
    Board 60
United Nations
  Economic and Social Council 57
  International Year of Homes for
    the Shelterless 209
United States
  Public Health Association 14
  Centre for Human
    Settlements 235
  Centre for Disease Control 36
Uranium 60
Urbanization 27, 231
Urea-formaldehyde foam 135
Urticaria 148

Vandalism 7, 12
Varicella 145
Ventilation 141-3, 149-54
  control methods 151-4
  health effects 150
Vermin
  infestation 7
  protectoin against 67-77
Vibration, protection against 61-7
View 43, 44-5
  intrusion of 21-3
Violence 11
Visual problems, special needs 206
Volcanoes 46, 47

Walls
  design 83-5
  thermal insulation 142, 165
Washing facilities, domestic 115-16
Washing, personal 116-20
Waste chutes 124, 125-6
Waste disposal 102-7
  control measures 103-7
  health effects 102
Waste storage chambers 127
Water
  clean 96-102
  contamination
    chemical 99, 100-1
    pathogenic 97
  control measures 99-102

Index